Ivy Compton-Burnett

Daughters and Sons

Panther

Granada Publishing Limited
Published in 1972 by Panther Books Limited
3 Upper James Street, London W1R 4BP

First published in Great Britain by Victor
Gollancz Limited 1937
Reprinted four times
Made and printed in Great Britain by
Richard Clay (The Chaucer Press), Ltd.,
Bungay, Suffolk
Set in Linotype Times

Ivy Compton-Burnett's world is the upper-middle-class family of the late Victorian and Edwardian era; the world of Galsworthy's *Forsyte Saga*—but viewed by a subtler and much chillier eye.

In the eccentric tradition of Laurence Sterne and Thomas Love Peacock she thrusts her characters onto the stage of her phosphorescent novels and then leaves them alone to outrageously talk and act their ways into and out of the dilemmas of living.

'She is probably the purest and most original of contemporary English writers.' *Rosamond Lehmann*

'A remarkable and unusual novelist who has, in her own well-tilled field, no rival and no parallel.' *Times Literary Supplement*

Daughters and Sons is the story of 85-year-old grandmother Sabine Ponsonby and her numerous progeny, of her autocratic grip over their destinies, and their dogged rearguard actions to preserve shreds of individuality. The whole novel is a comic delight and its climax—surely one of the most disastrous dinner parties ever given—would have had Groucho Marx splitting his sides. Could there be higher praise?

Daughters and Sons

One

'Well, gapy-face,' said Mrs. Ponsonby.

A girl of eleven responded to this morning greeting.

'I wasn't yawning, Grandma.'

'Do not lie to me, child; do not lie; do not begin the day by lying,' said Sabine Ponsonby, entering her dining-room and glancing rapidly round it. 'And it would be better to shut your mouth and open your eyes. You will have us confusing one part of your face with the other.'

The confusion would have been easy in Muriel's case, as her features were undefined, and seemed to occupy indeterminate portions of her face, and her tiny, blue, twinkling eyes tended to disappear in attacks of mirth. Sabine used to say that she wondered what she found to laugh at; and others could not enlighten her, as they were more struck than she by the absence of causes for spirits in her grandchild's life.

Sabine was a tall, lean, upright woman, with small, tired, acute eyes in a small, tired, acute face, and rather flat and formless features shaded by a fringe of dyed, dark hair, which had once taken from her years and now protected this period. Nothing about her, save perhaps the smallness of her steps, suggested her eighty-four years, but her face told their tale, and her pale grey eyes were the eyes of a woman of a hundred.

As she went to the bookcase, she gave a tap on the window, without pausing or turning her head. The response seemed as automatic as the signal. The French window opened and four young people entered, and stood about the room as if ill at ease under her eyes.

'Good morning, Grandma,' said a youth of eighteen. 'I am glad you are equal to taking prayers this morning. I do feel that Victor needs that start to his day.'

'Fetch me my glasses and my footstool, Chilton,' said Sabine, without moving a muscle of her face. 'You know I prefer them to be put ready.'

'Victor!' said the first boy, signing to his brother.

Chilton Ponsonby was as much like Sabine as a boy of eighteen could be like a woman of eighty, more indeed than could have been imagined without the proof. His brother, a bare year younger, bore no likeness to her, but had a share of normal good looks, which seemed to affect his demeanour. The two sisters were twenty-four and twenty-five, and both of the grandmother's type, the elder's face being darker and more defined, and the younger's fairer and purer in line. All the elder three had Sabine's small, pale, grey eyes, but Victor's were large and brown, and Muriel's, when they came into view, minute and the colour of the sky. The spaces in age were caused by the deaths of infant children, and Muriel had reversed the family rule and survived at her mother's expense.

Sabine never spoke against her daughter-in-law, though she was incapable of seeing her the fitting mate for her son, and had no scruple in speaking evil of the dead or evil of a mother to her children, indeed seldom spoke anything but evil of any human being. To marry a husband, live with him in intimacy and isolation, bear him children for survival or burial, and die in the effort to continue in this course, appeared to her an honourable history, dignified in life and death. So, prevented from speaking against her, she never spoke of her, and had established the rule.

'You ought to begin to read prayers, Chilton,' she said, in a vaguely wounding and threatening tone which revealed the general view of this office. 'You are the man of the family when your father is away.'

'But you are the woman, Grandma, and that is what counts. Victor, you may settle down and attend. Then I hope you will feel right all day.'

Muriel burst into laughter; Sabine did not admit a flicker to her face; the line of women servants entered, short for the size of the house. Sabine read a portion of the Scriptures in a colourless, recitative tone, as though she gave no particular support to the ceremony. She came to a pause for her audience to kneel, and led them in prayer, remaining in her seat. The Almighty would allow for her rheumatism, as his conception of her had in some way required its infliction, and would hardly be struck by any unsuitability in her abasing herself less than her household. She saw the matter as he would see it, as she assumed that she saw most matters. Her feeling for him was of such a nature that she only needed to have been born fifty years later than her date of eighteen hundred and ten, to fail to recognise him at all. When she ended and the servants were leaving the room, she addressed her eldest granddaughter.

'Did you take that medicine I measured out for you, Clare?'

'No, I did not, Grandma. It does not serve the purpose of medicine: it makes me ill.'

'When I give a direction, I wish it to be followed,' said Sabine, bringing her hand down on the table. 'Why else should I give it? What could be my reason? I do not care to have a member of my house with a dull complexion and a dull manner and a dull face. I do not desire it, for her sake or other people's.'

'Those are natural leanings, but the remedy aggravates the condition, and has even caused it. If I had not swallowed some yesterday, I might not present the appearance you describe.'

'I do not know what your father will think of you.'

'You should know,' said Clare, leaning back and letting her eyelids droop over her eyes. 'You have outlined the impression I produce.'

'Do not be self-conscious and conceited, girl,' said Sabine with a scolding hiss in her voice, thrusting her head forward in a manner which harmonised with it. 'It will not do; it will have to alter; I make no bones about telling you.'

'That is the case; I do not dispute it. But, though self-conscious you may have made me, conceited is not so likely.'

'What about my appearance, Grandma?' said Chilton. 'How does my complexion strike you? What of my appeal to Father? I have noticed it is less than it might be. Have you a remedy?'

'You look as well as you need to look. A boy's appearance is no matter.'

'But how about my expression? People can be made by their expression. "Plain but a sweet expression," they say. Is that how you would sum me up? "His expression made people forget his features." That might be a speech of yours.'

'"Manners makyth man,"' said Sabine. 'I hope you will remember it, Chilton, when you meet your father. I have been meaning to say a word to you. You are altogether too free and easy with him. You are an untrained boy, and he is a distinguished man. The difference cannot be simply passed over.'

'We are untrained certainly: that has been attended to,' said Victor in an undertone half meant to be heard. 'No one is to be blamed if the difference between Father and us is not as great as it can be.'

'Grandma has done what she could, and no one can do more,' said Frances, the second girl, known as France. 'It can only be said, even of her, that she has done her best.'

'Does that refer to your having had a tutor, instead of being sent to a public school?' said Sabine to her grandson.

'We shall have to refer to it soon, and to hear it referred to. It must be reckoned with before long.'

'It need not be reckoned with at all, except in so far as you have had a better education. And you need not be idle because your tutor had to go suddenly. You must be on the lines for Oxford by now, and able to work by yourselves.'

'And the departure was not so sudden,' said Clare in her dry tones. 'The final and intolerable insult had many forerunners. We were prepared.'

Sabine gave a spontaneous and almost pleasant laugh.

'Foolish young man! He repents of his folly by now. He was not important in the house, so why should he be treated as if he were? I hope he has had a lesson.'

'He meant to teach you one,' said France. 'He was, as you say, a foolish young man.'

'Lessons are not for me,' said Sabine with simple emphasis, as she came to the table. 'What should I do with them? I have long ago learnt all I needed. France, why are you and Victor giggling? Of course Muriel follows your example.'

'Would you wish Victor to leave the table, Grandma?' said Chilton, 'If so, I will just say the word to him.'

'He will behave better under my eye.'

'Victor, be a true victor, over yourself,' said his brother.

'Chilton, what is your age?'

'Eighteen and two months, Grandma. There are sixty-four years between us. It makes us such good companions.'

'Then must you carve a cold pheasant as if you were ten years less? Do you suppose no one wants any breast but yourself?'

'I hope no one does. Victor knows he has no claim to any.'

'Did it not occur to you to offer it first to your sisters?'

'I believe you see what occurred to me. There was not much of it.'

'And so you took it for yourself?'

'So I did. You tell me I must earn my bread, and that made me think of having some pheasant with it.'

'Did you suppose the others were tired of pheasants?'

'I supposed they were tired of these. In fact, I knew they were.'

'You may think you are funny, Chilton. I can assure you no one agrees with you.'

'Muriel does. I hear the sound of her young laughter.'

'She has the tricks of her age. Giggling happens to be one of them. It is a nervous habit which we must hope she will leave behind.'

'It is hard to see how we can leave behind nervous habits,' said Clare. 'Probably most of our habits are of that nature.'

'You are feeling in a sour mood this morning, my dear?' said Sabine, looking into her face.

'You know all to be known on that subject, Grandma.'

'Do not take that tone with me, girl,' said Sabine with her scolding hiss.

'Good morning, Mrs. Ponsonby,' said a voice at the door.

'Good morning,' said Sabine, after a moment's pause, her voice responding and doing no more.

'And good morning, everyone else.'

'Good morning, Miss Bunyan,' said Muriel with her eyes down.

'I feel a guilty person this morning.'

Sabine looked in silence at Muriel's governess, a short, square woman of thirty-eight, with bright hazel eyes, bright pink cheeks, roughly hewn features, and an expression consciously straightforward, as though she knew herself to be trustworthy and considered it an asset.

'I feel I do not deserve any breakfast to-day.'

'There should be no more difficulty in coming down for prayers, than for the meal to follow them,' said Sabine, with a piercing quality of tone which accorded with her meaning.

'Well, I would not quite say that, Mrs. Ponsonby, on these sharp mornings,' said Miss Bunyan, calling up a picture which would have been better vague in Sabine's mind.

'Will you have some bacon?' said the latter, as if the suggestion must naturally be an afterthought.

'Yes, please, Mrs. Ponsonby,' said Miss Bunyan, looking straight in front of her, as if the last object of her attention was her plate.

Muriel and Victor exchanged a glance, as Miss Bunyan's appetite was a matter for jest between them, which did not fail them on this occasion, though it had had no chance to be exhibited.

Sabine rather carefully put on a plate a portion which was liberal but not unreasonably so, and handed it to Miss Bunyan. It had not occurred to her that a governess should be treated except as a governess, an attitude more significant than it might sound. Feminine endurance is said to be higher than masculine, and no other explanation can be offered of Miss Bunyan's not having followed the tutor.

'Thank you, Mrs. Ponsonby,' said Miss Bunyan, looking fully at Sabine, as she received the plate.

The family waited while Miss Bunyan ate, having less to look at than was natural in the circumstances, as she made hardly perceptible movements of her mouth, as though seeing mastication one of those things which are inevitable but better passed over.

'It is really more wholesome to be up and about for a while, before settling to a good breakfast,' said Sabine, speaking as the situation suggested.

The movements of Miss Bunyan's jaws became less, so that the continued disappearance of her food was a ground for Muriel's mirth, as its normal disappearance was generally enough to cause it.

'What are you laughing at, Muriel?' enquired Sabine, with a rashness which was more apparent than real.

'Yes, pray let us share the joke, Muriel,' said Miss Bunyan, with less than her natural sincerity.

Muriel sat with eyes cast down and a congested face.

'Why were you so late, Miss Bunyan?' said Sabine, as though a question might be protected by its simplicity.

'I really do not know, Mrs. Ponsonby. I was very tired this morning. I awoke at the sound of the bell, but dropped off again unawares. We are not always our own masters—mistresses in these matters.'

'It is better to get up when the bell rings. That is the object of the bell. Someone has to be up to ring it.'

'Yes, Mrs. Ponsonby, I must take a lesson. I broke that good rule and my unwisdom found me out. I generally do make the effort at the warning, but to-day I was at the end of my tether for some reason. I do not know what I have been doing to exhaust me so much.'

'I do not know either. Exhaust you so much! I cannot throw any light upon it.'

'Well, every day a little bit of one's energy is drained away,' said Miss Bunyan, her manner bright for her words, as if it would compensate for them.

'Not more than should be made up by a good night's rest, a particularly good one in this case,' said Sabine, speaking with truth, as she caused her household to retire at ten, this being the hour she chose for herself.

'Yes, Mrs. Ponsonby, but I had some letters to write. I did not go to bed when we went to our rooms; I sat up for quite a while. The clock had struck twelve before I closed my eyes.' Muriel laughed at this term for repose, and Sabine passed over the lapse as if almost seeing it reasonable. 'I had fallen into sad arrears, and I have been in disgrace with my friends. However, I can hold my head up now.'

As Miss Bunyan made this movement, it struck her that she did not do so in her professional character.

'There is so little time for writing letters in the day, that I wait until I am in my room and master—mistress of an hour.'

'Master or mistress of ten and a half hours,' said Sabine. 'And you have the time between tea and dinner to yourself. We should work and play in the day and sleep at night. Then we do justice to ourselves and those we are responsible for.'

'I am always fresh for my work, Mrs. Ponsonby, if that is what you mean.'

'Yes, that is what I mean,' said Sabine evenly. 'How can you be that, when you continue your private occupations until midnight, and then are too heavy with sleep to rise for breakfast?'

'I am not even a very good sleeper, Mrs. Ponsonby,' said Miss Bunyan, looking at Sabine with dilating eyes, and then thinking better of her impulse and returning to her point. 'I am quite rested this morning. And I think a good catching-up is better than a series of driblets, which drain one's freshness and get one nowhere. I was really in bed before midnight, and I take care of myself at such times. I keep a tin of biscuits in my room.' She hurried on, sensing something in the silence. 'I do not believe in treating night as day in one way and not in another. That is an inconsistence one may pay for.'

'I do not believe in treating night as day at all. And your plan of eating at odd times is not wholesome for properly fed people.'

Muriel's gravity broke down over the subject of the nourishment of her governess, whose life she did not make an easy one.

'I do not call it eating between meals to eat when you are sitting up,' said Miss Bunyan with another note in her tone. 'That constitutes a little meal by itself. We are asleep when we go for many hours without food.'

'I do not need to reduce such things to a system. I find the established system enough for me.'

'Well, an educationist has to be a systematic person, Mrs. Ponsonby. So I do reduce them to a system, and keep a little store by me in case of emergencies. I have had some wakeful nights lately, and I find that sleep is induced more readily by a mouthful——'

'Have we all finished?' said Sabine, rising while Miss Bunyan spoke. 'I think we have sat about long enough, and if sleep is induced by mouthfuls, we shall all be snoring in our chairs if we go on like this. And Muriel must get her run before her lessons.' She turned to her grandchild and spoke with her scolding hiss. 'This will not do, Muriel; I will not tolerate it. If you do not improve, I must ask your father to find you a home elsewhere. My behaviour need not affect yours. We could not be further removed than we are.' She moved to the bell, confident that her grandchild would view with consternation a life passed under different conditions. 'Now let us all go about our occupations.'

'I think I will have some marmalade, Mrs. Ponsonby,' said Miss Bunyan, in a rather high monotone. 'I came down later than the rest.'

'Yes, I know you did; I thought we had waited for you; we seemed to be waiting. When Gertrude comes, she can leave your place and clear round it. Gertrude, you may leave Miss Bunyan's place. Clare, you may help Gertrude.'

'She has managed without my help every morning for seven years.'

'Feeling them but a day for the love she bare us,' said Victor.

'I don't like to see you mooning about from morning till night. It is not good for your nerves or your temper, or for the nerves and tempers of those who have to be with you. You are a thundercloud over the house.'

'Moving cups and saucers will hardly solve the problems of

my life.'

'Take care, Grandma,' said Victor. 'Thunderclouds burst, and you mentioned that this one was over the house.'

'I shall not take care in my own house,' said Sabine, who seemed to feel a complacence in demanding indefinite licence for herself in this sphere. 'I have no use for thunderclouds, and they will not burst under my roof. I should not tolerate it.'

'It seems extraordinary that we have lived so long in Grandma's house,' said Clare. 'I can hardly believe it.'

Miss Bunyan looked up with a little laugh that made light of the matter.

'Yes, you are all only fit to be laughed at,' said Sabine. 'Miss Bunyan is right.'

'Is there anything I can do for you before lessons, Mrs. Ponsonby?' said Miss Bunyan, rising with a briskness born of this approval and rolling her napkin.

'No, I like you to have this hour to yourself, so as to be ready for your work. Teaching demands the whole of a person's energy. You do not generally do things for me at this time: I do not know why to-day is an exception. And I do not know what you mean by saying you have no time for your letters, and so have to get up and camp out in the middle of the night. I do not understand it.'

'Miss Bunyan does not either,' said Clare.

'What are you doing to-day, boys?' said Sabine.

'I think I should devote myself to Victor, Grandma. I have somehow felt less hopeless about him lately, and my reward is the sweeter for being hardly earned.'

'What are you doing, Clare?' said Sabine in her even manner. 'I suppose nothing?'

'Why ask a question when you know the answer? As you say, nothing.'

'Clare and I can be together,' said Chilton; 'and I have a feeling that our combined influence may do something for our brother.'

'What are you doing, France?'

'I want to finish some writing, Grandma.'

'To finish it! That is good news, if the writing has made you so dull and absent-minded lately. You have hardly opened your mouth this morning, except to eat. But we will say no more about it, if it is coming to an end.'

'Then you will have two of us in my situation,' said Clare.

'Perhaps you congratulate yourself too soon.'

'You are sure I cannot help you at all, Mrs. Ponsonby?'

'Miss Bunyan, I told you I wished you to have this hour to yourself. Do not oblige me to repeat myself. I am tired this morning and I cannot stand it.'

'I should be glad to be of any use, Mrs. Ponsonby.'

Sabine put her hand to her head and hurried from the room, and so out of earshot of Miss Bunyan.

She left behind her a silence, which Miss Bunyan eventually broke in a bright tone.

'Well, now there is only my place left. I will clear it and save Gertrude the trouble. I am used to clearing tables. One of the results of our family misfortunes—reverses, I believe, is the word—is that I am more fitted to be left on a desert island than most people.' She gathered up cutlery and china, and with this furniture of a desert island in her hands, found herself face to face with Sabine.

'Grandma seems to alight like a bird,' said Victor. 'Poor Miss Bunyan, caught red-handed!'

Sabine advanced without a glance aside.

'What is all this rubbish in your room, France?'

'Well, it may or may not be rubbish, Grandma. I still hope it is not. It is the book I have written, and want to show to Father.'

'Well, finish writing it down here. Why must you creep away to do it?'

'I don't know why people creep away when they begin to write. I daresay they have every cause to be ashamed, but I am not sure that is their reason. I did not want Chilton to see it until it was done.'

'You could have told him not to look at it.'

'Grandma, you have always thought better of me than I deserved,' said her grandson.

'Why does it matter its being seen?'

'It does not matter now. I should like as many people as possible to see it, not stopping short of the general public. Would you like to read it, Grandma?'

'You shall read it to me some time,' said Sabine with indulgence. 'I can see you are excited at the moment. It should be an advantage to you to have your father a writer.'

'There are different results from talent running in a family,' said Chilton.

'Talent! Oh, we don't know about that. Hard and constant work is the thing, as her father will tell her.'

'Your instructions are inconsistent,' said Clare.

'I make no claim to consistency.'

'In your own house,' said Victor.

'Victor, remember you are speaking to Grandma,' said Chilton.

'Just fancy, two authors in the house! I feel quite proud of belonging to it,' said Miss Bunyan.

'Miss Bunyan, have I to put it into words, that I prefer to be left alone with my grandchildren sometimes? We must be allowed a little family life. No one can belong to another person's house to that extent.'

'Oh, I am sorry, Mrs. Ponsonby. I did not know—I had no idea,' said Miss Bunyan, hurrying to the door with a flushing face and somehow an inability to refer in words to the distastefulness of her presence.

'Grandma, you are ruder than is human,' said Victor. 'I almost admire it.'

'I do not,' said Clare.

'If you arrange for a woman to be in your house, having need of her in it, she must be there,' said France.

'I have no need of her; I have need of her services. She ought to know the difference. If she does not, she had better learn. You need not try to teach your grandmother anything.' Sabine became emphatic over her imperviousness to improvement. 'It will be of no avail.'

'Utterly fruitless,' said Clare, 'But if I were Miss Bunyan, I would leave you with your grandchildren for good.'

'No, you would not. That is how young people talk. You would be thankful for a good home, as she is. People do not want to find themselves without food to eat, Miss Bunyan least of all.'

Muriel laughed at the picture called up.

'It is not much of a home, where you are not allowed about,' said Chilton.

'There is always so much talk about what Miss Bunyan eats,' said France, 'and I never saw anyone eat so unobtrusively. She would be better off without food than most of us, as she has her own private stores.'

'And she has meals at home,' said Chilton, 'because she told us she cleared them. I like very much to hear about Miss

Bunyan's private life. I wonder why she writes all those letters. If she paid a yearly visit to each of her friends, she would not need to be here.'

'Oh, that talk about friends!' said Sabine. 'She does need to be here. Very few letters come for her, and those only from her family. Now I have something to say to you all, and I desire your attention. I will not have you answer me and hold your views against mine, as you have been doing of late. I am your grandmother and a woman who knows the world, and you are inexperienced boys and girls; and that gulf'—She brought her hand down on the table—'cannot be bridged. If you do not know when to be silent, I must see that you learn.'

'It sounds as if you have blamed Miss Bunyan unjustly,' said France. 'Family intercourse does not seem to have been hampered by her presence, or not enough for you to notice it.'

'It does not matter how it sounds. You have got into a habit of disrespect, and I do not care how soon you get out of it. Boys, would you like to go out with Muriel, as you are free from work?'

'Point out to us the connection, Grandma,' said Victor.

'As you will, as you will; I will not force your little sister on you. Clare, you can go out with her.'

'Would you force her upon me, Grandma? It is not worth while. She has gone into the garden, and her lessons begin at ten.'

'Then go into the garden with her. I have made it clear that I do not desire her to be alone. I do not know what you think is your place in the house, or why you think I want you in it.'

'We are clear that you do not want us in it. I claim no place.'

'You are all silly children,' said Sabine, taking up her glasses and the paper. 'Girls, go into the garden to Muriel. You seem to be unable to hear me.'

'We cannot make that claim,' said Clare, strolling through the window. 'Muriel, Grandma feels you will be the better for our presence. In what way may we serve you?'

'Why did Grandma come down in such a bad temper?' said Muriel. 'And Miss Bunyan made it worse, didn't she?'

Muriel's life with older people had led her to couch her remarks in the form of a question, as if she desired mature confirmation.

'You must not burst into laughter over Miss Bunyan's every

mouthful. Naturally we all eat.'

'Not as much as Miss Bunyan, do we?' said Muriel, with unusual gravity.

'She will be leaving, if you do not take care, and Grandma will not acquit you of guilt because she has been your accessory. Why should Miss Bunyan's every meal be made a burden?'

'Meals would never be a burden to Miss Bunyan,' said Muriel, with a confidence which justified a statement.

'I suppose she looks down on us all, and so puts up with us. I tremble to think what would be my opinion of this family in her place.'

This idea was strange to the pupil, who had assumed, perhaps perceived, that her instructress looked up to the employing house.

'Her meals are certainly difficult to-day,' said France. 'She is not to come to dinner because Father and Aunt Hetta are coming home. I don't know who is to tell her.'

'I could tell her, couldn't I?' said Muriel with a lift of her voice.

'You will not dream of it,' said Clare. 'It is Grandma's business, though that will not be much better. Your chief interest appears to be Miss Bunyan's inconvenience, and I admit that no one has provided you with any other.'

Sabine smiled to herself at the sisters' laughter, congratulating herself on the manner of home she gave them, and read *The Times* until interrupted by Miss Bunyan.

'I really must make it clear, Mrs. Ponsonby, that I require Muriel to come to me punctually at ten. We have only just time to get through our mapped out work, with the interruption for milk at eleven'—The speaker's attitude was clear towards this break—'and real luncheon's being at a quarter past one. It is so unsatisfactory to me not to see her do herself justice, and not to do justice to myself. There are certain things upon which I am justified in insisting.'

Sabine drew down her glasses with an easiness born of the retaliatory note in Miss Bunyan's tone, and leaned towards the window.

'Muriel! Come in at once to your lessons! Miss Bunyan is waiting for you. Do not keep her another moment. Girls, you should have sent her in at ten. You know that is her time.'

'It is eight minutes past,' said Miss Bunyan in an aggrieved manner.

'You might have come for her at ten,' said Sabine, 'or, better still, a few minutes before.'

'No, Mrs. Ponsonby, I do not really come and call my pupil to her work. I am at the table, waiting for her, prepared for her course, looking forward to seeing her acquit herself well; and I require her to be as punctual as I am, and as interested. I am disappointed that she was not waiting this morning, considering how enthusiastic we were yesterday, and how reluctant to close our books at the bell.'

'You can miss your break for milk to-day, if you like. You will hardly need it, with breakfast dragging on so late. That is what put the girls out in the time.'

'Now, that is very nice,' said Miss Bunyan, putting her hands together. 'We shall be able to go straight on and get our comprehensive views, without any pulling up. That is quite a pleasant little piece of news.'

'Your mid-morning luncheon need not disturb you as much as all that,' said Sabine, with the piercing note. 'Its object is not to distract you from your work, but to keep you up to it. I hope it does not fail of its purpose? You say yourself you cannot go for long without food.'

Miss Bunyan glanced at the window to see who was within hearing.

'And so it does keep us up to it. I am not suggesting any independence of the good things of life, the necessary things shall we call them in this case? I give them their own fair place, as is right and meet.'

'We can say good things, I think, without worrying about the term. We can claim that such things are good in this house. I am not quite sure they are necessary, in the middle of the morning.'

'Now I have caught you!' exclaimed Miss Bunyan, turning and laying hold of her pupil's shoulder. 'And you will not escape me again, so do not think it.'

She conducted Muriel from the room with a martial step, and Sabine smoothly returned to her paper.

'Grandma, you seem fated to talk to Miss Bunyan about her food,' said Clare from the window.

'Governesses are always concerned about what they eat,' said Sabine, giving the paper a shake to straighten it. 'They find themselves where the food is better than in their homes, and they have no other interest in their lives.'

'I shall begin to cry in a moment,' said Victor. 'To think that Muriel darkens a human creature's only joy!'

'Teaching is the highest of all callings. I am always teaching people myself,' said Sabine with her natural sequence of thought. 'There are grades in all callings, of course.'

'We are alive to the grades,' said Clare.

'You boys might go for a walk with France,' said Sabine. 'You are getting to be nice companions.'

'She is busy,' said Chilton. 'She wants to write this morning.'

'That does not matter in your holidays. She has her life to write in. You talk as if she were your father.' Sabine rose and rapped at the window and spoke without raising her voice. 'France, come and go for a ramble with the boys. They are waiting for you, and cannot wait any longer.'

'But for you, they would have gone on waiting, Grandma.'

'Why do you rap and call, Grandma, when you want anyone?' said Clare. 'Why don't you send a message? We are all with you, and if you are alone you can ring.'

'I have other things to do than ring, and the servants have other things to do than answer. I can't keep a large family in idleness, if we want waiting on, as well as several meals a day cooked and served and cleared and washed up for us. That in itself is a day's work.'

'It is odd how we always get round to meals.'

'It is not at all odd. Meals must always be a great part of life, the first object of a woman's thought, of servants' work, of a man's income. You may some day have a chance to learn it.'

'The promise of the future,' said Clare.

'Excelsior!' said Chilton, raising his arms.

'I have borne enough,' said Sabine, going to the door. 'I will bear no more. It is time your father took a hand with you. You are too much for me at my age. I don't wish to see you again before luncheon. You will turn up then, I don't doubt.'

'Meals are certainly the first object of a woman's thought,' said Clare.

'Why is it odd to turn up for them? Most people are fed,' said France. 'What good would there be in them, if we did not? I believe Miss Bunyan has a good deal to eat at home, as well as some over to bring away. She has the habit of it, though I would not say so to Muriel.'

'Are you going to give Father your book to read?' said Clare.

'I can hardly ask his advice, if I withhold it. He won't expect me to be sensitive about it. Writers don't judge other people by themselves.'

'I daresay not their daughters,' said Victor. 'It would not be natural.'

'Make him see that the matter is important to you, France,' said Clare, 'and so should be important to him.'

'Things cannot always follow like that,' said Victor.

'It is important in itself,' said Chilton. 'Clare has not read the book. It is better in its way than anything of Father's.'

'You can't have Father's books in your mind to that extent,' said his brother. 'Indeed, I know you have not.'

'I know just how far he can go.'

'You are too young to get right inside a mature brain.'

'But, Victor, you seem to think you are inside mine.'

'If Grandma knew, France thinks so much more is due to her than meals.'

'People are so sensitive about their relations' productions,' said France. 'I shall find myself Father's relation for the first time.'

'You may find yourself so in another sense,' said Clare. 'He gives full attention to any family matter. In his way he is the head of his family, and likes to be.'

'He could not hold his public without his popular touch,' said Victor. 'And we should be badly off, if he did not hold it. Why do we take this attitude, when we do not expect him to take it to France?'

'I wish the trouble were not just what it is,' said France. 'It would be nothing, if the work which holds his public, were just not the best. But it is not his best. He would have written better, if he had written for fewer and earned less. And it is for us that he earns; he does not spend on himself. It is all subtle and sad, and he is very pathetic.'

'My good girl, so are you,' said Victor.

'He is not pathetic,' said Chilton. 'He is an over praised, over sensitive, over successful man. We may suggest his pathos, so that France may be prepared for it. He has no real pathos. He has always had more of everything than he deserved, more praise, more money, more affection, more of everything. To have so much more than you have deserved, is not to be so unfortunate.'

'It will not happen to any of us,' said France. 'So we will keep our pity for our own pathos. We may need our own tears.'

'We shed them,' said Clare.

'How does Father see himself? Is his life a success to him or a conscious sacrifice?'

'Don't be absurd, France,' said Victor. 'What will your life be, if you meet his success? Not a sacrifice. Use the term where it is fit.'

'He wins so much affection,' said Chilton. 'That is what puzzles me about him. He clearly has Victor's, and Victor has very little affection to give.'

'And, as we see, has none over,' said France.

'And he has yours, France, and will continue to have it. Though he slay you, yet will you trust in him.'

'That seems to me a very odd sentiment. I require a service from him.'

'Frances does see him rather as the Almighty,' said Clare.

'The Almighty never had a daughter,' said her sister. 'He did not risk feminine insight. I see Father as a toiling, companionable man, oppressed by Grandma.'

'We all share that bond.'

'We have each other, Clare. And when people have each other, it seems to be recognised that other things do not matter. I suppose even each other's troubles. Indeed it seems to be those that do not matter.'

'It is so odd to me that France and Father are congenial,' said Chilton. 'I expect he thinks he is single for his daughters' sake; I daresay he was at first. I can hardly credit his being congenial to a wife and a sister and three daughters: I find him so uncongenial. And I believe Grandma would, if she did not see him as her son.'

'I hope I shall live to be old,' said France, 'and take advantage of it. My grandchildren shall have a governess. Shall we be in time for luncheon, or a little late? Which will cause us less humiliation?'

'Well, so you turn up like bad pennies,' said Sabine at the table. 'Now what was there in what I said, to send you all into laughter? You do not seem properly balanced. Miss Bunyan, what did you see amusing in my speech?'

'I do not know, Mrs. Ponsonby. The laughter was so infectious that I found myself joining in it unawares.'

'We do not want to laugh at nothing, any more than we want to talk about nothing, or to sit down at the table with nothing to eat. That last does not happen to us, does it?'

'Or to many other people,' said Clare.

'No, fortunately none of us has had that experience,' said Miss Bunyan.

'What kind of a morning's work have you had, Miss Bunyan?' said Sabine, leaving the subject at this spirit of dealing with it.

'Not at all good, Mrs. Ponsonby, I am afraid. I have to admit it to a question put straight like that. We did not begin to concentrate until the last hour, and then we had to break our only good spell.'

'Dear me, that is not at all good hearing. I was anxious to report good progress to Muriel's father. Between us all we must manage that the good spells come a little oftener. I do not know what we are to do about it.'

'I do not know either. We cannot undo the past,' said Miss Bunyan, who would have undone it, if she had foreseen this attitude. 'We cannot go back and live it again, as I was explaining to Muriel. She and I have been quite at a difference this morning.'

'It takes two to make a difference,' said Sabine, in a tone so even that the meaning seemed incidental. 'Would you like to have another hour's work between four and five?'

'Oh, now that will be very nice, Muriel,' said Miss Bunyan, turning her eye to her pupil. 'Now here is a chance to pick up and retrace our steps, and almost go back and live the past again after all. I may be able to eat my words, and very glad I shall be to do so.' Muriel gave a tremor of laughter at the choice of metaphor. 'We may redeem our day yet.'

'Well, if all is going to be well by ending well, we need not say any more about it. Will you have some more lamb, Miss Bunyan?'

'Thank you, Mrs. Ponsonby, I will have a little,' said Miss Bunyan, clearly not constrained to refuse by any feeling of discomfiture. 'I think an unsatisfactory morning's work takes it out of one more than a good one.'

'Yes, it must be like working in a mine, without striking a vein of coal,' said Sabine in her occasional genial manner. 'We must hope that history will not repeat itself on this occasion.'

'I don't think it will, eh, Muriel?' said Miss Bunyan, almost winking at her pupil, as she accepted her plate. 'I hardly think history made enough of a first impression this morning, for any repetition to be possible.'

'Well, we must see what an hour will do towards remedying all the omission. I fear it is but a short time for what it has to do.'

'Oh, an hour is an hour, Mrs. Ponsonby, and an extra hour is an extra hour and has all the possibility of an extra. An extra hour, an extra holiday, an extra treat, an extra opportunity'—Miss Bunyan modified the tendency of her ideas—'how different they are from ordinary hours and treats and opportunities! And this hour is an hour and a treat and an opportunity all in one. It is only of the nature of the holiday that it will not partake. And it will not partake of that indeed, I can assure my victim and my pupil.'

'It is almost time that Muriel had that hour as an ordinary thing,' said Sabine, giving her own account of it.

'Well, that would give me more scope, Mrs. Ponsonby.'

'Muriel will be the only one of us with a normal start in life,' said Victor.

'Father hardly had one,' said France. 'He began to write when he was almost a boy. Grandma would have had to give up the house, if he had not begun to earn.'

'That is quite true, France,' said Sabine, with a half-amused smile. 'It is right you should know, as it gives you the measure of your father. But there is no need to emphasise that side of things; it is a form of conceit and defeats its own object. Our rents went down and your father's income was a help, but he has never carried the full burden of his family. Your grandfather left me the place to manage for us all, and your aunt's being single has helped me to keep things the same. It may not always be so, and you may feel the difference. But as things are, it is silly to harp on that note. You are more without knowledge of the world than you should be at your age.'

'Father does not make any secret of his history.'

'It adds to him, but it does not add to you. You have no history. You have been lapped in luxury from your birth. To talk as you were doing is an affectation, and might be construed as a bid for admiration.'

'I have seen it that in Father's case,' said Chilton. 'And it serves its purpose. Admiration follows it.'

'It will not follow it in your sister's.'

'I think you are so right, Mrs. Ponsonby,' said Miss Bunyan rapidly. 'We have found it in my own father's case. It is parallel with what you describe. He had every advantage until his father died, and then it came to his taking up a most unsuitable profession, though he has done his best in it for all our sakes. And sight is always lost of his being what he is—lost in some cases to be fairer—and stand is taken upon his occupation, as if that bore upon his essential position or the personal touch——'

'Yes, that is how it would be,' said Sabine. 'But this case is different. My son has no unsuitable profession, though it was rather a departure in the family; and stand may be taken upon it, if it is desired. So the cases are not parallel. Now Muriel must get out for her walk, if she is to be at her books by four.'

'And she is certainly to be that,' said Miss Bunyan, rising from the table. 'So come, Muriel. We shall get as far as the woods if we are quick.'

'Don't hurry, and try to keep in the shade,' said Sabine. 'It is wiser not to walk fast in the sun after a solid meal.'

Miss Bunyan slackened her pace and then quickened it, adapting her energy to what had preceded it. Sabine went upon an errand of her own, not looking at her grandchildren. Chilton perceived her bonnet and cloak lying ready for the garden. He put them on, pulled some horse-hair from the couch and pushed it into the bonnet for a fringe, and walked up and down with a gait calculated to recall his grandmother's.

'Clare, your face has a muddy tinge. France, are you making a bid for admiration? Muriel, I do not like this report, but we will not talk about it after such a meal.'

Muriel broke into laughter; her sisters joined; Miss Bunyan returned and stood silent, prevented from joining by the last words; Sabine followed and, going to her grandson, stood simply with extended hands.

Chilton divested himself with awkwardness, dropping his eyes as he came to his fringe; Miss Bunyan maintained her gravity and beckoned to her pupil; Sabine went out with a slightly hurt expression, turning to cast a word behind.

'If you have nothing better to do than spoil the furniture, you may come and help me water my plants. You might have noticed I was going to do them alone.'

'Surely you were not?' said Clare. 'It would have been the first time within my memory. And the sun is on the flowers.'

'The sun is not on them any more because I ask you to help. You could have stopped me, if you thought I should do any harm. The sun will not hurt these large plants, if we keep the water to the roots. Chilton, take the heavy can and follow me. France may bring the smaller one.'

'Victor, Grandma does not ask your help,' said Chilton. 'Have you asked yourself the reason?'

'Clearly nothing would have stopped her,' murmured France.

'We ought to have another hose,' said Clare.

'No, we ought not, with four able-bodied young people in my little personal garden. Hoses have to be bought and paid for. You seem to think things are to be had for the asking.'

'If I thought that, I should have profited ill by my training.'

'You would have been very ill trained.'

'You are watering your skirt as much as the flowers, Grandma,' said France. 'But the sun on a wet skirt is better than on wet plants.'

'And Grandma's garden skirt seems ready for a little water,' said Victor.

'A drop,' said Sabine, glancing down at her dress. 'You have silly manners, both you girls. I must have a word with your father.'

'It may be well to direct his attention to us,' said Clare.

'I cannot bear it,' said Sabine, suddenly, putting her hand to her head. 'I cannot, the sun and the argument and everything. It is too much. I must go and lie down, to be able to face the evening. You can go on without me: I daresay you will be without me altogether before long.'

She went into the house, an upright, swift old figure, and her grandchildren continued their employment, as if at home in the position.

Sabine went up to the schoolroom, her air becoming one of mild purpose. She rang for some tea, observing to the maid who brought it that the room was in the shade. Then she rummaged gently on Miss Bunyan's desk, restoring each object to its exact place. When she came on a fresh, unposted letter, she put it with a smooth, automatic movement on the hot water jug, and when the glue melted, opened and read it without any touch of instinctive furtiveness.

'MY DEAR FATHER,

'I am indulging in an orgy of letter writing in my own room at night, and am greatly sustained by Mother's biscuits. I have less time as I become more valued, and I do not quarrel with the cause. My pupil is attached, and her grandmother, though an eccentric old lady, whom we all combine to serve, gives me her complete trust, though I say it as shouldn't. The grown up sisters and half grown up brothers are very kind, and I am made quite one of themselves. Indeed I shall soon be addressing Mrs. Ponsonby as "Grandma," if I do not take care. Not that she would mind, as I am already "my dear." Her son, my pupil's father, is returning to-night, John Ponsonby, the novelist. Mrs. Ponsonby seems to think that as members of intellectual professions we should be thrown together. I will leave this letter open in case of more to say to-morrow. At the moment my pillow invites.

'Your affectionate daughter,

'DOROTHEA.'

Sabine read the letter with experienced calm, finding no reason to move a feature of her face, and restored it to the desk with a sense of having had no need to open it. She met the governess in her ordinary manner, as she had found no occasion to change it.

Miss Bunyan and her pupil came to the table, looking self-conscious and expectant of question. They usually had tea in the schoolroom alone, but to-day there was domestic pressure, and the schoolroom and family meals were combined. Muriel yawned as she took her seat, her day having been more arduous than usual. The governess witnessed the action and involuntarily copied it.

'Well, gapy-face!' said Sabine, turning her eyes to her grandchild just in time.

'I wasn't yawning, Grandma.'

'Do not lie to me, child; do not lie.'

Miss Bunyan again and waveringly put her hand to her mouth.

'It is amazing how infectious yawning is,' she said, her manner less amazed than uneasy.

'We should be prepared for that, when it is a known thing,' said Sabine, raising her own hand, continuing the movement to her hair, and touching it before she brought the hand down again. 'Well, how did the hour's work go along?'

'Very well indeed, Mrs. Ponsonby. I feel we have quite re-deemed our day. I shall go to bed with a much lighter heart, than if we had not had our chance to recover.'

'Well, I hope you will really go to bed, and not sit up writing letters, especially as bed seems to be the goal of everything.'

'Yes, indeed I shall, Mrs. Ponsonby. I am very tired to-night and shall be glad to get my head on the pillow,' said Miss Bunyan, possibly dazed by weariness.

'I wonder what has tired you so much,' said Sabine, while Muriel giggled at the realistic phrase.

'Well, there was an unsatisfactory morning's work to begin with, a much more tiring thing than the other kind, and then a long walk, and then our energetic hour to retrieve. It all mounts up, you know.'

'It sounds an ordinary day's occupation. I am inclined to think it was writing letters late at night.'

'Well, well, then I must not write letters late at night, Mrs. Ponsonby,' said Miss Bunyan, with a change of manner.

'I am glad we have come to one mind about it. Now will you have another baked egg? You must need one after your walk, if it has taken it out of you, though they do say that the fresh air is very feeding.'

'No, Mrs. Ponsonby, I could not, thank you. One is quite enough, after a good luncheon and with dinner to follow.' Miss Bunyan made no mention of the item of the air, though Muriel's look at Victor included it with the others. 'One is enough indeed.'

'I think it would be,' said Sabine, continuing to insert the spoon. 'Indeed I do not think we should need one, with dinner to follow. I am not taking one, you see. But we are having a family gathering tonight, to welcome my son and daughter; so you must eat a good enough meal to carry you on till bedtime. You will not sleep, if you are hungry, and I don't suppose your stock of biscuits is proof against too frequent inroads.'

'Thank you, Mrs. Ponsonby, then I will have another,' said Miss Bunyan, with pleasant ease and a slow flush which con-tradicted it. 'I am quite glad of the opportunity as they are so good. And I shall have a chance to go over Muriel's books, and decide what work will best follow on. This is to be a catching-up day in every respect. And I am quite glad of it. It takes away that feeling of being a little out of breath that one has sometimes.'

'I should not work to-night. You must need an evening to yourself sometimes, especially if you find yourself out of breath. I believe I am the youngest person in the house at my age. What are you laughing at, Muriel? If there is a joke, let us share it.'

'Yes, Mrs. Ponsonby, let us. Be kind to us, Muriel, and don't leave us out.'

Muriel was kinder in merely gazing at the wall.

'I know your father's name so well, Muriel,' resumed Miss Bunyan, in a tone of general conversation. 'John Ponsonby is quite a household word with us.'

'It does not suggest her father to Muriel,' said Sabine. 'It is naturally not a household word here.'

'As a family we have unsuccessful names,' said Clare. 'I think Victor comes off the worst.'

'I think Victor is a charming name,' said Miss Bunyan, 'and it means just what it says, which is nice and straightforward.'

'What is your name, Miss Bunyan?' said Victor, who was aware of it.

'Dorothea.'

'And what does it mean?'

There was a pause.

'Come, come, where is your Greek?' said Miss Bunyan.

'Well, what does it mean?' said Sabine.

'The gift of God,' said Miss Bunyan in a light, easy tone, which was lost in her pupil's laughter.

'Do not be foolish, child,' said Sabine, laughing gently herself. 'We are all regarded as gifts when we come. I daresay even you were.'

Miss Bunyan looked in front of her.

'Miss Bunyan might have liked some notice, Grandma, that she would have an evening of her own,' said Clare.

'Oh, you need not both about her not coming to dinner,' said Sabine, with a final and reckless sloughing of convention. 'There is no need for it to be smoothed away and glossed over, as if there were something wrong in our having some family life.'

'I hope there is not anything wrong in it,' said France, 'for it is a temptation we often yield to. Indeed I think it is getting the better of us.'

'It is pleasanter for Miss Bunyan and all of us, for us not to be always tied up together.'

'It makes it more interesting to meet again,' said Miss Bunyan.

'That is so,' said Sabine. 'Do not begin to giggle, Muriel. It may not be interesting to meet a silly little girl, but that does not apply to anyone else, so be quiet.'

Sabine, having thus suggested the probable reason of her granddaughter's mirth, was silent, and Miss Bunyan looked about with a bright expression.

'There is not much hope that we may strike Miss Bunyan afresh to-morrow,' said Clare. 'For Father our companionship may have the charm of novelty.'

'Why do you suppose a gifted man like your father should so often wish for your company?'

'I do not suppose it: I was observing it was not the case. Even as I am, I have not avoided remarking that parents and children are in many cases thrown together.'

'We will continue this meal in silence,' said Sabine, putting her hand to her head.

'A good idea, Mrs. Ponsonby. It is sometimes quite a rest—— Oh, I beg your pardon,' said Miss Bunyan. 'Have you a headache?'

'We will continue this meal in silence,' faintly repeated Sabine.

They continued it in silence, and at its end, or what she saw as such, Sabine rose and left the room, turning at the door.

'You can pour out the tea, Clare, if anyone can drink any more.'

'I can drink some more and eat some more, can't I?' said Muriel.

'You are growing,' said Miss Bunyan, indulgent in this sphere, and also, it might have been felt, magnanimous.

'No, you cannot, Muriel,' said Sabine, looking back. 'Drink what you like, but remember you are to come to dinner, and only need a light meal now. I do not want your father to think you have no appetite; it would be such an unnecessary mistake. Miss Bunyan is the one who has to make a meal. You can look after her.'

'I have to compress two meals into one,' said Miss Bunyan, lightly. 'It sounds quite a feat of skill.'

Murial laughed at the probable suitability of the phrase.

'I shall have to make myself eat more than I want.'

Further laughter commented on the effort's likely result.

'We must not get into the way of feeling self-conscious over having reasonable appetites,' said Miss Bunyan, in an educational tone. 'That is a piece of foolishness which we have grown out of, which only exists in the lower classes now. I hope you are listening, Muriel. I should not like to have to tell you before your grandmother.'

Muriel giggled at the truth of these words.

'I should hate Miss Bunyan to have to tell me anything before Grandma,' said Chilton.

'Muriel seems unsteady to-day. If I did not know her, I should say she was hysterical,' said Miss Bunyan, who was certainly alive to genuine amusement in her pupil.

'She is at the tiresome age,' said Clare.

'Yes, we must put it down to that.'

'Muriel and Victor must go through these stages,' said Chilton with a sigh.

'She is at the age when it is usual for a child to need training,' said Sabine, returning to the room with a vase of flowers, an almost recognised pretext for her appearance at any moment, versed in the conversation. 'If she were perfect, there would be no need of it, or of anyone to carry it out. But I do wish, Miss Bunyan, that you could cure her of this trick of giggling at everything, at nothing. It is a silly habit.'

'I wish I could, Mrs. Ponsonby,' said Miss Bunyan sincerely, 'but it was a fixed habit when I came.' She spoke these words with a flush. 'But I will do my best.'

'Of course, I do not mind her laughing when there is anything to laugh at.'

'Of course not,' said Miss Bunyan.

Muriel strove anew with her mirth.

'What is the joke now, child?' said Sabine. 'Your father will anyhow find you in good spirits.'

'Nothing, Grandma.'

'Well, there you are, you see,' said Miss Bunyan.

Two

'Well, Mater; well, children,' said Henrietta Ponsonby, as she entered the house with her brother and cast her quick glance round the hall. 'Well, how have you been without us? How have you got through the last weeks? We can't help wanting a holiday sometimes, can we? Shut the door, someone! Cannot anyone shut a door? It does not seem an impossible thing, with all these able-bodied people about.' The speaker stood aside, as if to shut the door herself would have been unfitting. 'Well, are you glad to have us back again? Or would you like us to leave you for good?'

'No, Aunt Hetta,' said Muriel.

'You would not like it? Well then, perhaps we won't do it this time. Take those books from your father, Chilton. Don't stand about empty-handed, with older people laden. I can see you want me back: I expect you feel it. Girls, have you spoken to your father? Are you not glad to see him? You have been thinking of his coming, I suppose? Or have you no feelings on the occasion? I do not believe in feelings that are not expressed. They say that still waters run deep, but in my experience they do not run at all.' Hetta's tone had significance beyond the occasion and took on the piercing note of Sabine's. 'You hardly seem the sort of daughters people would expect. But you need not hang on his arm, France. That won't make him any less tired, will it? The weight of a grown young woman is not an advantage. Or do you think it is? Now, John, you have had your word with them. You can come away until dinner. It will be on the table in an hour, and you will have them all round you again.'

Hetta Ponsonby was a pale, fair, upright woman of forty-eight, who was vital without being physically vigorous, and stately without being tall. She had the family flattish features and pale grey eyes in so much finer a form, that she seemed as good-looking as Victor in another way. Her brother was a tall, top-heavy-looking man, a few years older, with a dark, ruddy face, dark, clear eyes, a wide, nervous nose and a deep, square head which linked him with his elder children. He resembled on the whole his father, whose type he had transmitted to his younger son, without great likeness to himself.

There was a touch of the conscious artist in his clothes and his pointed beard, the result of his break with tradition and service to the pen. His mother surveyed him with controlled, maternal eyes, as if she would have seen him differently, if he had not been her son. His face was old for his years, and had a look of exhaustion beneath its colour and constant change.

'Well, here are my reasons for life and work,' he said, with the rather laboured liveliness which had become his manner. 'I would not have only my public to serve. They are all equally my children, those and these.'

'Too large a family,' said Clare. 'The attention cannot go round.'

'Do not begin to whisper at the moment we arrive,' said her aunt. 'Look about to see if there is anything you can do. Chilton, there are your father's books. I have spoken before.'

'I made a sign to Victor, Aunt Hetta.'

'Well, my fellow men, how is the world with you?' said John. 'Is it an easier place than for your father?'

'It is at the moment, I fear,' said Sabine. 'But I have a tutor in my mind. In the meantime they are working by themselves.'

'In the meantime!' said Hetta. 'We must put an end to that. We can guess what will be the result.'

Hetta Ponsonby had cast in her lot with her brother's on the death of his wife, and for eleven years he had lived under her control, finding his dependence and gratitude becoming constraint and doubt. It took all his effort to maintain his name and do his part for his family, and she shared his aims and steered the course for them both. Sabine regarded her daughter with a proud, possessive eye, admiring her powers, seeing her above any ordinary mate, submitting or no to her absolute direction, according to her own mood. Hetta was the only person who did not fear Sabine, and Sabine alone was normally at ease with her daughter; but they were both the only people in much of what they did.

The grandchildren saw their aunt with feelings which had grown with themselves, and which they hardly defined. She was an influence at once dubious and powerful, at once natural and sinister, an authority at once lower and higher than Sabine.

'Well, is it all as usual?' said Hetta. 'Nothing for me to be told? It is pleasant to see these fresh country faces. I wonder if you all feel you are fortunate?'

'I would as soon have a London face,' said Clare. 'And my face has not been described as fresh to-day. Grandma took another view of it.'

'Now, Clare, don't begin to be foolish,' said Sabine.

'What is it, Mater?' said Hetta, who had almost established a rule that nothing was to escape her.

'Clare says she is tired of the country. I don't know why her feelings towards it matter more than other people's.'

'Well, she may as well be tired of life. There is nowhere but here for her to live, and no one but her father to support her.'

'It comes to being tired of life,' said her niece.

'We could all put an end to our lives, if we wanted,' said Hetta, who had entangled her wraps, and who vented all irritations. 'The fact that we do not do it shows we do not want to. We prefer to be kept in luxury at other people's expense. Chilton, give me a hand with this cloak: don't stand there looking at someone struggling single-handed with something too much for her, and don't offer to help. And don't make any silly joke about Victor; give me a hand yourself.'

'It does want a delicate touch,' said Chilton, doing as she said.

'The girls do not cost us much,' said Sabine. 'It would not be right that they should, but it is a fact that they don't.'

'Don't take me up in that absurd way, Mater,' said Hetta, almost with violence. 'You knew quite well what I meant; you are not an idiot. Muriel, are you always yawning? You were yawning when I left three weeks ago, and you are yawning still! You must try and conquer the habit; it is ugly and self-indulgent. I don't know what is the good of Miss Bunyan, if she teaches you nothing but that.'

'It is because of what Miss Bunyan teaches her, that the poor young girl is exhausted,' said Victor.

'I don't know why Clare and France cannot teach her. I presume they remember what they were taught themselves.'

'Why do you presume that? People never do remember it,' said Clare.

'And if they do not, what was the good of it? It is absurd to have two grown women in the house and keep a governess. There is no better cure for being tired of life than regular occupation. Seriously, Mater, can't we get rid of Miss Bunyan, and kill two birds with one stone? I don't know what I should do, if I mooned about all day. I should have no self-respect; I could not hold up my head.'

'We do not need the girls' self-respect to grow beyond a point,' said Sabine in a grim tone, going into the drawing-room. 'Come to the fire, my dears. You find us quiet as usual.'

'We are naturally quiet, when anything else would add to expense, and we are only just able to keep things going.'

'Hetta, pray make some contribution to the talk, that is not couched in this vein,' said her brother. 'Let the girls see some other aspect of you. Clare will be inclined to your tone, as it is.'

'I should be only too glad for her to copy me in any way. It would be an advance on what she is. I should be thankful to see the change.'

'It would not make her you,' said Sabine.

'Let her go further in my line and stop doing nothing. Shall we consider the question of the governess? I have not been answered there.'

'I don't care for the girls to do that work,' said John, lifting his eyes from the fire. 'Why should I work myself? What would be my reason?'

'France has her writing,' said Sabine, 'and Clare is often with me. You know I do not care to sit alone. So you have been answered, Hetta, as it was proper you should be. Your suggestion is a good one, and you had every right to make it, but it is not practicable. Now dinner is at half past seven and you have not too much time. The girls are already dressed.'

'It would save the girls' dresses if they did not put them on so soon,' said Hetta to her brother with Sabine's grimness, as they went upstairs. 'But it would be taken ill if I suggested it, so I hold my peace. There is something cropping up every moment to be put right, but it gives offence if it is done, so there is an end of it. I should like to save your money, but it just has to be spent.'

John walked at her side in silence.

The young people came into the drawing-room when it was free, looking round the door to assure themselves of this condition.

'It is a good thing Miss Bunyan does not know that someone grudges her support, even more than Grandma,' said France.

'One gets used to having one's support grudged,' said Clare. 'It does not take away the support.'

'It seems it may take away Miss Bunyan's.'

'Even to Miss Bunyan life may be sweet,' said Victor.

'I wonder who thought of its being sweet,' said Clare.

'It is sweet to Miss Bunyan,' said Chilton. 'Bread is the staff of it.'

'If Muriel laughs so loud, she will be heard,' said France. 'It is Father's life that is threatened. Aunt Hetta is planning his end much more surely than Miss Bunyan's.'

'Grandma is the only one of us in a strong position,' said Chilton. 'She cannot be sent into her grave out of due time.'

'It would be good to have power,' said his brother.

'No, we should use it,' said France. 'No one can stand it. None of us could: think of the stock we come of.'

'I don't want to come to dinner,' said Muriel. 'I would rather be with Miss Bunyan.'

'So would we all,' said France. 'And it is Aunt Hetta's excuse, that she would be surprised if she knew.'

'And her fault that we do not dare to tell her,' said Clare.

'Yes, so perhaps there is no excuse. We would rather think there is none.'

'How a governess must know life!' said Chilton.

'Not as much as a daughter. Life is less deep when you are not related.'

'Does Father like Aunt Hetta?' said Muriel.

'He used to,' said Clare. 'After Mother died, he could not let her out of his sight. But his feeling is changing. I can see it day by day.'

'Grandma likes her too, doesn't she?'

'You are not struck by a third phenomenon?' said France.

'Why does not Aunt Hetta have a husband?'

'Someone else would have to like her,' said Clare, breaking off at the sound of the door.

'Because she does not want one,' said Hetta in a light and lively manner, coming in with the almost open intention of effacing her first impression. 'And a nice thing it would be for all of you, if she did, and decided to leave you to your own devices. How would you like all your life to be like the last three weeks? Well, you make me look an old woman, you two young ones, but youth is not everything, is it? Or do you all think it is?'

'It must seem a small thing at the moment,' said Victor.

'When there is only one thing to be said, Victor can say it,' said Chilton.

'So Muriel is to sit up to dinner? You others never did at her age.'

'Victor and she are both sitting up, Aunt Hetta.'

'Grandma wanted Father to see her,' said Clare.

'She has already been in his full view.'

'A sight that is not easily forgotten,' said Victor, turning Muriel to the light and causing her considerable amusement.

'I do not want her to feel her father is a stranger,' said Sabine, coming in with her son. 'She will be no trouble. She is a very easy-tempered child.'

'She has not much to make her anything else,' said Hetta. 'When everything is done for her, it is the least she can do to be pleasant.'

'It is the most she can do as well. Everything has to be done for children, of course.'

'Well, Clare,' said Hetta, as they came to the table, 'so you have managed to while away the week?'

'I have not done so. It has dragged away.'

'You have found nothing to do from morning till night?'

'Those are the seasons which embrace my waking life.'

'Can you not find some occupation in the house?'

'The house is my province,' said Sabine.

'You could give Clare your directions.'

'I have given them. They are, that she is to leave it to me. It cannot do with too many mistresses.'

'She need not be its mistress because she gives her help.'

'She would be,' said Sabine with a grim smile. 'She is more your niece than her sisters.'

'I do not see the likeness.'

'Neither do I,' said the niece.

'I have seen you both grow up, and I see it,' said Sabine.

'How about your week, France?' said Hetta.

'Have you earned the right to enquire into our affairs?' said Clare.

'Earned the right? Do you hear that?' said Hetta in a shrill tone to her brother. 'Earned the right! I have the right; the right is naturally mine! Earned the right! Who would trouble to earn it, or to use it, if it were not necessary? Well, what pitiful thoughts they have in their minds! What do you say to it, Mater? Have you brought them up for this?'

'Clare does not show the best of herself, and does not go the way to get it from other people. She is not getting it from you, or deserving to get it.'

'How about your week, France?' said Hetta, repeating her former words.

France glanced at her father's face.

'I am following in Father's steps and writing a novel.'

'Well, that is a rather ambitious plan. Wouldn't it be better to choose something more likely to come off?'

'Less ambitious things need training,' said Sabine. 'We will leave her her own occupation, as it costs us nothing.'

'It does not save us anything either. But I am glad she has some occupation, and is not too sunk in black sulks to mention it. We will leave her to waste her time in her own way.'

'There is no alternative,' said Sabine.

'What of the boys? Now I am going to ask these questions, so you need not gather yourselves up and look offensive. It is clearly my duty to ask them; I see that more and more. The fact that you are so reluctant to answer them, tells its tale. Now what are you both reading? Your future begins to loom large. You would not want to be supported like the girls, would you?'

'I am sure they would not,' said Clare.

'What about the other side of our lives,' said Victor. 'Does Aunt Hetta desire a complete view? Would she like an account of our relaxations?'

'Spare time can look after itself in the country.'

'That is a contradiction in terms,' said Clare.

'Does Miss Bunyan not sleep in the house?' said John.

'She is having an evening to herself,' said his mother. 'I thought we would be a family party.'

'Your purpose is fulfilled,' said Clare.

'Do you want to be sent out of the room like a child, girl?' said Sabine with her sudden hiss.

'I have no feeling on the matter, Grandma.'

'Would you like me to have a word with Miss Bunyan, John?' said Hetta. 'And judge if she is a suitable person for Muriel?'

'I have judged that she is suitable,' said Sabine, 'or she would not be here.'

'You don't make things easy for me, Mater.'

Sabine did not reply.

'You look tired, Father,' said France.

'Was your holiday free from worries?' said Chilton. 'Victor was not at all on your mind?'

'There are a lot of you to keep going,' said Hetta. 'He could not take a full holiday, as you seem to be doing.'

John turned to talk to his daughters, and his sister watched for a minute and then interposed.

'That is not the way to get rested, John, if you are so tired; and not the way for France to help you, if she is so concerned. Leave them alone, at any rate until to-morrow. They will drain every ounce of energy out of you. I know they have drained it out of me. I am as tired as you can be.'

'It is a mercy Miss Bunyan was not at dinner,' said Clare, under cover of the move to the drawing-room. 'Grandma was very wise.'

'It is more than you were, girl,' said Sabine, looking back.

'I cannot pretend to like Aunt Hetta. She gives too little reason.'

'Why do you not pretend to?' said France. 'It would be better for Father. Perhaps you do not pretend to like him?'

'We have so little to do with him. He seems to have been pushed out of our lives.'

'You need not push him further out.'

'I believe it would be better for him. He has to suffer for any share in them.'

'Let us keep him apart from Aunt Hetta to-night.'

'We can try to entice her away from him.'

'You may try to be enticing to your aunt, my dear,' said Sabine. 'I think it is time.'

'You do seem to need some practice, Clare,' said France. 'I see it is an art which requires it.'

The evening passed without further strain. Hetta made an effort to retrieve her position, and talked with the conscious fluency and liveliness which she felt to be charm, prevented as she was by her life from turning her eye on herself. The brothers exchanged their banter, or rather Chilton bantered Victor without response, and Sabine and her son withdrew their influence by falling asleep.

The next morning, which was Sunday, Sabine looked pale and withdrawn. The day, as she had lived it, had been too much. While her son read prayers, she sat with her hand over her eyes, making no sound or sign of response. When Miss Bunyan entered with a touch of bustling and breathlessness, she seemed to sense it with closed eyes and met it with a frown. She watched the family take their seats for breakfast, with an air of holding herself in readiness for cause of irritation, and raised her hand to repudiate morning greetings, with a fluttering movement which suggested a fear that she would not be in time.

'We will take this meal in silence,' murmured Victor.

'We will, as far as you are concerned, boy.'

'We shall miss his innocent, mindless chatter,' said Chilton.

'And as far as you are concerned, Chilton.'

'We did not see you last night, Miss Bunyan,' said John. 'You were tired and had gone to bed.'

'Yes, Mr. Ponsonby, I remember I was very tired. We had had a long day, Muriel and I.' Miss Bunyan stumbled as she recalled that her pupil's retirement had not been hastened, and Muriel marked the hesitation in her usual way.

'You may follow the others' example, Muriel.'

'It will not involve much change,' said Clare.

'So may you, Clare.'

'Miss Bunyan, you and I will now embark upon our dialogue,' said France.

'You will take part in the general conversation or be still.'

'I don't see how we are to manage general conversation.'

'Then you have the alternative.'

'Good morning, Mrs. Ponsonby,' said Miss Bunyan, as if she had been waiting to achieve her greeting.

'Good morning,' said Sabine, just moving her lips.

'Good morning, Miss Ponsonby.'

'Good morning,' said Hetta, with a hint of a smile.

'Well, gapy-face!' said Sabine.

'Miss Bunyan, Muriel's manners!' said Hetta. 'We must see what can be done. We ought to begin to see some result of all her advantages.'

Miss Bunyan recognised the allusion to herself, but hardly knew how far to be flattered by it. Sabine gave Hetta a repressive glance, aware of Miss Bunyan's view, that criticism should come from herself, and caused her daughter to continue.

'We were talking about her education last night, and I was asking her sisters if they were prepared to give any help. But they did not seem to care for the idea. And it may not be wise to have that sort of thing within a family.'

There was a pause.

'But I think it is a very interesting question, Miss Ponsonby,' said Miss Bunyan, in a fluent, social tone, which somehow held a new, equal note. 'I have often thought upon the subject. It is interesting to an educationist. I must tell my uncle your view, as it coincides with his own. He has often said I ought to live with him, and undertake his household, and put an end to such problems in his case. I do not know, of course'—She gave a little laugh—'how much his desire to have me is a determining factor; but I think there is an element of sincerity in his view or—I am sure you will agree with me here—he would not voice it; and there may be an element of truth. May I have some more coffee, Mrs. Ponsonby? And just a thought weaker, if it is not fussy? You are rather generous with the coffee-pot. Thank you so much.'

Sabine was more generous with either pot than she would have been.

'Who is going to church to-day?' she said, showing that her thoughts were not with her eyes, on Miss Bunyan's cup.

'I am staying at home,' said Hetta. 'I feel I want a little time alone.'

'So do I, Miss Ponsonby,' said Miss Bunyan, as if struck by this similarity.

'I cannot go,' said Sabine, speaking more faintly. 'I should like to, but I cannot.'

'I should like to go too,' said Chilton, 'but I cannot.'

'I do not need to go to church to worship,' said Sabine, using a vaguely reproachful tone. 'We can do whatever is worship for us, wherever we may be.'

'I think I will go,' said Clare. 'It is better than doing nothing at home, and nothing else is worship for me.'

'I don't want anything better than the first,' said Miss Bunyan, lightly.

'Neither do I,' said Chilton. 'But perhaps Victor should go. Something might come home to him.'

'Clare and Muriel can go,' said Sabine. 'The boys and Miss Bunyan may do as they please. France can go for a walk with her father.'

'France can go to church with the others,' said Hetta. 'There is no reason to make an exception.'

'I have said what is to be done.'

As the family stood about the table, Miss Bunyan suddenly

rose and approached Sabine, with her eyes set and prominent.

'May I speak to you for a moment, Mrs. Ponsonby?'

'Yes, certainly,' said Sabine, her own eyes becoming bright for a moment and then going down.

'I should have said, might I speak to you privately.'

'There can hardly be anything private in what you have to say.'

'This is both private and important, Mrs. Ponsonby.'

'I think it surely is not. It is only that you wish to leave, isn't it?'

Miss Bunyan looked at Sabine and did not speak.

'That is not important. And it can hardly be private. People will have to know that you have left. They may notice it.'

Miss Bunyan did not dispute this possibility, but held to her purpose.

'I thought you might wish to know—I thought I might tell you my reasons. It is usual to do so.'

'No,' said Sabine, possibly feeling that these might as well be private. 'They are not my concern; they are your own.'

'That is not quite so, Mrs. Ponsonby. They are really yours as well, if you will excuse me. You will be having another governess.'

Sabine was silent upon her affairs.

'Unless Muriel's sisters are really going to teach her.'

Sabine was silent.

'You will wish to know—it would be wise, well for you to know—you might find it convenient——'

'No, I should not. My manner of dealing with one person does not bear upon my dealing with another. Each person determines her own treatment; it is indicated by the individual.'

Miss Bunyan stared in front of her, as the extent of her responsibility was brought home.

'What is the good of Miss Bunyan's leaving, if she must meet the same treatment everywhere?' murmured Clare.

'Then I will leave at the end of the term, Mrs. Ponsonby.'

'Yes, that will be the usual time.'

'I shall be sorry to leave Muriel,' said Miss Bunyan, indicating the line of her feeling to a certain extent.

Sabine did not speak.

'I shall, of course, take as much pains with her, as if I were going to stay.'

'Of course, as you say. It should really go without saying.'

Miss Bunyan was silent, as silence seemed to be indicated.

'I shall not be needing a testimonial, as I shall be living with my family.'

'Then that is all we need say,' said Sabine, as if further words would have been suggested in the other case.

'Thank you, Mrs. Ponsonby,' said Miss Bunyan, turning and walking to the door with a gait needlessly stiffened by her sense of watching eyes, as all were averted but Muriel's.

'She wanted to make a scene,' said Sabine.

'And does not know how well she succeeded,' said France.

'It does seen that the turn in her fortunes has been passed over rather easily,' said John.

'I am glad she did not ask a testimonial, Grandma,' said France, 'as she would not give you one.'

'What she wanted to give Grandma,' said Clare, 'is better passed over, as Grandma passed over it.'

Sabine gave the genuine laugh, which had a note of Muriel's.

'Muriel is the only one who has had a testimonial,' said Chilton, 'so unjust are the rewards in this world. I half expected Miss Bunyan to speak in Victor's favour.'

'Are you sorry she is going, Muriel?'

'I don't mind, Aunt Hetta.'

'Here is a chance to further your own suggestion, Aunt Hetta,' said Victor. 'We honour your forbearance.'

'I should be more worthy of honour, if I did further it. I cannot face the struggle.'

'The woman has several homes,' said John in a dubious manner. 'There is no need to be in trouble over her.'

'Certainly not, in that case,' muttered Clare. 'It would be absurd in us. But I wish one of the homes was not here.'

'Would you like to teach your little sister, Clare?'

'I should not mind, if I had the education, Grandma.'

'Would you, France?' said Hetta, looking at her niece.

'No, not at all: it would try my patience too much.'

'More than you tried people's patience when you were a child?'

'I daresay not, but I remember that was too much.'

Miss Bunyan opened the door, wearing her coat and hat.

'You do not mind my going to church, Mrs. Ponsonby?'

'No, not at all. You decided not to go, yourself.'

'I feel I should like to go,' said Miss Bunyan, pausing after these words and then closing the door.

44

'I think Miss Bunyan wants a little comfort,' said France.

'For not being allowed to speak her mind to Grandma,' said Victor. 'It must be a disappointment. I can't think how she can bear it.'

'She evidently cannot in her own strength.'

'How came she to conceive the project?' said Chilton. 'There must be a lion heart in that little body.'

'That will do, all of you,' said Sabine. 'Clare and Muriel, you may start for church. It is a most undignified thing to be late. Go and sit with Miss Bunyan, as if nothing had happened. We don't want to advertise our every little household disturbance.'

'Certainly we do not,' said Claire. 'I can't remember one which we should want to advertise. But Miss Bunyan may want to advertise this one. She seems somehow to be another woman.'

'Boys, go out into the air,' said Sabine. 'France, get ready for your walk with your father. John, you need not stand there looking upset. Nothing has happened. Go out with the girl and think of other things. Hetta, my dear, come and sit with your mother. I shall forget that you are my daughter.'

'Well, France, well!' said John with his conscious lightness. 'So things go smoothly with you all? The ruffles are on the surface? It is the surface that I must see.'

'It is a pity that is the case. That is where they show.'

'And that proves they do not go deeper? The surface is their place?'

'I don't wonder Grandma forgets Aunt Hetta is her daughter. It seems such a subordinate position for her.'

'Ah, your aunt is one by herself, France. We don't meet others like her. I hope her life is the right one; I hope she is doing well by herself as well as by her family.'

'It is difficult to do much for both. I always wonder that living for others stands in such good repute.'

'There is no greater pathos than that of the person, who gives her life for too little, and feels it.'

'A good definition of living for others.'

'After all, what is the difference between giving service and taking it?' said John, with his swift change of mood.

'Not much in Aunt Hetta's case. So perhaps it is well after all.'

'And so there is nothing amiss? There is nothing below the surface? You would not keep things from your father?'

'Do you keep things from us, Father? Is the family rushing to ruin as quickly as Aunt Hetta would suggest?'

'Well, I have not a steady profession,' said John in a sharper tone. 'The human brain is not a machine. I worked hard as a young man, and look to work hard as an old one; and when you burn a candle at both ends, you can't do so much in the middle. You must be content with the lean years while they last.'

He walked on, striking the hedges with his cane, and moving his lips as if he would have talked to himself, if he had been alone. France led the talk away, but could not bring it to herself.

They returned to the house to find the family at luncheon. Sabine had never relinquished the head of the board to her son. It was her natural place, as the opposite one was her daughter's. John sat at the side by his sister.

Sabine raised her hand to ward off the attack on her nerves, made by the general entrance. Miss Bunyan came to her seat with a briskness and ease which were somehow unfamiliar, though these were qualities she cultivated. Sabine gave her a glance, and under it she drew forth her napkin, laid it on her lap, and gazed at nothing.

'Are you too warm, Miss Bunyan?' said John, observing her colour. 'Would you like a seat away from the fire?'

'No, thank you, Mr. Ponsonby. I always make for the fire. I am a most catlike person. Wherever I am, I seem to make my own a place near to it.'

Sabine looked up in almost open recognition of the change, and Miss Bunyan seemed impelled to maintain it.

'Are you with me, Mrs. Ponsonby, in preferring a place in the full heat?'

'I like to be warm enough: I am not with anyone in particular over it.'

'He that is not with me is against me,' murmured France.

'What is that, France?'

'Nothing, Grandma.'

'Tell me what you said.'

'I said, "He that is not with me is against me." '

'Oh, how did you enjoy the sermon?' said Sabine, allowing herself to be diverted. 'Was it a suitable sermon for Muriel?'

'Yes, more or less,' said Clare.

'Was it about foolish virgins then?' said Chilton.

'It was about hiding talents in the earth.'

'I wish Victor had gone. He could have taken a lesson from the man with one talent.'

'Did you like it, Clare?' said Hetta.

'No, it was stilted and lifeless. I think it came out of a book.'

'Did you, Miss Bunyan?'

'Well, yes, Miss Ponsonby, I was sufficiently held. For me it served its purpose. I was not so struck by its bookishness. That is really a new idea to me. Were you struck by it, Muriel?'

'No,'

'Were the usual people there?' said Sabine.

'I do not know,' said Clare. 'I did not look.'

'You must have seen some of them.'

'I tried not to, for fear I should have to talk to them.'

'Why should you object to that?'

'Because it is time for us to ask them here.'

'I could not bear it,' said Sabine, putting her hand to her head. 'I am past all that: I have indeed done my share.'

'I could hardly tell them you could not bear it.'

'No, they would have been quite startled,' said Miss Bunyan, causing Sabine to frown.

'Whom do you want to ask?' said John to his daughter.

'Everyone whom we call by the name of friend, or once called by it.'

'Are the friends proving fickle?' said Miss Bunyan.

'It is we who are proving that.'

'There are too many,' said Sabine. 'I am not equal to a crowd of people in the house.'

'It sounds as if it would be quite a reception,' said Miss Bunyan. 'It would be quite a change.'

'Miss Bunyan,' said Sabine, rounding on her with her hiss, 'we will not have any difference, if you please. We will go on in just the same way while you are here.'

'I do not know what you mean, Mrs. Ponsonby.'

'Oh, yes, you do, though I daresay you dislike to hear it said. You cannot suddenly change in a moment without knowing. You are not any more one of us, because you are leaving; rather less.'

'Miss Bunyan has decided not to be one of us at all,' said John.

'I am sorry if my going inconveniences you, Mrs. Ponsonby.'

'I am sorry it inconveniences all of us,' murmured Clare.

'It does not, as you know, but your staying will, if you are going to be like this. It is not a suitable thing.'

'I am quite at a loss as to your meaning, Mrs. Ponsonby.'

'Muriel, don't sit there laughing at nothing. You need not listen to grown up people's talk,' said Hetta, hardly assigning her niece's amusement to nothing.

'There is no other talk for her to listen to,' said Clare.

'I could not resist listening to it myself,' said France. 'I suppose it to be quite unique.'

'Don't whisper; don't whisper,' said Hetta.

'Will you have some more chicken, Miss Bunyan?' said Sabine, with her eyes on carving the bird, and an assumption that she was retrieving her position. She had not reckoned with the change in Miss Bunyan, though she had discussed it.

'No, Mrs. Ponsonby, thank you,' said the latter, rising to her feet. 'I will not have any more; I will eat and drink no more in this house. I shall be leaving this afternoon and going to my uncle at the vicarage. Strictly speaking, I should not go without notice, but as you render my remaining impossible, the question does not arise. I will take the opportunity of wishing everyone goodbye. Goodbye, all'—The note of equality was so pronounced that it touched something further—'goodbye, Muriel; I hope you will do well.'

She stalked to the door, putting her napkin down unfolded, in token of no further use for it. Victor opened the door, and she gave him a short, definite bow and vanished without looking back.

There was silence for a second, and then Sabine gave a sigh of weary indifference, which expressed her feeling, if not all of it.

'Come, come, this is going too far,' said her son. 'The woman is in our house and under our protection. Someone must go after her.'

'No one will go,' said his mother, foretelling the truth.

'She will eat and drink no more in this house,' said France. 'Miss Bunyan's oath of farewell! True to herself to the last.'

'And not false to any man,' said Victor. 'She met Grandma in open fight.'

'Now you are going to make a heroine of her, I suppose,' said Sabine, 'and talk about straightness and pluck and the other admirations of boys. But I beg you will wait until I have left the room.'

'Now Victor must feel very self-conscious and uncomfortable,' said Chilton.

'I hope he is glad to suffer for Miss Bunyan,' said France.

'It is her triumph that she left in the middle of a meal. No calculating waiting until it was over! With Grandma's hands actually on the chicken, she went.'

'What will she do without luncheon?' said Victor. 'I suppose she will pack the biscuits last of all.'

Muriel burst into laughter in anticipation of her own words.

'Or—or finish them,' she said.

'This is a very stale joke,' said Sabine, 'and in bad taste, if you were sincere in what you said.'

'We shall never live down letting slip a word in favour of Miss Bunyan,' said France. 'But I am not ashamed of taking a stand for the right.'

'Grandma, you have gone too far,' said Clare. 'Let it be a lesson to you.'

'Lessons are not for me, my dear.'

'Clearly not, if you have not taken one.'

'What are we to do, Hetta?' said John. 'The woman is our responsibility. She is related to our friends. She cannot go like this.'

'What can we do, since she refuses food?' said France.

'You need not appeal to me,' said Hetta. 'My suggestions are taken so ill, that I am ceasing to make them. You can get out of this difficulty in your own way. But I hope you see my point in wanting to give up a governess.'

'That is quite a different point,' said John.

'There is a sameness in the result,' said Victor.

'Miss Bunyan sees it,' said Clare. 'She has come to know us, and shakes the dust of our house from her feet.'

'I daresay knowledge of most families would lead people to that,' said France. 'Governesses often change their posts.'

Sabine raised her hand to impose silence, and motioned Victor to the bell. When the table was cleared, she spoke.

'Her salary can be calculated up to date, and taken up to her in an envelope. The trap can come round for her luggage later. Tea can be taken to her room, and she can send it down or not, as she pleases. She will hurt no one but herself.'

'She will hurt me,' said France. 'I cannot bear Miss Bunyan to go hungry from our door.'

'I cannot bear her to go hungry to her uncle,' said Clare. 'It is most embarrassing.'

'Clare, you can teach Muriel until we get another governess.'

'You are responsible for her being without one, Grandma. Why do you not teach her?'

Muriel looked up with her eyes surprisingly wide.

'I teach you all enough. And I have no modern education.'

'Neither have I.'

'I have said what is to be done.'

'It cannot be done, but it does not matter.'

'It does not matter much,' agreed Sabine. 'Governesses exaggerate their importance. I had very little education myself, and I have seldom felt the want of it.'

'Other people have done that,' said Chilton to France. 'No educated person would dare as she has dared.'

'People's disadvantages generally fall on other people.'

'Don't whisper, don't whisper,' said Hetta. 'How often am I to speak? Don't behave as if you were ashamed of what you have to say.'

'It is often the only way to behave,' said John, smiling.

'What was it? Make it a rule to speak so that everyone can hear.'

'We should never speak in Grandma's house,' said Clare, 'and she tells us we should be received in no other. We have not Miss Bunyan's choice of abodes.'

'Her uncle may come in after the service,' said Victor. 'He often calls on his way back from church.'

'I hope Miss Bunyan will not be going just when he arrives,' said Sabine, with simple sincerity.

'You are right that her going is a disgrace to us,' said Clare.

'Well, well, we must learn how to deal with the next governess,' said Sabine in an almost amiable manner. 'Governesses are touchy people. They are situated just where touchiness is natural.'

'I should not describe Miss Bunyan as touchy,' said France. 'If she is, she is a heroine and a martyr.'

'Well, you have decided she is both,' said Sabine. 'Do this sum for me, Clare.'

'I don't know why I am equal to all these mental demands. Grandma! Is this all Miss Bunyan was paid?'

'She had a good home,' said Sabine, her voice less full than usual.

'We have learned to-day that she did not think so.'

'We must count board and lodging in a resident post.'

'Did Grandma count board?' said France. 'She always seemed to see it as an extra.'

'You are a set of stupid, inconsiderate children,' hissed Sabine. 'I get no help and support from you at all. You might have some grievance against me, instead of great reason for gratitude. I simply don't understand your frame of mind.'

'Oh, don't try to, Mater,' said Hetta. 'I have long given up the effort.'

'I will leave you all,' said Sabine. 'I can bear no more. No one is to go up to Miss Bunyan. She has said goodbye.'

'She has,' said Chilton, returning from the door; 'and never shall I forget the moment of her saying it.'

'Naught in her life in this house became her like the leaving of it,' said Victor. 'We can say it now that Grandma is not here to put us to shame.'

'Things did not generally become Miss Bunyan, did they?' said Muriel.

'Let us leave the subject,' said Hetta. 'Have you no other interest in life?'

'No other,' said Clare.

'Well, this is our chief one at the moment,' said France.

'Surely it is yours too, Aunt Hetta,' said Victor. 'If it is not, I can hardly credit the scale of your experience.'

'You ought to be resting, John,' said Hetta. 'You have been in a crowd all day.'

'I must appear a feeble old creature, always retiring to recover from an hour with my family.'

'This was no ordinary hour,' said France.

'Well, I have personal work to do, and must be prepared for personal effort,' said John, looking round with a flash in his eyes. 'Your aunt is not wrong there. I wish one of you had chosen my path, the path of the man who makes the thing he gives. I wish I had a child who would follow me.'

'You have one,' said Chilton. 'France has set her foot on the path. She has reached the first natural halt, the end of her first novel.'

'Has she? Has she got as far as that? So my wish is granted, and I am to have a companion. But the first halt is the hard one. It is then we go back and begin the climb again. We reject our first effort and forget it. And then the road winds uphill all the way. I shall not complain, if she has not courage to climb it.'

'That is what he was complaining of,' muttered Chilton.

'I have the courage to start,' said France. 'That is generally forthcoming, and it may as well be used while it is there.'

'But have you courage to start a second time?' said her father, almost with challenge.

'What has been done can be done again,' said Chilton.

'That is not what is before her. She has to do something different, climb up another way, starting from the same place.'

'What is that noise?' said Hetta, willing to turn her brother's mind.

'Miss Bunyan's luggage on the stairs,' said Victor. 'I suppose Miss Bunyan is following with noiseless tread.'

'I suppose she must go?' said his father.

'Clearly she must,' said Clare, 'Grandma being what she is. Grandma has not altered in the last hour. What eighty-four years have not accomplished, is not done in a moment, even a moment such as this has been.'

'Miss Bunyan's voice sounds just like it always does, doesn't it?' said Muriel.

'Did she have her tea?' said Victor, breaking off as a maid entered and looked about for some possession of Miss Bunyan's. 'Gertrude, has Miss Bunyan had any tea before her drive?'

'I took it up to her, sir, but she did not take it. It was rather soon after luncheon.'

'We know it was not, considering her part in that meal,' said France. 'Her food is to be a problem to the end. Her two last meals have been the most difficult.'

'Indeed, have not come off at all,' said Chilton. 'It is the first time we have had to say that.'

Muriel laughed at this circumstance.

Miss Bunyan's voice was heard in the hall, distinct, pleasant, thanking the maids. Her luggage, bulky in proportion to her personal display, was piled on the trap. Muriel was pulled from the window. Miss Bunyan mounted to her seat and settled her gloves and her bag, and continued to settle them under her sense of the eyes of Sabine openly watching from above.

'A ship that passes in the night,' said Victor.

'A ship that will frequently pass in the day,' said Clare. 'She is only to be at the vicarage, and very difficult we shall find it.'

'Grandma will not,' said Victor. 'We must leave all dealings with Miss Bunyan to her. Such is the irony of life.'

'Will Miss Bunyan think we don't like her?' said Muriel, in an uncertain tone.

'Do we all bear these marks of the last hour?' said France. 'Will Muriel never be the same again?'

'She may think you do not, Muriel,' said Clare. 'She does not know of the change in you. It has come just too late. That is what things do.'

'We have no comfort on the score of Miss Bunyan,' said Victor, 'who has shared our ups and downs for a year.'

'A little chapter of your life has gone, Muriel,' said Chilton, 'a chapter you will never be able to go back and live better.'

Muriel looked at him with tears in her eyes.

'Don't be silly, Muriel,' said Clare. 'You have never been fond of Miss Bunyan, or been anything but tiresome to her. It is of no good to try to be upset.'

'I think it is very suitable,' said France. 'I could not have borne it, if no one had shed a tear for Miss Bunyan.'

'I have had to wink mine back,' said Chilton. 'But I know it is nothing to be ashamed of. Victor, these are not the tears that are unmanly.'

Muriel went into hysterical mirth.

'So this is the sort of laughter that is near to tears,' said France.

John looked on and listened, amused, proud, uneasy; Hetta did the same, wearing a tolerant smile; and the two soon went to the library, where they often sat alone.

When the family were at tea, a visitor called, who combined the characters of a family friend, the vicar of the parish, and the maternal uncle of Miss Bunyan. The Reverend Dr. Chaucer was a large, loosely-built man of fifty-four, with round, pale, speckled eyes, a pendulous neck and chin, and a nose and mouth of an oddly infantine mould. If people were inclined to pity him for this appearance, the pity was, as so often where appearance is concerned, needlessly bestowed, for he had a confidence in his poise and stateliness which almost gave him these qualities. His voice was full and without tone;

his hands and shoes and linen were all but impossibly clean; his eyes went over his friends with an almost emotional expression. He had a consciousness of his doctor's degree, and the acceptance of the work he had presented for it, had at the time occasioned criticism. The criticism had died away; the work had died also; and as the degree remained, his attitude was perhaps incredulous towards it. He advanced and bent over the hands of the ladies, with a deliberate smile for each, making no exception of Muriel.

'Well, Chaucer, you see me with my mother, my sister, my three daughters, and my two sons,' said John. 'You know me to be a person who practises many relationships under his roof.'

'Chaucer sees me with my grandmother, my aunt, my father, and my three sisters,' said Chilton, 'and also with my brother, whom I may as well mention.'

Chaucer gave a smile to John, but continued his way to Sabine, as if concentrating on the most significant greeting.

'I am right, Mrs. Ponsonby, in assuming that I have my usual welcome?'

'Indeed you are. How could it be otherwise?'

'I am glad,' said Chaucer, allowing himself to smile, 'that the sins of nieces are not visited upon their uncles.'

'There is no question of sins. Your niece had every right to leave my house.'

'The occurrence has been a shock to me,' said Chaucer, shaking his head. 'I could not have anticipated such an incident between your house and mine.'

'It is hardly between ourselves or our houses.'

'I cannot think my niece was clear in her mind about the step. I was sensible of the advantages of your post to a girl in her position; and accordingly bowed to her earning her support in the place where, in my own sphere, I earn my own. As a bachelor, I can find a use for her, but I feel that a dependent girl tends to be like a prophet, without honour in her own house.'

Muriel, who had been striving with the emotions aroused by this description of Miss Bunyan, was conquered by them, and Chaucer looked about with a broad smile.

'Muriel, you may take round the cups,' said Sabine.

'Stay, Mrs. Ponsonby,' said Chaucer, hastening forward. 'Neither I nor your grandsons can submit to such ministrations from a lady, however young. To her performing the office for her father I make no demur. That relation covers a multitude of irregularities.'

'Boys, come and take the cups,' said Hetta. 'You should not go to sleep.'

'Instructions short and sharp!' said Chaucer, going into laughter, with his eyes on Hetta. 'And, I will wager, just as sharply to be obeyed. Well, boys'—As he took his cup, he glanced to see that the sisters were supplied—'may I enlist your support in a petition to your father? We hope he may address us on the occasion of our village dramatic effort. Or, if you doubt yourselves as intermediaries, I will solicit the office of your sisters, knowing that the persuasions of a daughter have a particular potency.'

'I think my brother would like it,' said Hetta in an easy tone, 'if you don't want too much of an address. I can't regard his time as his own.'

'Miss Ponsonby, I should have known the quarter in which to lodge my appeal, and am grateful you will regard it as so lodged. I hardly know whether to express my gratitude to you or your brother, and will therefore solve the problem by expressing it to both.'

'What play are you acting?'

'That, Miss Ponsonby, remains a question. We are somewhat in the position of Shakespeare's day, in that our ladies have to be acted by the choir-boys. And the play has to suit the capacities of the young and the tastes of their elders. So far, the choice has eluded us.'

'France,' said Chilton, going to his sister, 'part of your book would make into a play, and would be something of what is wanted. It would be a chance to make Father notice your writing. We can't do anything with him in his present mood. Shall I say a word to Chaucer, or shall we discuss it together?'

Chaucer was drawn into the younger group, and appeared to relish the position. He sat with his hands on his knees, leaning forward into the midst, wearing an elated, conspiratorial air and glancing at the elders of the family with simple furtiveness. When the conference ended, he rose to his feet and, after bare, smooth farewells, went with a suggestion of tiptoeing to the door, seeming to feel that this interest excluded any other.

'What was all that confabulation?' said Hetta.

'Oh, nothing,' said Victor.

'My dear boy, don't talk like a child. Clare, what was all the talk?'

'Nothing that need be said.'

'Of course it need not be said. I did not say it need. I simply asked what it was. And as I happened to ask, I will be answered.'

There was silence.

'It cannot be a private matter, with a family of you involved. And Dr. Chaucer would not have a secret with you.'

'Answer your aunt, one of you,' said Sabine.

'We were talking among ourselves,' said Victor. 'You will all know in the end.'

'Know in the end!' said Hetta, her voice rising. 'Why should we know in the end? Why should we want to? It cannot be anything we should want to know. But as I asked a simple question, I will be answered. When people make casual conversation, other people should respond. I cannot have this custom of secretiveness and mystery making. It is silly; it is empty; it is impossible.'

'Let it be, let it be,' said John. 'Do not let me see my children harried in their home. This has been a day to give me heart.'

His sister threw him a glance and rose and left the room. She went to the table laid with the cold Sunday fare, assuming that she would be followed, and naturally right in the assumption. She did not speak through the meal, except to dismiss the maids, as though seeing the conditions unsuitable for witnesses.

John spoke at last in a weary manner, seeming to hear his own words.

'Hetta, is this what it has come to? Is this the way to go on with the work so well begun? Why cannot we live in ease and goodwill, glad of our lives and of each other?'

His sister heard him in silence, with her head held back, and her eyelids nearly covering her eyes in a way which recalled Clare. While he still spoke, she rose and moved to the door, beckoning slowly and vaguely to her mother. John signed to his children to follow them, and sat with his head buried in his hands. Hetta left the others in the hall and went upstairs. The young people went to the drawing-room and sat in silence round Sabine. Later Hetta came to them and spoke a cold, curt word.

'Your father is busy and wants to be by himself. Do not go

into the dining-room and disturb him. He is in the mood when nothing he says means anything, and he does not like it heard. You know these moods and are old enough to respect them.'

'We are debarred from one room, and hardly dare to remain in the other,' said Chilton, moving aside.

'Why is Aunt Hetta getting so much worse?' said Muriel.

'She tried to live for others,' said France, 'and people try to improve what they live for, and that is the end.'

'Most people live for themselves,' said Clare, 'Grandma among them. Do they try to improve what they live for?'

'Grandma showed no embarrassment in meeting Chaucer,' said Victor. 'I was cringing with shame for the gross conduct of my family.'

'She knew he would rank himself with the person in the superior place,' said Chilton. 'Miss Bunyan, taking refuge in his house, is not in it.'

'Is she not?' said Clare.

'Chaucer really thinks he is a chivalrous man,' said Chilton.

'Chaucer keeps staring at Aunt Hetta, doesn't he?' said Muriel.

'Don't let Grandma hear you call him that,' said Clare. 'I rather like Miss Bunyan; I don't know why she is so absurd.'

'I know many reasons why she is absurd,' said France, 'but I like her too. We are more absurd, and we are not surprised if people like us, on our rare occasions of contact.'

'She is anyhow accorded an adult place.'

'Not by Chaucer, is she?' said Muriel with mirth.

'What are you laughing at, Muriel?' said Hetta from her seat.

'Dr. Chaucer called Miss Bunyan a girl, Aunt Hetta.'

'Well, that must seem funny to you, of course.'

Miss Charity Marcon walked up her garden path, crossed her hall, and entered her plain little drawing-room, her great height almost coinciding with the door, and her long neck bending, lest the experience of years should prove at fault and it should quite coincide with it. She stood inside the room, an elongated angular figure, with her prominent, opaque, brown eyes looking out from her deep, jutting head over her strong, elaborate, slightly ludicrous face.

Her brother looked up with eyes of comprehension and companionship, and lifted from the sofa a length equal to her own, but less on a man, and a frame at once more willowy and with more weight. He had a face and head of the same jutting shape, lighter, narrower, sharper eyes and the same shock of drab, grizzled hair, apparently transferred from the head to the face, as he was bald and wore a beard. Miss Marcon had observed that it was somehow absurd that they should be twins of fifty-seven, and she was right that it was somehow absurd.

She began to speak in her deep, dry monotone.

'I have been up to London to get the book I am writing, out of the British Museum. I have got a lot of it out, and I shall go again presently to get some more; and when I have got it all, there will be another book.' She slung a strap of notebooks off her arm, and advanced to the fire with the smooth, unswaying motion of a figure drawn on wheels. 'So many people were there, getting out their books. It doesn't seem to matter everything's being in books already: I don't mind it at all. There are attendants there on purpose to bring it to you. That is how books are made, and it is difficult to think of any other way. I mean the kind called serious: light books are different. Mine ought to be quite a success. It will be just like the ones I am getting if out of, and they are standard books. I put things from several into another, and then it is called a biography. What have you done to-day?'

'I have paid a visit to Mrs. Ponsonby,' said Stephen, in a voice which was as high for a man's as his sister's low for a woman's. 'And I have begun to weed the garden.'

'I saw you had, and you have got beyond the weeds, and Mrs. Ponsonby is a host in herself, so you have done more than it sounds. I shall soon have to weed my book. Books are very like plants. They are better, the more they are weeded, and they come up out of each other and are all the same.'

Stephen Marcon had had an early scientific bent, and desired to give his life to research, replying to his father's objection that there should be a safer support for the family of a younger son, that he had no intention of supporting anyone but himself. The father had insisted on a normal career, and Stephen had chosen medicine as the nearest to his own line, viewing its practical side with deprecation, its human contacts with distaste, its system of fees as displeasing and unfit; and, naturally overcome by these feelings, had ended as an obscure country doctor, with his science the pursuit of his leisure, which was the greater part of his life. He was a contented, disappointed man, happy in his own disappointment, living simply on inherited means, making the friends he fancied, preferring his sister to other women, and indeed to other men, and seeing his small advance in science the reward and reason of life, to which he did not assign any great reward or reason. Sabine was of those who chose him as a doctor, because of his easy fulfilment of the duty and indifference to their choice.

'What is wrong with Mrs. Ponsonby?'

'Nothing. Or everything. She is eighty-four.'

'She is a wonderful woman.'

'No, she is not: she is just what she ought to be at her age, or must be, life being what it is.'

'Stephen, of course she is wonderful. People over eighty always are.'

'It is what they are not. They are more wonderful at any other age.' Stephen's high voice became a squeak, when he felt what he said. 'Unless you mean they are not blind or deaf, or actually dead, which is what you do mean.'

'Actually dead is what I mean, I suppose. It is what is meant. You see, you knew my meaning.'

'Not actually dead after eighty years and therefore wonderful! With the knowledge of a child, because they have had no time to increase it! How can things advance? Why should they? I wonder people are not afraid of the truth.'

'They are afraid of it, terrified, as you are. You have put their fears into words. You are much bolder than most people; I think you are too bold. I said that people were wonderful, and it is better than not being blind and deaf and the other things you say of them. And I can't think Mrs. Ponsonby has the experience of a child; I am sure there is something unchildlike about her.'

'Was it cold and stuffy in the reading-room?' said Stephen, his voice descending to its normal pitch.

'Yes, it was both. I moved about it, a grotesque but dignified figure. Many people looked up to wonder who the tall, strange woman was.'

'And did you tell them, Aunt Charity?' said another voice, as a young man entered and sank down at Miss Marcon's feet.

'No, I am a woman who seldom speaks of herself. It would not fit with writing lives of other people.'

'And with opening your doors to your ne'er-do-well nephew, and keeping them open.'

Miss Marcon rose and loomed towards the mirror in the chimney-piece.

'Ah, Charity, rightly named!' she said, and resumed her seat.

'Are you tired by the day? I am exhausted by striving with a man's simplicity to manage my life.'

'I suppose I have the pleasant tiredness which comes after a day's work. It is not so very pleasant; it is too much like the ordinary tiredness which I should have thought a day's work would cause. I am only just beginning to like it, and even now hardly enough. Of course, doing nothing is the most exhausting thing in life. A lot seems to be known about exhaustion, but I think myself it needs more study.'

Alfred Marcon leaned his head against his aunt's knees, considering his own tiredness rather than hers, as it was of the more exhausting kind she mentioned. He was a tall, supple man of thirty, with a straight, dark face, which had a foreign look without any cause, and rather large, slate-blue eyes, which had the opaqueness of his aunt's brown ones and gave him an unplaceable likeness to her. His face had an obvious hand-someness, which faded as it became familiar. He was a nervous, versatile man, accomplished rather than gifted, more unstable than indolent, who did not so much grow tired of successive kinds of work as simply tired by them, and repaired for periods of rest to his uncle's roof. His aunt welcomed his company and enjoyed his facile gifts, and neither found him a burden. Their means were enough for their needs, and this ended their concern with them.

'Are we not to have tea, Aunt Charity?'

'This is the time when it usually comes. I hope there is not going to be any exception to prove the rule. Rules don't need the proof, if they don't have it. Will you rise with your unconscious grace and ring the bell?'

'I have something to confess,' said her nephew, as he obeyed in every particular. 'I am going to do some new work, and I feel shy about telling it, much shyer than about living at your expense, though I know that is shameful.'

'It is the things that are not shameful, that make us shy. That is why we are warned about it, and work is one of them, anyhow honest work.'

'The honest gain is often shameful,' said Stephen.

'This is not honest work, Aunt Charity. It is work done under false pretences: I am not fit for it. I am going to educate Mrs. Ponsonby's grandsons.'

'Has she asked you to do it? Does she know you are not fit?' said Stephen in his highest tone. 'Must they not be nearly educated?'

'She is going to ask me. Chilton and I have arranged it. She is not to know I am not fit. Remember that, Uncle Stephen. It will be less dishonest, as they are nearly educated. I must do something to earn my support.'

'And doing something nearly done is a good way,' said his aunt.

'Chilton says she respects me too much for being related to you, to insult me as much as the last tutor. He left because of the insults. Foolish youth! As if a rough word hurts anyone!'

'There is a governess as well as a tutor there,' said Stephen.

'Yes, yes, but I am not going to be both. Muriel is not nearly educated.'

'It is true that the last tutor was driven away by insults; I heard from Clare,' said Miss Marcon. 'Alfred is going to be him. Of course bread is all the sweeter if it is hardly earned.'

'It does sound as if the tutor was foolish to leave,' said her brother.

'It is a privilege to hear any word from Mrs. Ponsonby,' said Alfred, going to the piano. 'The tutor could not have been a civilised man: I remember he was not.'

'How about the salary?' said Stephen.

'That will be between Mrs. Ponsonby and me.'

'You will still live with us, I suppose?'

'No, I think I live in the house with the governess,' said Alfred, moving his hands with effect and ease. 'I flinch at nothing; I will no longer be a burden.'

'The governess has left too,' said Miss Marcon. 'I noticed she was not there, and pried into the matter. She bore the insults with a woman's courage, but at last rebelled. Mrs. Ponsonby had a woman's courage too, and it all leaves them without a governess. But some other woman will soon come, and Clare is teaching Muriel for the time. One does see what women are.'

Alfred heard his aunt with his hands held over the keys, and now brought them down with a crash.

'We have a tea party this afternoon,' he said, softening the music to speak above it. 'I met the Seymours and saw that Jane wanted one. I cannot resist the appeal in a woman's eyes.'

'I will go and get rid of the dust,' said Miss Marcon. 'There is no reason why everyone should not try to please. To be careless about it is only a different kind of conceit, though I do think it is very different.'

The guests arrived as their hostess returned, a short, fair man about fifty-six, with a wide, weathered face, kind, bluish eyes, a broad nose and lips, and a look of breeding; his sister, a few years younger, tall and thin and pale, with larger eyes, narrower features, and the look of breeding less definite; and his son, a tall, spare man of thirty-four, with a long, oval face, a high, hooked nose which seemed to overshadow his short upper lip, and the look of breeding so pronounced, that it blunted his other attributes. They lived in the large house of the neighbourhood and formed the whole family.

'I hope you do not mind my arriving with my two stalwart men!' said Miss Seymour, in her usual tone of exclamation, summing up her party in her own terms. 'I could have done with a single escort, if I could have left the other helpless man hanging about at home.'

'Men ought not to be stalwart and helpless,' said Miss Marcon. 'It is quite unnecessary.'

'I am glad for my aunt to hear you do not approve of that, Jane,' said Alfred. 'She has left me all day and gone off on her own concerns.'

Miss Seymour was generally addressed as Jane, and did not dislike the custom, as she had an inability to be intimate with anyone, and felt it was disguised by an appearance of intimacy with everyone. Miss Marcon, who was easily intimate, was given the formal address, which tended to be pronounced in one word, as if it were a Christian name. Jane was much affected by the circumstance of living with her brother and his son, seeming to consider that the assignment to her lot of two members of the male sex had significance, though it was explained by her brother's having lost his wife and her nephew's not yet having chosen one. Sir Rowland saw his sister with affection, because their relationship involved this sentiment, and she believed that she sufficed him for the outlet of his gentler emotions. Rowland and Evelyn knew that it was Evelyn who sufficed him, and that no one aroused and held his feelings as did his son.

'Well, Charity,' said Rowland, in the ordinary, pleasant voice which had a permanent note of sympathy in it, looking at Miss Marcon with eyes in which the sympathy was also permanent. 'I saw you going by yourself to the early train. I tried to catch you up, but your legs were too long for mine. And you like walking by yourself. You like going along alone.'

'Well, you might have managed that, Rowland!' said his sister with a note of serious reproof. 'That was not much for a full-sized man to undertake.'

'Next time you go to London, Miss Marcon,' said Evelyn, 'I will call for you and the notebooks, and we will swing along, two tall figures in step, the books dangling from my hand.'

'Miss Marcon has her own escort, Evelyn,' said his aunt, still with the note of reproof. 'I don't know what was happening to her two active men.'

'I don't get up for breakfast,' said Alfred. 'Aunt Charity forbade it after my last breakdown. You would not have me disobey my aunt?'

'Well, no, I would not. You have me there, with my large nephew all ears at my side. I am put in a tight corner.'

'Jane seems to meet a high standard of physique in men,' said Stephen to his sister. 'It makes her expect a good deal of them.'

'I am going to be a governess,' said Alfred suddenly. 'I am going to educate the Ponsonby boys, whom so many people have educated. It seems silly not to try a thing which is so generally tried, before I give myself up and become a burden on my relations.'

'And they are not the nearest relations!' said Jane.

'No, so it will not matter very much if he does become a burden on them,' said Miss Marcon. 'They will mind so much less.'

'It is a good, self-respecting idea!' said Jane. 'A little bird told us about it.'

'I wish the little bird had told my uncle and aunt, and saved me the embarrassment. It always tells the last people it should. Uncle Stephen hates my being hired in the same house as he is.'

'Ideas that show you respect yourself don't bring you the respect of other people,' said Miss Marcon. 'And Alfred is to sleep in the house. We wish he would become a burden.'

'When you can do so many things, Alfred, why do you have breakdowns?' said Evelyn. 'They are for people who find things difficult.'

'I don't know, Evelyn; I don't know. They are just part of me,' said Alfred, getting up and spreading his hands. 'I don't find anything difficult, and I am always a success for a time, but nothing averts them. I don't know anything about them; it is enough just to suffer them. With me nothing fails like success.'

'You would be poorly off without your aunt!' said Jane.

'That is a matter of opinion, Jane. I should be in the river. It would do Evelyn good to have to support himself.'

'You think so well of the river?' said Stephen.

'No, you are right, Uncle Stephen. Evelyn can be the man he was meant to be.'

'What were you meant to be?' said Rowland, gently, looking into Alfred's face.

'What Evelyn is, only with more gifts.'

Rowland looked from his son to Alfred, as if it was not for him to decide between them.

'That is half true,' said Evelyn. 'I am so glad an unjust fate prevents it. But, of course, half the truth is the blackest of lies.'

'Who was the little bird? Chilton or Victor?'

'Clare,' said Evelyn.

'How does Clare come to be chattering about?' said Stephen. 'I thought she was shut up at home.'

'That is how she came to it,' said his sister. 'She could not bear it any longer, and so she did not. She felt she must have something different, and so she had it, sensible child!'

'Does her grandmother know?' said Jane.

'No, no, no, that would not be sensible,' said Rowland, more quickly than usual. 'And no one else knows. No.'

'How nice of Clare to think about having me with her!' said Alfred.

'Now, now, is that the kind of thing you have in your mind?' said Jane.

'So Mrs. Ponsonby wants to have you, likes the idea of having you on her staff?' said Rowland, smiling.

'I don't know if she knows about my being on it. Chilton was to suggest it to her. Did the little bird mention if he had?'

'Yes, he had,' said Evelyn. 'And she is calling this afternoon to talk it over. That is why we are here. I want to hear you say that you will do your best, and that she will not regret her decision, if you can help it.'

'You did not tell me she was coming here, Evelyn!' said his aunt.

'No; you might have thought we should not be wanted.'

'I should certainly have thought it! Was there ever a woman who had to manage two such monsters?'

'Why two?' said her brother. 'I am not guilty of anything.'

'Oh, but you will be before long, if I take my eyes off you. I make no mistake about that.'

'Come and look, Alfred,' said Miss Marcon from the window. 'They say that to look at some people is to love them. What do you think about Mrs. Ponsonby?'

Rowland laughed.

'I always think there is a lot of good in her!' said Jane.

'That is not at all what I mean.'

'Alfred has never learned to obey,' said Evelyn. 'How will he be able to command, when you have to obey first?'

'That is quite untrue,' said Stephen. 'The one hardly ever leads to the other. There are no two things more apart. People who obey may go on doing so.'

'Then it has been clever of Alfred to refuse to do it in all his posts,' said Miss Marcon. 'And he has not gone on doing so.'

'How do you do?' said Sabine, entering the room and glancing round with an openly appraising eye. 'It's nice to have a fire on the first chilly day. We were taken unawares. You must have very thoughtful servants.'

'One of our two servants is thoughtful, and so is my brother,' said Miss Marcon. 'If they had known you were coming, they would have shown some more thoughtfulness.'

'We surely could not have more than this.'

'But if we had known you were coming, we would have. Mary and my brother would have arranged it. We never tell our friends we are not going to make strangers of them. I wonder who found out how sensitive strangers are to discomfort. We would have made a stranger of you, if we had had the chance.'

'The guests you prepare for must be fortunate. But enough is as good as a feast.'

'A feast is better, and much more suitable when you are here,' said Alfred, displacing his aunt and taking a seat by Sabine.

'We prepare for guests ourselves, but our ordinary standard is perhaps not so high.'

'Plain living and high thinking are best,' said Alfred, 'but our standard of thinking is not high enough to warrant the living's being too plain. I am sure in your house things are properly balanced.'

The opening was made; the talk was soon under way; the outcome was plain from Alfred's lively bearing and fluent speech.

'And you won't find the living omitted in our house,' Sabine was heard to say. 'We attend to that side of things as well. It would not do to go in only for thinking. That would not be the way to get the best out of anyone. I have too much experience for that.'

'Get the best out of anyone,' murmured Rowland to himself.

'So Alfred is a tutor now,' said Miss Marcon to her brother, 'and people will get the best out of him. I wonder what that will be. People are always at their worst with their families, so we can't have any idea.'

'There are Clare and Chilton walking up and down outside the gate!' said Jane.

'They came to walk with me,' said Sabine. 'I naturally do not walk alone. They are waiting to take me back. We need not consider them: there is no hardship in waiting: it is what they are there for.'

'But will they not come in and have some tea?' said Stephen, not observing his sister's silence.

'No; we were too many to come to tea. We settled that. It was quite clear between us. It was silly of them to wait where they could be seen. It looks like attracting notice: I hope it was not that.'

'It doesn't seem to have turned out very differently,' said Evelyn.

'They are coming up the path,' said his father in an appreciative tone. 'Stephen beckoned to them.'

'They lost no time in responding,' said Sabine. 'I don't know what good my words were: I must put things more plainly. Clare, why did you walk where you could be seen, when we arranged that you should keep out of sight?' Her tone implied that she had no scruple in bringing the matter into full light.

'We forgot, as the time went by, that our office was a guilty one. And it began to rain, and we were casting wistful glances towards the porch.'

'Of course you could not stand in the porch, when we had come to that arrangement. You could have waited under the hedge on the sheltered side; the rain would not have hurt you there. There is nothing to be ashamed of in waiting for your grandmother.' Sabine's tone became ruthless. 'There is no need to be self-conscious about it, if that was the trouble.'

'Of course Alfred will have a breakdown,' murmured Evelyn, while his father silently regarded Sabine.

'It is natural to be self-conscious about waiting beyond a point,' said Clare. 'If you suspected it, why did you not put us out of our misery? And about waiting where we seemed to be concealing it. It looked as if someone was self-conscious about it.'

'We arranged it in order that you should not come to tea,' said Sabine in a distinct tone. 'You knew that.'

'I am rather glad the arrangement fell through,' said Chilton, stirring his cup. 'It hardly took enough account of Clare and me.'

'Fancy being a tutor to Chilton!' said Evelyn. 'And for a man prone to break down.'

'I hope Mr. Marcon will not think my words are generally ignored like that,' said Sabine. 'It would be a most misleading beginning.'

'I tremble to think what he must think of you, Grandma,' said Clare. 'I wish the beginning had been more misleading.'

'Your words were not ignored, Grandma,' said Chilton. 'We

lurked in the lanes until human nature rebelled, and the heavens wept in sympathy.'

'Boy's talk, boy's talk,' said his grandmother.

Rowland looked at Sabine with the startled expression which had withstood a lifetime's knowledge of her.

'And we are not strangers in this house.'

'You certainly do not seem to be.'

'Oh, do you see that you are not? I am so sorry,' said Miss Marcon. 'I am afraid it does seem as if we knew you very well. It is dreadful to have to take people as they are. No wonder they apologise for making it necessary. If you will come again, we will be quite different, not in the least like ourselves.'

'I will be going, if you have both finished,' said Sabine, coldly to her grandchildren. 'And I suppose you have. You must see that we have taken enough kindness.'

'From the tutor's family,' murmured Miss Marcon.

'I am going to take a little more,' said Chilton.

'I will not impose my commands to have them disobeyed. I will go home alone, and will speak to you when you have followed me.'

'Will you not be afraid to go home?' said Rowland to his son, in desire to know.

'Miss Marcon will have to adopt them. She said she wanted to treat them as strangers, but that will not be possible.'

'Will you let me walk home with you, Mrs. Ponsonby?' said Alfred, as Sabine was leaving without word or sign. 'You will have to get used to having me about.'

Sabine relaxed, and turned and performed her farewells, and left at Alfred's side.

'It is extraordinary that anyone can choose to live in our family, when he has met us,' said Clare.

'Alfred likes to be scolded by women,' said Stephen.

'Yes, it is true,' said his sister, 'especially by old women. He lost his mother as a young boy, and has worried over what he has missed. He likes a family atmosphere.'

'Missed,' said Rowland to himself.

'He will have it,' said Clare. 'And perhaps he will cease to worry.'

'We must return to it,' said Chilton. 'We do not dare to stay away. It will be wise to have our meeting with Grandma, in his presence. It is wonderful that so much of our lives will take place in it.'

'I have so liked having you,' said Miss Marcon. 'You have such nice ways with each other, just as Stephen and I have. You really almost treat each other as strangers. It is the only way to keep family affection. One must never feel that one is in one's own home.'

'We never do feel it,' said Clare. 'Grandma makes it clear that our proper condition is homelessness. She is herself very much at home.'

'I hope Alfred will not be at home,' said Miss Marcon. 'I think he has that tendency. It may be wise for him to leave us, before he begins to be at home here. He has spoken to me more than once lately as if I were his aunt.'

'What will be the end of those children?' said Jane.

'Mrs. Ponsonby can't live for ever,' said Miss Marcon. 'There will be an end, and we can't always say that.'

'She is a wonderful woman!'

'That is what I tell Stephen, but he does not believe it.'

'He likes to be original!' said Jane. 'Most people do like to have an individual view. What I like is to form my own opinion and state it. You can't be the one woman in a family for long, without seeing a good deal of the other kind of originality!'

'I am the one woman myself, but I have not seen much.'

'Well, you are one of the original ones too. I should not go up to London to research.'

'That is not a thing an original person would do. You don't understand about research. It is rather natural that people should keep it to themselves.'

'Well, it seems quite odd to be at home again,' said Alfred, returning. 'It shows how readily I shall settle down. My position in the house will call for all my qualities; and I almost meant that, the whole variety of them. Do you know who are the most pathetic of the Ponsonbys? Miss Ponsonby, Mrs. Ponsonby, John; in that order. Then Clare, Victor, Chilton, France, Muriel; in that order. Muriel reaches the point where there is no pathos.'

'Born with the gift for a happy childhood, she simply uses it,' said Evelyn.

'It is a rare gift,' said Stephen. 'if not so rare as is thought. I did not know it was even recognised to-day.'

'What will you be paid, Alfred?' said Evelyn.

Rowland looked up in interest.

'If you will come up close, I will whisper it.'

Rowland turned away so as not to hear.

'Not so bad,' said Evelyn, 'with treatment as one of the family.'

'No, it is much more than the governess is paid. You would hardly believe that.'

'I should not, but Clare says it is true,' said Miss Marcon. 'You would hardly believe in treatment worse than that of the family either, but that is true too.'

'Does Mrs. Ponsonby realise how Clare talks behind her back?' said Jane.

'No, she does not,' said her brother, 'and that is best.'

'A good deal is done to her face,' said Alfred. 'Clare has her own courage.'

'Yes, courage,' said Rowland.

'I believe you are in danger of admiring Clare, Alfred,' said Jane.

Rowland turned his face quickly, as if to confront the same accusation.

'I admire France, Clare, and Chilton intensely,' said Evelyn; 'and I rather admire Victor and Muriel.'

'Dear me, you young men are in danger.'

'I should like to teach someone,' said Evelyn, 'and give the best of myself to him. That is what teachers are said to do. It is true that you would hardly believe in their treatment.'

'What I can't understand about that family,' said Rowland, 'is how they say what they like all the time, and yet seem to be afraid. Can anyone explain it?'

'No one yet,' said Miss Marcon. 'Alfred may be able to presently. But families can seldom be explained, and they make better gossip without any explanation. To know all is to forgive all, and that would spoil everything.'

'You don't ever think, Evelyn, you don't ever think about Clare?' said Rowland, as he left the house behind his sister, hurrying to keep up with her rapid steps. 'You don't ever give a thought to it? I think, if I were a young man—I think she would like a change in her life, would like to have things different.'

'I am not a young man, Father. I am one of those strange people who are born old. It is only to the superficial eye that I have the gift of perennial youth. The life of the ordinary man is not for me.'

Four

'Now, the sooner we face it, the sooner it is past,' said Alfred, guiding Sabine's steps to the carriage. 'I know that dread of facing the unknown at night. My aunt says I am an old woman, and I tell her it is a good thing to be, and I wish she could contrive to be one. It is silly of Chaucer to put his celebration so late. He thinks it is more impressive at night. But I begin to feel excited; I love a village show; it entertains in the extra ways.'

'It is better to start in a mood to be pleased, and not with dour faces, as if nothing in the world could satisfy us,' said Sabine, with allusion to her grandchildren. 'It is fairer to those who will be exerting themselves for our entertainment. People who never put themselves out for others, do not understand the point of view of those who do.'

'I am glad we are offending blindly,' said Clare.

'Your grandmother is right,' said Hetta. 'Do you want to go, or do you not? Make up your minds and tell me. It is absurd to go in the spirit of martyrs. Come to your decision; I am waiting.'

'We have not been in any doubt,' said her niece. 'We do not reject the week's dissipation.'

'They misinterpret our anxiety for France,' said Chilton. 'We must throw it off and live each for himself.'

'I hope you will do so,' said France. 'I shall be setting you the example.'

'I am waiting for the rest of you,' said their aunt. 'You did not say Clare was to speak for you all.'

'We say it now,' said Chilton.

Sabine took her place in the carriage, motioned her daughter to her side, and her granddaughters to the opposite seat, ignoring the latter's discomfort in sitting three abreast. Alfred put his head through the window to see that all was well, and satisfied, if rather easily, withdrew.

'Grandma will think less and less of us in comparison with Marcon,' said Victor to his brother.

'I don't grudge him the reward of Grandma's preference. Of the four women in the house Grandma is his choice: it is fair that he should be hers of the men.'

'She has never taken so to a tutor.'

'No tutor has ever taken so to her. I don't remember the others showing any weakness for her. Here is Marcon's scroll of music, by which he will perform between the acts. I expect he will wrest away France's success. The talent seems to come from our house.'

'It does not matter about her success. It will not alter the play.'

'It will alter it in people's opinion, though I daresay not in Father's; he ought to know what he thinks.'

'Now follow your father and me,' said Alfred, setting out with John, without taking his music from Chilton. 'We shan't be much behind the carriage.'

The brothers obeyed, as they found themselves obeying Alfred. He was a successful tutor, with a learning which was sound if not deep, and never presented as deeper than it was. He worked with a nervous force which threatened to exhaust him and explained his frequent collapse. Chilton respected his accomplishment and Victor emulated his general address.

They reached the village hall to find Chaucer welcoming Sabine, with his eyes held from other distractions, until he had honoured womanhood in age.

'This is a privilege, Mrs. Ponsonby. I had hoped against hope that you would bring yourself to tolerate our effort. Subject to your criticism, the seats in the middle of the front row are yours. The position should be a convenient stepping-off ground for your son, against his moment of taking the platform. I trust the anticipation of that ordeal will not interfere with his enjoyment of the preliminaries, which is the rightful term for what leads to such a culmination.'

The party took their seats; the audience settled about them; Rowland found places for his sister and himself and took possession of them; Evelyn stood among the choir-boys, straightening a collar or a coat, talking almost on equal terms and meeting a chorus of response. Jane wore garments which were a somewhat confused compromise between afternoon and evening dress. Miss Marcon wore a gown which was entirely evening, not seeing why charity functions should be treated with less honour than those not meant to do good, and making this observation to her brother. Miss Bunyan handed the programmes in new, cheerful, awkward clothes, which were entirely afternoon, and chosen of this nature owing to her conception of herself rather than the occasion, and with the support of her uncle, who shared the conception. Sabine always dressed as a widow in tribute to her husband, who was entitled to this amount of recognition, as he had been an excellent man, and was accorded no other. Sabine had regarded him first as her husband, then as her subject, and since his death as a conventional character, unrelated to the truth. Clare and France wore good dresses which were out of date, and their aunt a better one which was up to it.

Miss Bunyan came up and shook hands with a cordial ease, keeping her eyes from Sabine.

'How are you, Muriel, and how are you doing? I hope you are two months further than when we were together.'

Muriel, taken aback by allusion to dubious occurrences, looked at her in silence, and Sabine, respecting her for it, exchanged civilities, bearing her no malice, and characteristically neither expecting nor meeting any.

'Now, Chilton and Victor,' said Chaucer, modifying his tone for masculine youth, 'you have a choice before you. Do you elect to sit in the front with your family, or at the back as younger members of the audience? Either position is equally honourable in its way.'

'Alfred is in the front with Mrs. Ponsonby,' said Stephen. 'Is that position honourable? I suppose in its way.'

'I hope, Chilton'—Chaucer glanced about in apprehension of hearers—'that no breath has come to your father of the revelation awaiting him? Our little plot was well laid and hatched?' He laughed at his sustained metaphor.

'No; we are successful conspirators. But our party is too prominent in the first row. Victor and I will retire from it.'

'Stay, Chilton,' said Chaucer, checking the latter's movement, 'nothing is further from my thoughts than cavalier treatment of your family. I think your ladies may prefer their escort with them. I spoke without due consideration.'

'The programmes are running short, Uncle,' said Miss Bunyan in clear, conscious tones.

'Two will be enough for us,' said Victor. 'We can pass them about.'

'You do not think, Victor, that that arrangement might convey a hint that the play was not unknown to some of you? We want the truth to break upon your father, not to creep upon him unawares. It were better and more telling in that way. I think your aunt's clear judgement, if we could ask it, would be with me.'

'The play is late,' said Rowland.

'You, Sir Rowland, cannot be accused of not being prepared for it,' said Chaucer, laughing at his parishioner's capture of his seats. 'Seriously, is there some hitch?'

'Something has gone wrong with the dresses of the women,' said his niece.

'The women!' said Chaucer, going into further laughter. 'That is a hitch indeed, when the "women" depend on their dresses for their very nature. Can anyone be of service to us?'

Evelyn disappeared behind the scenes, and the stir of uneasiness subsided. The curtains parted and the play was under way, Chaucer standing as near as possible to the Ponsonbys, with his eyes on their faces.

The play was a succession of scenes taken from France's book and following its thread. They were imagined in the family sphere which comprised her experience, and the parts less within her knowledge were those omitted, so that the play gave an impression of a book better than it was. John sat in growing interest, and at length covered his eyes and gave himself to listening, as if shutting out the blur imposed by the actors. At the end of the first act he applauded fully, at the next more gravely, and at last sat up and looked about, as if to seek and recognise his fellow. Chaucer stood with an air of resolute self-control, and the young people kept their eyes from each other. Sabine sensed something in the air and looked about with impatient question.

'What is it? What is the mystery? Let me be told without any beating about the bush. I do not choose to ferret it out; I do not choose to wait for my answer.'

'Stay, Mrs. Ponsonby,' said Chaucer, leaning towards her and lifting his hand; 'stay. There is no mystery. The truth is unfolding itself in its own way; let it do so.'

'It is our way,' said Chilton to France. 'The truth did not save us so much trouble.'

'It would have done its best to remain hidden.'

'Someone has written the play, I suppose,' said Hetta; 'perhaps one of our boys. It is to break on us as a great surprise. They would feel it was very important, and we must play up. We shall have to work as hard as the actors. But it is much better than I should have expected.'

Sabine, too old to consider the play, and conscious of her son and daughter at her side, so that her grandchildren were at a distance, subsided at this and permitted the play to take its course, or felt that she did so. John became excited in its progress, and in the interval walked about and began to question.

'To whom do we owe this? It is a clear and vital thing. I did not look for anything on this level.'

'I am more than gratified to hear you say it,' said Chaucer, standing before him and slowly moving his head. 'Personally, I am not qualified to criticise such productions, but I accept from a higher tribunal a verdict which gives me great pleasure.'

'I should be interested to meet the author.'

'You would; I can take upon myself to confirm it.'

'He is an interesting person, is he? Is he here to-night?'

'I hardly know how to answer that question. The answer will out in its own good time.'

John glanced at his sons.

'No, you are not so very warm, Ponsonby, not so very warm. At least, I think not to your own mind.'

'Not so very warm?' said John in a lighter tone. 'Well, I should not want so much for myself; I am ashamed of my passing thought. I will meet the author with the greatest pleasure; I have a great desire to meet him.'

'I have seldom listened to words which broke upon me with greater illumination. Truly there are strange and natural affinities.'

'You like the play?' said Chilton to John.

'So much that I was guilty of the egotism of fathering it on you. I am put in my place. I am not to be the founder of a line.'

'I should not write a play: it is not within my scope.'

'My dear boy,' said John, putting his hand on his shoulder, 'I should not like you better if you wrote a thousand.'

'That is true,' said Stephen.

'Are people really as wicked as you think?' said his sister. 'It is no good to think it, if you feel it may not be true. It would take away all the pleasure.'

'And you are my reader and belong to my larger family,' continued John, 'and so are doubly my son. All my children are my children twice.'

'And if he had written the play, in what relation would he

75

stand to you?' said Chaucer.

'Ah, then he would be my fellow and my equal. I confess that for a moment the conception pulled. But I am a foolish man; he is nearer as my son.'

'Ah, Ponsonby,' said Chaucer, looking after him and speaking half aloud, 'something of what you would ask is coming to you. It is not only on a son that such a weight may fall: there are shoulders more frail that may sustain it.'

A signal recalled the people to their places; Sabine and her daughter had remained in theirs; Chilton took France's and no one noticed she had not returned. John gave himself to the play, almost as if some obstacle had rolled away and left him magnanimous and free.

'A good thing,' he said at the end, 'coming, I hazard, from a young mind, and promising things beyond itself. But I should not be talking. Who am I upon the occasion?'

'The judge whose verdict we awaited,' said Chaucer, leaning towards him, and then drawing back with a still guarded air.

The curtains met; the clapping ensued; the actors were summoned and applause was bestowed in proportion to their popularity, which seemed, as so often, to coincide with their gifts. There was the call for the author, and Chaucer held himself tense, and John supported the call and sat ready to acclaim, glancing to see if he was noticed. He dropped his hands and stared at his daughter, and renewed his clapping in a steady, even manner, seeming to compose himself under its cover. When France was recalled, Sabine sat up and joined the applause, in a way of one not according excessive praise to her own. Hetta did the same, becoming suddenly vivacious, bending to her nephews and calling attention to the nearness of her guess.

'Well, so she wrote it,' said Rowland. 'Yes, so she is her father's daughter. Or to-night he is her father. Yes, he must be very proud.'

'He must indeed. I wish I had something to be proud of in my family,' said Jane, looking reprovingly at her nephew. 'I begin to think I never shall have. Evelyn, are you going to allow yourself to be beaten by a girl?'

'Oh, yes, by a girl, but I am glad it is not Alfred. I was so afraid it was. He makes me feel competitive, and it is a feeling so unworthy of me. He played the piano just as if he had written the play. Of course I knew he was not capable of it, but

I am relieved I am not wrong. Anyone may make a mistake, and one never knows with Alfred.'

'So it is nice to know now,' said Miss Marcon.

'I had no suspicion of it!' said Jane. 'Most people would like to claim that they had known it all the time. But I enjoy any excitement in life too much to worry about the personal credit.'

'It is absurd of Alfred not to have written the play,' said Miss Marcon. 'To be a tutor and give solos between the acts, and then not write it would make anyone ridiculous. And that wonderful child! To write that, sitting at home, and not to have to go by train to get it! I do look up to her. But why do they call for the author last instead of first? The author is really the cause of everything. If I wrote a play, I would come and bow at the beginning. But perhaps I don't understand the modesty of greatness. If they are arranging for that, it is different.'

'I wonder what her father is feeling,' said Stephen.

'You are not wondering. You have made up your mind. I am talking to cover your thoughts. I hope they are covered.'

'Yes, yes, we both know how to cover them.'

'When anyone has any success, it is natural enough to feel you would rather it were yourself. There is not anyone who would not rather.'

'That is not what I meant.'

'I know it is not. But don't say it in public; wait until we are at home; I shall love to hear. Ah, Charity, rightly named!'

'Why was it done in this mysterious way?' said Sabine. 'I should have taken more pleasure in the play, if I had known. I do not like mysteries in my house; I have said that nothing shall be kept from me. And France should have had a dress for such an occasion. She looked ridiculous, bowing in one she has been known by for years. It shows what happens when I do not manage things myself. I desire that in future I shall have the opportunity.'

'It was known that we should appear in these dresses, if not on the platform,' said Clare. 'Aunt Hetta must have realised they were behind the mode, when she attained it herself.'

'Young people are always mysterious over such things,' said Hetta, watching her brother's reaction to the light upon his daughter. 'We have to remember how large it looms in their minds. This is not a trifling thing to France. We must put ourselves in her place.'

'It is not a trifling thing in itself,' said Chilton. 'It is a good piece of work, an unusual thing to achieve.'

'That is a good brother,' said Hetta, smiling at him, but still looking at John.

'It is all a compliment,' said Chilton to Clare. 'Aunt Hetta is afraid that Father will think too much of France.'

'Whispering here!' said Hetta. 'And at your age, Clare! I must break you of these home habits, if they are to catch you out in public. They give you away too much.'

'Our home habits are our only ones. And when that is the case, they do give people away.'

'Smartness, smartness!' said Hetta, still looking at her brother. 'I get so tired of it.'

Chaucer came up to John, his eyes moist, and his hands maintaining the act of applause, while he subdued the sound to allow of his speech.

'You said, Ponsonby, that you would be interested to meet the author. How much more interested are you than you foresaw! You caught yourself hoping it was your son. You find it is someone fully as near. You said you were not the founder of a line. It comes to you that you may be even that. I envy you your feelings upon the occasion.'

'Then you understand them,' said John, in a light tone. 'I am taken by surprise; I did not know the ambitions had taken such a definite line. And I must be careful what I say, if my words are remembered.'

'I think I congratulate you even more than your daughter. Yours, if I mistake not, is the greater joy.'

'I expect it is,' said John in a tone of recollection. 'My poor girl! Of course she is overwhelmed by a rush of doubts. I know how it is, before custom has dulled the feelings. And I am not a foolish father; I feel the criticisms springing to my mind; I have a high standard for my own. Now that the young man has not materialised, I must have what I can from the young woman.'

'That is the tone; that is the bracing note; and I will warrant the heroine of the day has the grit to stand it. Here she is, coming to receive your congratulations. If I am not unwelcome, I will stand by and see the authoress becoming the daughter.'

Chaucer was not so unwelcome as he might have been, as both John and France were glad of his presence.

'Well, little leader of a double life!' said John, drawing her to him. 'So you make your beginning without consulting your father. You follow the old, old line. Well, why should you strike a new note, after all? But didn't you feel me at your elbow, when you wrote those scenes without welding them into a whole? Did you think they were a string of beads? But on the whole, well done, my child, well done.'

'The scenes are taken from a book,' said Chilton. 'That is why they give that impression. You must read the whole thing as it is.'

'And when am I to read it? When we get home to-night? Do I not burn enough midnight oil? But I will read it, never fear.' John stroked France's hair. 'There is something in it that appeals to me. Chaucer bears me witness that I spoke my word for it, before I knew that I spoke in a way for myself.'

'And you must not go further and say what is in your heart,' said Chaucer. 'That must not be at the moment. And in the meantime our occasion must run its course.'

'Indeed it must, indeed,' said John in a tone of compunction. 'We are making it into an occasion for ourselves; we must hang our heads. Boys, remember you are part of an audience; do not conduct yourselves as guests. When it comes to my speech, it shall contain no word to do with my own family.'

The occasion did not seem to be suffering. Alfred was rendering a solo, to which the Seymours gave attention, and inviting support in the chorus. Chaucer withdrew to assume his doctor's gown for the presentation of some prizes; and returning with a conscious flush, which marked his relation to his niece, waited on the platform with his lips still moving in his own contribution to the sound, until his voice was at his own disposal. John made a considered, clever speech, praised the performers, recognised the efforts behind them, made a light allusion to his daughter, paused with amused deprecation when her name aroused applause.

The people dispersed for supper and became themselves. Sabine was tired and autocratic; France was nervous and aloof; John talked without pause to friend after friend, almost as if to prevent their replies.

'Well done, well done,' said Rowland, coming up to France. 'You are a real writer like your father. What does he say to it? Authors and such people are said to be jealous of each other.'

'Sir Rowland, what a very untoward speech!' said Chaucer,

laughing. 'You do not suggest that our friend, Ponsonby, could so fall short in gallant and fatherly feeling?'

'Men are said to be especially jealous of women in their own sphere.'

'Especially jealous! Surely ordinary jealousy would suffice?'

'That is not true,' said Evelyn. 'Men are especially jealous of men in their own sphere. I should have been jealous of Alfred, but I am quite pleased about France. Not so very pleased, of course: I have done nothing myself.'

'Is writing your sphere, then?' said his aunt. 'I am glad to hear you have one! There is a second surprise to-day.'

'Of course writing is my sphere, when it is everyone's. You must have noticed that everyone talks of writing as if he were a writer. It is because people think it needs brains and no training.'

'That would certainly help them to recognise themselves,' said Stephen.

'Yes, you were so ashamed of being trained,' said his sister. 'The play is good, France, my dear, and it is done by brains and not by training; we all know you are quite untrained. It is so nice for you to have it really known. I have trained myself to be accurate and industrious and other low things; trained myself; that is the pity of it, for I began by being as untrained as anyone. I am not one of those people who are born trained. And Stephen is even better, for he was impossible to train.'

'Ah, Miss Marcon, we can't all do our work on your level,' said Chaucer. 'Even Miss France does not aspire to that. The British Museum cannot be the sphere for us all. It is a good thing there are lighter matters for lighter efforts; we will not say lower.'

'Wouldn't he say lower?' said Miss Marcon. 'I am surprised.'

'He heard what you said,' said her brother. 'He thinks they are lower.'

'I am proud of having lived in the same house as the author,' said Miss Bunyan, referring easily to past conditions.

'I have enjoyed your father's books,' said Stephen to France; 'but I am going to like yours better.'

'Stay,' said Chaucer, lifting his hand, 'we will have no comparisons, if you please, and pitting of one against the other. Mr. Ponsonby is our guest, and as such he has addressed us; and we have listened to him, I hope, without placing him in one side of the scales, with his daughter opposite. The fact that she is his daughter, deters us in her presence. As her father she will prefer us to speak of him.'

'Now Stephen must be trained,' said Miss Marcon.

'It was kind of Dr. Chaucer to use your play, France,' said Sabine. 'Have you shown him that you think so? I hope people won't tire of kindness.'

'When people say that, they hope they will tire of it,' said Clare. 'There is no hope in this case. People can't be tired too easily.'

'Victor, you may wait upon your friends,' said Chilton. 'Don't be afraid. We all go through these awkward stages.'

Chaucer went into laughter, standing with his hands thrust into his pockets and negligently displacing his gown, his eyes consciously twinkling on the brothers.

'Chilton, your father is well and in full work?' he said, rather suddenly recovering. 'It must be wonderful to have such power with the pen. My recent effort in the field of words'— He flushed as he recalled his own speech—'has helped me to gauge his position, and unhesitatingly do I take my place behind him.'

'I am so enjoying the evening,' said Miss Marcon.

Alfred, who was carrying a coffee-pot, dropped and broke it.

'Dear, dear!' said Chaucer. 'That is a breakdown as great as I suffered in my worst dreams.'

'It had no handle,' said Alfred.

'Then it may be said it was not prepared for its part,' said Chaucer, continuing his figure. 'So I need not perhaps rank myself with it.'

'Do somebody pay Dr. Chaucer a compliment,' said Miss Marcon.

'We enjoyed your speech very much, sir,' said Evelyn.

'How came the pot to be posing as qualified for its purpose?' said Chaucer, looking at nothing and speaking at once.

'It had been dropped before. One of the women—it was let fall on the floor,' said Alfred.

'It was let fall; that is better. A petticoat should be able to shelter behind so many pairs of trousers. And if the corresponding pairs of hands collect the debris, it will not devolve upon feminine hands, a climax which does not appeal to us.'

'Victor!' said Chilton, signing to his brother.

Evelyn and his father stooped to the ground, and were not left without assistance.

'Stephen, you can get a piece if you try,' said Miss Marcon, looking on.

'It was too hot to hold,' said Alfred, also a spectator.

'Too hot to hold!' said Chaucer, throwing back his head in mirth. 'A pretty word for six foot one of English manhood! Come, Marcon, it has cooled for some time, so face the risk, unless you are afraid it will freeze you now.'

'If I were afraid it would either freeze me or scald me, I would not touch it.'

'I don't see how you are to touch it,' said his aunt. 'People are always so selfish over risk.'

'I was the first to push in,' said Rowland, standing up.

'There should have been a holder,' said Evelyn, who was versed in the arrangements.

'A holder!' said Chaucer. 'Do you all keep one in your pockets, may I ask, in case of coming upon something too hot?'

'It belongs to Miss Bunyan.'

'Does it indeed?' said Chaucer, shaking from head to foot. 'And you purloined it from her, in case you should need it more than she?'

Alfred gazed at the fire.

'You do not take me, Marcon, to be guilty of anything beyond a jest?' said Chaucer, laying his hand on his shoulder.

'No, I knew you meant it for a joke.'

'I am convinced that any real demand upon your fortitude would find you up and willing.'

'Why is he convinced of that?' said Evelyn.

'I make no claim to that kind of fortitude. They say that women feel pain less than men.'

'Do the women say it?' said Rowland. 'Do people want to feel pain?'

'Women have more self-control,' said Jane.

'A man would drop a hot plate fifty times to a woman's once.'

'That may be the reason why my niece has provided this china,' said Chaucer. 'Crockery would, I believe, be the term.'

'Oh, is the crockery yours?' said Alfred. 'I am sorry about the pot, but it was without a handle.'

'Would you have held to it, if you had known it was mine?'

said Chaucer, with rallying eyes.

Alfred leaned against the wall, as if unaware of what was said.

'Come, Marcon, join in the laugh against yourself,' said Chaucer, tapping his shoulder. 'It is a further height to reach than may be thought, but you will show it is not beyond you.'

'It cannot be higher than is thought,' said Stephen. 'Surely we have made enough of it.'

'We are to base our evening upon a coffee-pot and a play,' said Victor, 'and neither of them complete.'

'Come, Marcon!' said Chaucer, his tapping becoming rhythmic.

Alfred turned on him the faint frown which marks the partial catching of a speech.

'Can no one change the subject?' said Stephen.

'I hope no one will,' said Evelyn. 'I do enjoy Alfred's discomfiture.'

'I wonder why Chaucer was a parson,' said Alfred, leaning against the wall and seeming to suppress a yawn.

'I might say, Marcon, why were you a tutor,' said Chaucer, as if the words were addressed to himself, as indeed in a sense they were.

'Because I like teaching and am interested in boys.'

'Those, Marcon, are the right reasons,' said Chaucer, gravely. 'I am glad you are not ashamed to state them. It is a strange thing how many of us keep our better reasons to ourselves.'

'Not if you think how we are despised for them,' said Miss Marcon, 'though not generally as much as by Dr. Chaucer. To be surprised that someone is not ashamed of them, is going almost too far.'

'Alfred will not bear much more,' said Stephen.

'What will he do then? I thought he was not bearing any more already.'

Chaucer was continuing on his own line.

'We might say, why was Ponsonby a writer. You and he and I, Marcon, must use our gifts, if such a word may be applied to us as well as to him, in the medium in which they find their outlet. I a clergyman, he a writer—or the other order would better become me—as such must we live and move and have our being.'

'Alfred is bearing some more,' said Miss Marcon. 'If I were he, I would not.'

'The other order would sound quite wrong in these surroundings,' said Chilton.

'That may be your view, Chilton,' said Chaucer with a gratified flush, 'from your position, as we may put it, near the sun.'

'Is the evening never going to end?' said Alfred, turning from the group. 'Mrs. Ponsonby will be worn out.'

'Alfred is not ashamed of his position,' said Miss Marcon. 'In my heart I am as surprised at it as Dr. Chaucer.'

'I am ashamed of it,' said Stephen.

'Our good Marcon!' said Chaucer, looking after Alfred. 'His is not an easy spirit and brooks but little. I trust I have not been guilty of tactlessness.'

'What does Dr. Chaucer call you, Stephen, as he always calls Alfred Marcon?'

'He never speaks to me; I have seen to that.'

'What does he think of your seeing to it?'

'He does not know; I have seen to that too.'

'Girls, how often am I to say it is time to go?' said Hetta. 'I speak and speak, and you might all be deaf. You all look as if you were settled here for life. People won't think we are very used to going out.'

'They will be right,' said Clare, 'and they know we are not.'

'We shall seem as if we could not tear ourselves away.'

Victor was talking to strangers and apparently could not do so; Sabine, in a state of exhaustion, was being supported by Alfred; John was walking up and down, as if aloof from the occasion, and the departure seemed as doubtful as Hetta thought. Alfred did not find it beyond him. Keeping his hold on Sabine, he gave the sign for the carriage, summoned the sisters, roused Muriel, and was soon closing the carriage door upon its occupants.

Sabine would not have brooked the delay of her men, and her family soon assembled in her hall.

'It was kind of Dr. Chaucer to use your play, France,' she said, using words she had used before, and unconscious of it. 'I hope people won't tire of kindness.'

'Oh, my girl's play was up to them,' said John. 'They did not want a better. A better would not have done so well. I feel it is we who have done the kindness, and that I should soon tire of it.'

'Did you not think the characters good?' said Chilton.

'I was so glad to see them differentiated. Young authors do so little in that line. There was no wondering who was who tonight. I hardly found myself held up.'

'The actors could not do it justice. That could not be helped.'

'Well, well, if it were not for the actors, it could not have been put on at all. We must not complain there.'

'You must read the novel when you can.'

'I will read it when it is put into my hands. And I hope some day to read one that others will read.'

'This one ought to come to that; I am sure you will say so. Clare and I are quite agreed.'

'It is much better than I expected,' said Victor.

'What you expected is nothing to do with it. The point is that it is good in itself.'

'It is better than I expected too,' said John, looking mildly from one to the other, 'if I can say so when I did not expect anything. It was a good idea to spring it upon us, and let us judge it as strangers. I found myself saying it could not be by anyone here.'

'I should have known that by the first line,' said Chilton.

'The first line does not tell much, and you know the others better than I do.'

'I do indeed, if you could put that play down to the neighbours for a second.'

'Well, I did not put it down to them; I have told you. But it is good to see my son supporting his sister. No family striving or man and woman struggle in my house!'

'France must work hard and achieve something worth while,' said Hetta. 'She has all her life to herself. She could not have more opportunity.'

'Working hard seems to give such a heavy aspect to it all,' said Victor.

'And I cannot have my girl do that. Why should I work myself?' said John.

'There is work in this book,' said Chilton, 'in so far as work makes a difference. The main thing is talent.'

'The elders will think it soon to talk about that,' said Victor.

'No, they will not, if the talent is there. Why should they?'

'We will leave it until to-morrow, when I shall be myself,' said Sabine, in a voice which did not seem personal to her, as it told simply of weariness and age. 'Everyone talks and talks and does not tell me, so that I do not know what it is all about. Good night, gapy-face.' Her tone hardly changed, and she repudiated Chilton's arm and accepted Alfred's, and mounted the stairs.

'Well, where is the book?' said John, stretching his arms as if in sympathy with her. 'Someone give it to me, and then we must to bed.'

'Won't you wait until the morning, when you will be fresh?' said Chilton.

'I have other things to do in that state,' said John, putting the manuscript under his arm without looking at it. 'And why not, when I am the father of you all? I have to pay for my privileges. And I can see you and France want to get this behind: I know what it is to wait for a verdict.'

'We don't want a bemused one,' muttered Chilton.

'We want verdicts because we expect them to confirm our own opinion,' said Victor.

'If we did not expect that,' said his brother, 'we should not have an opinion.'

'You won't have one from me, if you don't release me soon,' said John. 'And don't talk as if you were ten years older than you are; I don't want to lose my boys. I have one finished young man in my house, and find it enough.'

The next day John came to breakfast late. He paused in the doorway, signing to his family to ignore his entrance, and passed his mother's chair on tiptoe with a humorous gesture of guilt.

'You look as if you had not slept, my son,' said Sabine, passing over these proceedings as utterly as he could have wished.

'Ask that young woman why,' said John, looking at France. 'What a manuscript to put on a man in the dead of night! And when he had had the gist of it before his eyes! The book contains the play, my child, and that is what I have to say for it. You gave us the cream last night, and that was wisely done. I give you the congratulations I have given; and I give you also my sympathy for not doing as well without experience as you will with it.'

'Don't you think the book should come out, Father?' said

Chilton. 'We wanted your advice about that.'

'No, you don't want advice. No one does that. You want to give advice to your sister, and I want to give it too. But I will not do so, for I know how unwelcome it is.'

'Don't you think the book should come out? We wanted to know just that.'

'Of course I think the book should come out, when I think of what I felt about my first book; and of course I think it should not come out, when I think how I wished I had kept mine back and used it later. But as it cannot come out under my name, I may not be the person to consult. I shall not get the credit or discredit.'

'Do you mean that another writer of your name would do you harm?'

'My dear boy, do you want to find yourself without bread to eat? Or, literally, without the advantages you are depending on? It is because I am myself and by myself, that you have been taught they will be yours.'

'It would do you as much harm as that?'

'That would be harm, wouldn't it?' said John, laughing. 'Never mind, my son; we all of us measure things by their effect on ourselves; and it is a good way of gauging them, the way that has our heart.'

'Do you not want France to be a writer, as you are?'

There was a pause, and then John spoke more sharply.

'Do I want her to be a worker, as I am? Why should I want it? What is there to want about it? Can I leave them all to your support?'

'I had not thought of the matter in that light. We must consider it in every light, of course.'

'Your own light will do. If we all do that, we get the light all round in the end.'

'Well, we will leave the matter for the moment.'

'No, we will not: that would mean we should recur to it; and that will not do; you make me see that. We will leave it until one of you can take my place. That is how it sums up. Then we will return to it, and I shall do so gladly, glad to lay down my burdens.'

'What do Grandma and Aunt Hetta think?'

'The women dependent on me,' said John, with a light laugh.

'We are not dependent on you,' said Hetta. 'You know that

is not the truth. We should have to leave the house if you did not earn, but that is all. And in a way I should not mind. It takes my energy as much as it takes yours. But the boys know what you mean. Why they all pose as being stupider than they are, passes my comprehension. We are all quite stupid enough; that is a good basis to go upon. France has had her play acted; and she must do something more, if she wants to go further.'

'Father's meaning is simple and clear,' said Victor. 'I don't know why we make a fuss about it. We should not ask him things, if we don't want him to answer. He is speaking a truth which we might have arrived at by ourselves. Of course his work for us all must come before anything else.'

'I had better go and get on with it,' said John, rising with a faint sigh. 'I think it has never been so hard to me as at this moment. You understand I am ready to yield my place to anyone who can take it. That is all there is to the matter. But as in the meantime it has to be filled, I must give it what energy I can muster. My night hours were not my own.'

He left them, waving his hand in his usual way, and his sister followed. Sabine and Alfred continued to talk, but the young people felt there was a silence.

'Well, there is an end of it,' said Victor.

'Of course there is not,' said his brother. 'There are other names.'

'You must consult Father before you do anything.'

'We have consulted him, and he made us regret that we did so. We are dependent upon ourselves.'

Victor sauntered up and down, humming in his father's manner.

'Father has his own way of being the opposing parent,' said France. 'The cases on record may have their explanations. I daresay they are natural ones.'

'Are you of the stuff that martyrs are made of?' said Chilton. 'I hope not; it is useless stuff.'

'She is of the stuff young women writers are made of,' said Victor. 'That is quite different.'

'What are little boys made of? Well, we thought Father would be a help to you, France. And you will have no help.'

'It is the common lot,' said Clare, 'and it may be better than a lot moulded by her family. It is probably a good thing that is rare. But it is a pity that Father's mantle has descended on his favourite.'

'Doesn't Father like France to write books?' said Muriel.

'He would like you to write one,' said Victor. 'Go and attend to the preliminaries.'

'I am to have a holiday until I have a governess. Clare does not like to teach me.'

'I told Grandma I could not bear it. A good-tempered pupil is impossible.'

Muriel looked acquiescent.

'What are little girls made of?' said Chilton.

'Authors have often kept their beginnings secret,' said France. 'Who knows what their reason has been? One is criticised for the tendency to secrecy, but the instinct is a true one.'

'Father likes the book enough to feel what he did, and actually to say it,' said Chilton. 'You have had great encouragement.'

'It is a piece of sound advice that the book should be boiled down and made more like the play,' said Clare. 'If France takes it, Father will have helped her after all. But to take advice, and such advice, may be more than human.'

'I have already taken it in my mind,' said her sister. 'It seems dishonest to let Father help me, when we accepted his refusal.'

'Oh, the family moral standard admits of that.'

Five

'I don't want to hurry you,' said Sabine to Miss Marcon, who was paying her a call, 'but Muriel's new governess will arrive in a few minutes.'

'If you really don't want to hurry me, I will stay and see her arrive. I have never seen a homeless woman coming among strangers before.'

'You may have to wait some time. That train is often late.'

'Well, you said you did not want to hurry me. I suppose it is just like a governess to begin by giving trouble. But it may be better to begin as you are going on. Does the station master know she is on the train? He always shows his knowledge.'

'I hope he will be polite to her.'

'Yes, I think he will be polite. Do you think it natural not to be polite to a governess? Perhaps that is why you have one; it might make it very easy. But I thought people were always so careful to make no difference. This will be a tiresome hour for her to want tea, won't it?'

'Do you suppose she will want tea?'

'Yes, I do suppose so. Governesses have that habit of ringing bells. But wouldn't you want some in her place? I know I should, because I am in her place.'

'Oh, will you ring the bell? I forget how early I have my tea. We will soon have some for you. I don't know why I should ask you to ring, except that I am an old woman.'

'I expect you were thinking of the governess. I am afraid I am not glad you did not wait. I wish you had waited; it looks as if the tea was just for me. I hope it will not upset the maids; that is so unpardonable. People must do something the maids cannot pardon, to do it, and maids pardon more than anyone else, I always think. What a pleasant face this maid has! I hope she does not think the tea is just for me. What is her name?'

'I do not know. We call her Gertrude. We always use the same name. It makes it easier.'

'But not for her, does it? For the first one, I suppose. It hardly seems fair that the first to leave should have the most consideration. What was the name of the last governess? Do you want to call this one by it?'

'Her name was Miss Bunyan; Bunyan, I should say. Of course we shall have to call this one by her own name.'

'Miss seems part of the name of a governess, but she would not pardon the other part's being anyone's but her own. I said that maids pardoned more than anyone else.'

'Here is the governess!' said Sabine in the low, conspiratorial tone of speaking to an equal of a different being. 'Do not look as if we were talking about her. Speak of something else.'

'Would it matter our talking about her, when we are just expecting her to arrive? I think that would be an excuse——'

'How do you do, Miss Hallam?' said Sabine, offering her hand from her seat. 'You see I have not forgotten your name.

I am afraid your train was late.'

'How do you do, Mrs. Ponsonby? You see I have not forgotten your name either. We do not often forget names we have seen written.'

'No, but my memory is not what it was,' said Sabine, her tone as even as before, but betraying to Miss Marcon that her idea of the newcomer had undergone a revolution. 'You must forgive my not getting up; I am a very old woman. Let me introduce you and my friend.'

'You think I am nearer to an old woman than you expected?'

'I think you said you were forty-six in your letters. Perhaps you do look a little more.'

'You have not forgotten that either; I do not think you are forgetful.'

'I thought it was pathetic, when women seeking employment concealed their age,' murmured Miss Marcon for Miss Hallam's ears. 'I see it is not.'

Edith Hallam was a woman of medium height and rather heavy build. She had a broad, bare brow, a pale, straight-featured face, delicate hands and limbs, and little, clear, brownish eyes, which showed a sudden, passing light. Her speech was blunt and easy, her voice natural and dry. Her clothes were rather worn and rather good, and she looked older than her age.

'My memory is up and down,' said Sabine. 'I cannot depend on it.'

'I was forty-six last month. I have brought my birth certificate.'

'I would have taken your word.'

'Yes, but I would rather you believed me.'

'She did not mean you would doubt her,' said Miss Marcon. 'Are you fond of teaching?'

'I have come to see it as my life. I began to teach when I was seventeen.'

'Then you are almost a born teacher,' said Miss Marcon.

'That was very young to begin,' said Sabine.

Very young, so I said I was twenty, and of course they took my word. That must have been the beginning of my looking older than my age.'

'I hope it began then,' said Miss Marcon.

'Did you make the choice yourself?' said Sabine.

'No, I am the classic governess, driven by necessity. When my father died, I found myself without a home. He had speculated and lost all he had.'

'And I expect he had such a good reason,' said Miss Marcon. 'I had a brother who speculated and lost all he had, and it was because he wanted to treble it. I don't think his reason could have been more sensible. And it turned out so differently from what he hoped, that he shot himself. Of course it could not have been more different.'

'I have not heard of that brother,' said Sabine.

'Haven't you? I thought it was the kind of thing that inevitably leaked out. People told me it was. He was Alfred's father, and Alfred is situated just like Miss Hallam, and dealing with the situation in the same way.'

'Miss Marcon's nephew is my grandsons' tutor,' said Sabine to Edith. 'It is strange that your cases should be parallel.'

'I think a tutor's and a governess's case might easily be.'

'Your father did not think of you, did he?'

'But it was of her he was thinking,' said Miss Marcon. 'It was for her sake he wanted to treble all he had, just as my brother wanted to for Alfred's. My brother left a note to explain it, and it seems that that is best. And then he would not be a burden. It would not have done for anyone to be a burden on Alfred.'

'Were you an only child, Miss Hallam?'

'Yes; I had no brothers and sisters to support.'

'And your father was a widower?'

'Yes; I did not even have to support a mother. You feel I am fortunate?'

'And the life has proved what you hoped?'

'No; I hoped to be able to provide for my old age. I did not know at first that teaching was its own reward.'

'I believe there are homes for worn out—for governesses who have retired,' said Sabine, looking away as she ended.

'If you think, there would have to be,' said Miss Marcon.

'An aunt left me some money, and I am letting it accumulate until it is enough.'

'You would like to treble it,' said Miss Marcon, 'but do be warned.'

'I should like to treble it so much that I am afraid it must be a family trait.'

'But it is wonderful that money gets more by being left. We

are really rewarded for not spending it, as we ought to be.'

'That does seem astonishing, when you think how things generally are.'

'I am sorry I could not agree to the salary you asked,' said Sabine to Edith; 'but I have no aunts to leave me money as you have.'

'People are nearly always left their money by somebody nearer,' said Miss Marcon, 'and they do not seem to count that. I am glad we are to leave our money to Alfred, and have it counted.'

'Am I to see my pupil this afternoon?'

'Would you like to see her? I can easily send for her,' said Sabine.

'I think I must go now,' said Miss Marcon. 'Goodbye, Mrs. Ponsonby. It is so kind of you to let me make a friend. I make one very seldom, but when I do, it is for life.'

'Is there anything to tell me about the child?'

'She is eleven and a half, the youngest of my grandchildren by six years, a merry, good-tempered child. She is not very forward, but you may alter that; and she is young for your teaching, perhaps, but she will mend of that by herself.'

'People do have to alter their pupils. Can I tell her that I was a governess when I was six years older than she? Or is that the sort of thing you would not wish to come near her?'

'It would not do her any harm. She will certainly not be capable of it. I will ring and have her fetched. No, don't let me trouble you; I can reach the bell.'

The sisters appeared, and Edith shook hands with her eyes on their faces.

'Have you had a long holiday?' she said to Muriel.

'Her sister taught her for a time, after Miss Bunyan left,' said Sabine.

'Then if I see their natural affection reassert itself, teaching will be its own reward.'

'Are you having a second tea, Grandma?' said Clare, for the sake of speaking.

'I am not having any. Miss Hallam needed some, of course. Muriel, pick up Miss Hallam's handkerchief.'

Muriel did so, showing no amusement at the mention of refreshment for her governess.

'Did you hate Miss Bunyan, Muriel?'

'No—yes—no,' said Muriel, looking at Edith.

'You already have more respect for me, haven't you?'

'Yes.'

'Well, we will learn to respect Miss Bunyan together. It will be the first change I shall make in you. I always respect the person who did what I am doing. I know what her difficulties were, and if her methods were obsolete, it was reasonable in one who was to be superseded. Now you may come and help me to unpack.'

'Muriel,' said Sabine in a low tone, as her granddaughter was following, 'come here and listen. Now Miss Hallam is a very clever lady, and is very kind to teach you, so do not let us have any nonsense as we had with Miss Bunyan. Do you understand me?'

'Yes, Grandma.'

'You may run after her and ask if she would like a fire in her room. She may be unpacking for some time.'

Muriel returned with the message that Miss Hallam would like a fire, and Sabine rang and gave the direction.

'Thank you very much,' said Edith to the maid. 'I like to be warmed in the same way as other people. Did Miss Bunyan feel the cold?'

'I don't know, ma'am, but you need a fire after your journey.'

'You already know more about me than about her. I must be easier to know. We should not go on seeing the same face day after day, and never know what lies behind it. You will tell me some time what lies behind yours.'

'Yes, I will, ma'am. Do you want any help in unpacking?'

'Only a little, and Miss Muriel will give me that. Did you help Miss Bunyan to pack, Muriel?'

'No, she packed by herself. She went all of a sudden. She—her uncle wanted her.'

'She sounds to have been as much of a stranger when she went, as when she came. I have never known that really happen before. I must see that you write to her.'

'No, I don't want to,' said Muriel with shrillness.

'Well, well, what would be the good of writing to a stranger? Did you like learning with your sister?'

'No, she was impatient and she did not know anything.'

'So you are a pupil who needs patience. I hope you made her difficult task as easy as you could. Do you come down to dinner?'

94

'No, but I am coming to-night.'

'And do I come down?'

'Yes; that is why I am coming.'

'Of course, to get to know me. Don't we have any meals together?'

'Yes, schoolroom tea at half past five.'

'Why don't we get to know each other then? That is when we shall do it. Do you mean a real schoolroom meal with real things to eat? Do I have dinner as well?'

'You do not—you need not—Miss Bunyan—you need not eat more than you want at tea.'

'I am glad of that. Did Miss Bunyan eat real food at half past five, and then dinner at half past seven?'

'She often did,' said Muriel in a tone of confidence.

'And so you had no respect for her? You found her a person of a gross habit?'

'What?'

'You thought she ate more than was proper?'

'She kept things in her room as well,' said Muriel, lowering her voice.

'Well, perhaps she needed them with that habit. You see I keep nothing. I expect to be given all I want to eat, and I find I am. I have heard it is astonishing what governesses expect, and I think it was astonishing if Miss Bunyan expected what she had. Now we must go down. Do you have to change your dress?'

'I changed it when I came upstairs.'

'Yes, of course, it is a different one. How do you know which to wear first?'

'One is older than the other,' said Muriel, laughing with comprehension. 'They look more different in daylight.'

'It is in daylight that we see the other, isn't it? Wouldn't it be better to change them round, to fit in with the lights?'

'I am not allowed to wear what I like; Grandma tells me.'

'Of course. How fortunate you are to have a grandmother! Now we shall never be strangers again.'

A group on the drawing-room hearth fell silent, as Edith entered.

'If you stop talking because I am here, you will be able to talk so seldom. The drawback to a governess is that she is always there. You cannot get rid of her when you would like.'

'We are all regarded as having that drawback here,' said Clare.

'Did you have a good journey?' said Victor.

'Well, I had that familiar feeling of approaching the unknown, and it was prolonged, as the train was late. But I enjoyed it very much, thank you.'

'You will find us different from other families,' said Chilton.

'Families are different. I did not know at first about the difference. You have a grandmother instead of a father and mother?'

'We have a father and an aunt as well.'

'Yes, it is different. Do you keep everything from all three?'

'Everything from two. Not always everything from Father.'

'It is very different; that would very seldom happen. I somehow feel you are all my pupils.'

'There is a great deal they may all learn from you,' said Sabine, coming in with Alfred. 'Well, boys, have you had a good day's work?'

'I shall enlist you on my side when that fails to happen, Mrs. Ponsonby,' said Alfred. 'So, Miss Hallam, you and I do what is best worth doing in the house. We stand a little superior and apart.'

'We stand a little apart. But the worst of things worth doing is that they are worth so little else. I don't think we are seen as superior. But I am glad not to feel alone.'

'You will certainly not be that here,' said Sabine, catching the last words. 'I hope you will not find all these young people too much. I confess I often do myself.'

'It is good to hear that as a confession,' said France. 'It tends to be a statement.'

'Miss Hallam is not so much older than I am,' said Clare. 'I am twenty-six.'

'Twenty years,' said Edith. 'It is true it is not as much as you think, but I expect it is not as little as I think, either. Would you like to die before you are forty-six, Muriel?'

'I think I should like to be as old as Grandma.'

'Then you will be a little more than forty-six.'

'Yes.'

'What was that fuss you were making over the post?' said Sabine. 'Was there some exciting letter?'

'No, Grandma; we were having an argument,' said Chilton.

'No, you were not. I know your voices when you are doing

that; I have reason to. But I do not desire you to lie to me. I would rather hear nothing than a pack of ugly lies.'

'Miss Hallam is seeing us as we are,' said Clare. 'Do families often stand revealed as soon as this?'

'Yes, fairly often,' said Edith. 'You would hardly believe about families. Or many people would not.'

'We have to belong to a family to believe it,' said France. 'But everybody does belong to one. It seems so odd, when you think of what is involved.'

'There is nothing so revealing in my not desiring to hear lies,' said Sabine. 'Miss Hallam can hardly be surprised at it.'

'Miss Hallam's faculty of surprise must be already exhausted,' said Victor.

'I think it must,' said Alfred, smiling. 'I thought when I came here, "What an astonishing family! What an inexhaustible fund of surprise!" But it is all held together by the hand at the top.'

'Do you like lies, Miss Hallam?' said Sabine in her ruthless manner.

'No, I like to know the exact truth about the smallest thing. It is the result of a narrow life. I hope the truth will come out about the letter.'

'I daresay it will to you. I am a lonely old woman and do not count.'

'How many of us would dare to say that?' said Alfred. 'We should be afraid of the power of words. We do not count enough.'

'Did you really live with your grandmother before Mr. Marcon came?' said Edith. 'All your lives until the last weeks?'

'Well, here is the breadwinner come to join you!' said John at the door. 'The most harmless, necessary member of the house.'

'Let me introduce my son, Miss Hallam.'

'Another strange face!' said John. 'You must be tired of the procession. And another unfamiliar name.'

'Your name is far from unfamiliar.'

'Well, that may be a help. You have one acquaintance in the family, even if a shadowy one.'

'It is interesting to see him take a definite form.'

'It is supposed to be a shock to see someone in the flesh, whom you have known in the spirit. But only one of us has that effect upon you?'

'I am not so sure,' said Sabine. 'Clare said our family stood revealed, and I am afraid it did.'

'I have a book about the origin of the family,' said Edith, 'and it is based on property. It seems so tangible.'

'It has its tangible side. A family has to be fed and housed and clothed and educated. It is not all so intangible.'

'It must be based on a good deal of property.'

'Well, is this a case of keeping the best for the last?' said Hetta, coming in prepared with her effect. 'I am sorry I could not be here to welcome you. I was detained by manifold duties.'

'Families are even more surprising than you thought, Miss Hallam,' said Alfred.

'I ought to be prepared for anything in them.'

'But you were not prepared for this? You cannot boast that you were?'

'I hope Miss Hallam is prepared for her dinner,' said Hetta, going to the door. 'She ought to be after the effort of grappling with a family of eight.'

'Aunt Hetta's talk is so much more ordinary than she is,' said Victor.

'Do we never have any talk suitable for Muriel?' said Edith. 'Ought I to be guiding it into that channel?'

'It will do her good to listen,' said Sabine. 'It is a treat to her to be downstairs.'

'Well, it is no good to keep too much from children. They begin by belonging to a family.'

'Her family is incomplete, poor child,' said John. 'She cannot remember her mother.'

'Gapy-face,' said Sabine, in a low, warning tone.

'I thought the talk was too heavy for her. When it is a treat too! It cannot be much of a treat to hear you have no mother, and have to be fed and clothed and educated. Being educated is never a treat; they ought to have some other word for it than advantages. No, I will not have any more, thank you; I feel I have just had tea.'

'Your predecessor would have frightened you,' said Hetta.
Muriel laughed.

'This is more of a treat, I see. But she would not have frightened me, only brought back my old self. My nurse used to say it was a treat to see me at meals, and Muriel would have found it so, I see.'

'We must try and feed you up,' said Hetta.

'No, no, it is too early in the term for treats. It can be something for Muriel to work for.'

'Shall we go to the drawing-room?' said Sabine. 'Muriel, you can say good night, unless Miss Hallam will let you stay a little longer.'

'Do I have absolute power over Muriel? It seems dreadful to want to be a governess; but I don't think anyone ever has wanted it. Human nature always has a certain decency.'

'Come and talk to us,' said Victor. 'Marcon is taking our place. As long as he will be a son to Grandma, we are free.'

'There is a great bond between you all. I have never met such a bond in a family. The bonds I have met have been outside. I said I was prepared for anything, but I was not prepared for that. Had I better settle on which side I am, yours or your grandmother's?'

'On ours,' said France. 'Grandma declares everyone is against her, and we accept anything she says.'

'But she does not know it is true. She must not know it about me. By the way, I see Muriel cannot talk, but can she listen?'

'It does not matter, as she cannot talk,' said Clare.

'Did Miss Bunyan improve her much?'

'Muriel has been the same ever since she was born.'

'That is what I thought, and, of course, if people do not improve her, she has to remain the same. But the rest of you have altered since you were born. The little daily events will help me to understand it. What about that lie you told to your grandmother? I see a lie is a little daily event. You know I am on your side.'

There was a pause, and then Chilton answered in a tone of saying all that could be said.

'The letter was for France from a publisher, offering her terms for a book. It may not lead to anything, and it is to be kept a dark secret.'

'It is to be a complete surprise?'

'No, no, it is to be a permanent secret in the house.'

'But is it to be a secret from the public as well? Isn't it giving the house rather a large place, compared with the rest of the world? I don't mean it is not more important; I only mean I am inclined to take the weaker side.'

'It is like this,' said Victor. 'My father read the book, and said something for it; but he felt that another writer of his name might do him harm, and so do harm to all of us. So my sister is in a quandary, and feels there is no way out. It was really no good to submit the book to a publisher.'

'How different you are from when you were born! And when you were born so lately!'

'My brother is a very imitative boy,' said Chilton. 'And he is a great deal with me.'

'France could use another name,' said Clare, 'but even then the letters would attract attention. Letters get a deal of attention here; Grandma always sorts them.'

'And publishers' letters have the name of the firm on the back,' said Edith. 'You can't always manage as you did to-day.'

'We are so little different from when we were born, that we don't know how to manage at all,' said Chilton.

'Would your sister like to use my name? I must be here for a time; I can hardly be dismissed at once. And I am never dismissed; I only leave of my own accord; and I shall not leave here yet; I take too deep an interest in everything. It is nothing to anyone if I correspond with a publisher, and it is a good enough name for the purpose.'

'Thank you!' said France. 'It is a great solution. You can open the letters, and give them to me, if they are mine. I have no private correspondence, or only private from Grandma and Aunt Hetta. The way is smooth.'

'And if the veil is withdrawn, the explanation is good,' said Chilton. 'It is the best of ideas, as it comes from whom it does. It would have been no good if it had come from Miss Bunyan. Grandma would have been on the scent.'

'What would Grandma have been on the scent about?' said Sabine, crossing the room.

'About any correspondence of Miss Bunyan's that followed her here,' said Victor.

'Correspondence is private, and no one would be on the scent of it in this house, I hope. It is in my own family that I have to be a sleuth hound. And Miss Bunyan only had letters from her relations.'

There was laughter.

'My dear children, I had to get to know the writings, when I sorted the letters and saw them regularly for months. And Miss Bunyan told me she heard from her family.'

'Miss Bunyan told you many things, Grandma. Shall we

start this train of memory?'

'That will do, Victor; I do not need another word. I am speaking to you, and not you to me. I think you all seem brighter to-night. Miss Hallam will be a companion for you. I should think you may have a good deal in common; I hope she will find it so. You must do what you can to be companionable.'

'I have never felt less alone among many, on a first night,' said Edith. 'I have hardly remembered about being as if I were not there. I believe I have simply been here.'

'You are talking nonsense,' said Sabine, smiling. 'Have you made up your mind about your pupil?'

'I have said some nice things about her, but they would sound foolish repeated.'

'Well, I think I will say good night. You will understand that I am an old woman. I have seen you are happy and at home. Good night, my dear; good night, all of you.'

'Good night, Mrs. Ponsonby.'

'Good night, Grandma.'

'So I already have my rush of compunction,' said Edith. 'I have taken kindness from someone I have wronged. It is supposed to be generous not to mind that, but I do not mind at all. I really appreciate the kindness more; I must be very generous. I almost think it is the wronged person who is generous. I will go and say good night to Muriel, as that is an action loyal to your grandmother.'

'Well, this is better than Miss Bunyan,' said Victor.

'We need not put it in terms of Miss Bunyan,' said his brother.

'France is safe,' said Clare; 'and not only from the world, as Father wished her to be, but from Father. And when you have to be safe from the world, it is wiser to include your family.'

'That is a needless tone to take about Father,' said Victor. 'I notice France never takes it.'

'I never understand about France and Father,' said Chilton.

'You would, if Father had taken to you as he has to her,' said his brother.

'I daresay I should. A lot of little favours from childhood may mean more than one large things that alters a life. But they do less.'

'Father has done nothing to prevent France from writing, and publishing what she has written.'

'I wonder if he thinks he has. I think so.'

'He has been especially nice to her lately.'

'I have noticed that.'

'You take a good deal from Father yourself.'

'Not more than I must, considering my age and condition. It is what you take, and I have heard you complain of it.'

'You had better go to bed,' said Hetta, coming up to them. 'When Miss Hallam comes down, I want her to find you gone. She has to learn we are an early house, and we cannot say it to her face.'

'Actions speak louder than words,' said Clare. 'We could have said it to Miss Bunyan's face. Miss Hallam's being better treated is not going to be much advantage.'

The next morning Edith missed prayers and joined the family at breakfast. Hetta was nervous after a sleepless night, and chanced to stumble as she took her seat.

'You do not mind my saying, Miss Hallam, that it is our custom to meet in the morning at prayers.'

Edith looked at her with the light in her eyes.

'I do rather mind your saying it. I do not know why you say I do not. And I never come to prayers; I do not find them congenial.'

'They would do for you what they do for other people.'

'They would do nothing for me. I don't take any comfort in religion. I always live in my own strength.'

There was silence, apart from an indefinite sound from Sabine.

'You do not mind reading the Bible with Muriel?' said Hetta. 'I am afraid that is part of the duty you undertake.'

'No, not at all, if you don't mind her reading it. I think it is an unsuitable book for a child, but I like it very much myself. I am glad she is to adapt herself to me, and it is good for children to read unsuitable books.'

'I did not say anything that annoyed you, I hope, Miss Hallam?'

'You make up your mind rather readily. I thought I admitted that I was annoyed.'

'What are you all laughing at?' said Hetta, almost with violence. 'I might be sitting with a lot of grinning idiots instead of human beings.'

'Let us leave Miss Hallam her own ways,' said Sabine. 'She has had a great deal of experience.'

'I certainly cannot do that, if she is at all like anyone else I have had in the house. I always have to guide and influence people. If they do not like it at first, they soon come to depend on it.'

'But I am not like those other people,' said Edith. 'I can tell I am not by Muriel's expression.'

'You certainly strike your own note,' said Hetta in a casual tone, 'or do your best to strike it.'

'I have done my best and I have struck it. And you may have done the same. I think we both have that something which marks us as ourselves.'

'My daughter means she would like to help you in any way she can,' said Sabine.

'I did not quite catch her meaning. And I do not need any help. I said that I lived in my own strength. I don't think the other people can have done that.'

'They lived in mine,' said Hetta with nonchalant coldness. 'I am only too glad to meet someone who does not need to do so.'

'I think they ought to have come to prayers, if their own strength was not enough. They should have allowed as much to be taken off you as possible.'

'I am glad you feel enough at home to do as you please,' said Sabine.

'Is that a speech with a second meaning?'

'No,' said Clare. 'If Grandma had a second meaning, it would be the first.'

'I don't think that is Miss Hallam's reason,' said Alfred. 'She would not call it one. It is just that she does not adapt herself to the family. There is always a little touch of the guest about her. Now I adapt myself in every way. And I have never enjoyed anything as much as adapting myself to this family, or been so much improved by it.'

'Will you be able to manage on the books Muriel has?' said Hetta to Edith.

'Yes, I shall, thank you.'

'You have had time to look over them?'

'No, but I always manage on the books people have. Wanting new books is resented more than many graver things. And all books say the same about their subjects. If you think, they must, or they would not be the usual books.'

'You make me feel a very ordinary person, Miss Hallam,'

said Alfred. 'I wanted new books; I came to prayers; I behaved just like anyone else. I made no attempt at all to be original.'

'Neither did Miss Hallam,' said Chilton.

'Have you nothing to say this morning, John?' said Sabine.

'Nothing, Mater, unless you want me to say what is worse than nothing. I have had a publisher's account, and although I did not look for much from it, I looked for more than is forthcoming. It is not a bright chapter, the one before us; I was not eager to talk of it. I have not been working on my own level, and if I give people less, they give me less. But they did not at first; their faith in one dies hard. But it recovers hard too, and I shall not pull at once to my place. There is a lean time ahead.'

'People do not realise, when they see things there, what it means to keep on making them,' said Edith.

'They do not, Miss Hallam,' said John, swiftly turning his head. 'Their part is different as readers. Their yoke is indeed easy and their burden light.'

'And a good thing, the ordinary creatures!' said Alfred.

'I can't have my readers disparaged. They are much of the meaning of my life. I have been meaning less in theirs. Is it a forward or a backward step to say it?'

'A wonderful step anyhow,' said Edith.

Sabine turned and smiled at Edith.

'We shan't have our time in London this winter, Hetta,' said John, seeming to take advantage of a stranger's presence. 'You can have the convenience of certainty about it.'

'That will be a great saving of expense,' said Clare. 'To cut off one big thing is better than snipping off trifles everywhere and making life a continual strain. It is a good piece of news.'

'For you, my dear,' said Sabine, 'better than perhaps it should be. You are not giving up anything. It is your father and aunt who are doing that. It is one big deprivation for them, instead of the many little ones for you. We are to be clear that you like it better?'

'Much better, because it is better. It is better for Father too. If it is not for Aunt Hetta, she has had what none of us has shared, for a long time. She would not expect it for ever.'

'It is not for you to say what she would expect.'

'I should expect it, if it were good for your father,' said Hetta. 'It is for him we have had it; I have never wanted it for myself. It has been an extra strain in a burdened life.'

'Then it is not a deprivation for you either, and we can all look forward to a better life together.'

'I wish I could say we could,' said John, who had heard with a clouded face. 'I hope we can in time. But as things are, we must keep our tight hand. It is what we cannot afford that we are cutting off, not one extra instead of others. It is good to have a daughter to tell of my troubles.'

'I should hardly have thought so,' said France, in a low tone to Clare. 'It might be better.'

'We shall have nothing that Clare does not share, anyhow,' said Hetta. 'That should put her mind at rest. It is a good thing we are not going away. The house can do with my eye over it; I can see that, or rather I have been shown it.'

'It hardly can, my dear,' said Sabine, in her grim manner. 'It only just does with my eye. The children will not have any more. I am not defending them or saying you could not improve things. I merely state the fact.'

'It would mean our improving ourselves,' said France, 'and self-improvement is always terrible.'

'What would you say, Miss Hallam?' said John, lightly. 'Do you not advocate self-improvement in your profession?'

'I have never met it. People are always improved by others. That is what gives rise to the profession.'

'It is hard to see how the word, self-improvement, arose,' said France.

'You must have great knowledge of people. And it is the greatest of all knowledge. Shakespeare had only to be himself and use it.'

'That is all,' said Edith.

'We have sat an hour at breakfast,' said Sabine. 'I can sit no longer. Say grace, gapy-face'—She stumbled at the juxtaposition of the words—'Muriel, you may say grace.'

Muriel obeyed, and Sabine left the room, followed by her son and daughter, the latter turning to cast a cold, appraising glance behind, as though with some private purpose.

'Are you afraid of your aunt?' said Edith.

'Only me,' said Muriel. 'The others are not afraid of anything.'

'I always feel we do not know her,' said France.

'She has no life of her own,' said Chilton. 'And she is not a person to live in other lives. I can't think why she tried to.'

'Having no life of one's own is often the reason,' said Edith;

'and it is the best one. It would be seldom done for any other.'

'Religious people may do it for their eternal welfare,' said Victor. 'Aunt Hetta may be religious.'

'Well, that is a life of their own.'

'She goes to church,' said Muriel. 'And she does not have to go, does she?'

'If she were religious, she would not go,' said France. 'She would have thought about her religion and lost it.'

'Father seems to be very poor,' said Clare. 'If the London visit is to be cut off and not make any difference, he must be earning much less.'

'He said he was,' said France. 'And we know he is.'

'I don't think I ought to be afforded,' said Edith. 'I don't think your grandmother should run to me, as well as to Mr. Marcon. Your aunt looks at me, as if I ought to be cut off. Of course, he has become a necessity.'

'I am thankful you are here,' said Clare. 'Grandma can't let herself go beyond a point.'

'Unfortunately Aunt Hetta can,' said Chilton.

'People believe in the sanctity of the home,' said France. 'It makes them let themselves go. They think the sanctity is over everything, and it is astonishing how it seems to be.'

'What home do you know but this?' said her sister.

'This is where I have noticed it. And you do not seem to have been blind.'

'You observe that my sisters are outspoken, Miss Hallam, where a normal self-respect would keep them silent,' said Victor.

'If silence were a protection, we would be silent,' said Clare.

'I rather wonder that your grandmother welcomes strangers in the house.'

'I can't think how she dares to,' said Victor. 'It is sheer impudence and dare-devilry. It comes of a lifetime of having her own way.'

'Miss Hallam has not seen her yet,' said Clare. 'Grandma has kept herself under a tight hand. I can't think how she knows about her.'

'Even the degree of silence we have observed, has been useless,' said Chilton.

'I would not let Muriel hear this talk,' said Edith, 'if I could not see it has never done her any harm.'

'She must be one of those people who cast off evil,' said

France. 'I think she casts off everything.'

'Muriel, look me in the face,' said Victor, 'and tell me you got no harm from Grandma's dealings with Miss Bunyan.'

'She was a little brutalised by them,' said France. 'No one could touch so much pitch and not be defiled.'

'Tell me about that,' said Edith. 'I have wanted to know.'

'Miss Bunyan went at a moment's notice,' said Victor.

Muriel began to laugh.

'At whose notice?'

'Oh, at her own,' said Chilton. 'We had no unworthy triumph.'

'Not one of those victories which are more painful than defeat,' said France. 'I think Miss Bunyan had that.'

'I believe we did have an unworthy triumph, very unworthy,' said Clare.

'But tell me how it came to a climax.'

'How much you know!' said Chilton. 'Well, Grandma and Miss Bunyan indulged in some conversation, and "indulged" is the right word in both cases, and it came to Miss Bunyan's saying she would eat no more in this house. And so she went that afternoon. It was really the only thing.'

'But what did your grandmother say to her? You have only told me one side.'

'No, no, we have not come to that. If you have not guessed, you shall not know. Even Muriel would hardly put it into words.'

Muriel was making an effort to do so, impeded by her mirth. When she recovered, she did what she could.

'I don't remember,' she said.

'Evil rolls off her,' said France. 'You would think the words would be engraved on her heart.'

'The London visit should have been given up long ago,' said Victor. 'I suppose Aunt Hetta dreaded the prospect of her life without it.'

'I see her point of view,' said Clare. 'Such a life is not un-familiar.'

'You did not go up to London with them?' said Edith.

'No. Father is supposed to be happy with Aunt Hetta. And Aunt Hetta will now be supposed to make his happiness here. That is, she will seek out points for minute economies, and take away Grandma's interest in life.'

'When Grandma is dead, Aunt Hetta can do it,' said Muriel.

'When do you think your grandmother will die?' said Edith.

'I don't know, but she is very old.'

'I knew a woman who lived to be ninety-eight.'

'Grandma is eighty-four,' said Muriel, mentioning a similar age.

'The mother and child must manage together somehow,' said Victor.

'Is Aunt Hetta Grandma's child?' said Muriel. 'Oh, yes, of course she is.'

'Well, what is all the talk?' said John, opening the door. 'I am not so often seen in my family circle. I ought to learn the life of my house, if I am to spend all my time in it. You won't mind another member of the family, Miss Hallam? One more or less cannot make much difference.'

'Miss Hallam has already ceased to be surprised at the number of her following,' said Victor.

'She is surprised at nothing, ignorant of nothing, puzzled by nothing. I shall come to her in my doubts about human life, and thank her in my prefaces and say that without her help the books could not have been written. Well, you have a sad, weary fellow for a father. You have to do with less at a time when you are needing more.'

'We have Miss Hallam and Mr. Marcon,' said Muriel, 'and we have you always at home now.'

'So you have, my little one, so you have. And you have said a word your father needed, at a time when he needed it. You may look back one day and remember.'

'It is a pity that things roll off Muriel,' said France.

'It is Aunt Hetta who will not profit by the change,' said Victor.

'My son, I should have fared but sadly without my sister. In my dark hour I had no one else. If I do not requite her sacrifice, it will be because I cannot.'

'Sacrifice does recoil on people,' said Edith, 'and most of all on those who make it. In our resentment of it we should remember that.'

'People say someone regrets a sacrifice, as if it were against her,' said France. 'As if she could do anything else, when she comes to consider! People repenting at leisure are not at their best.'

'Ah, the words, her and she!' said John. 'Sacrifice has been the woman's privilege.'

'There, the word privilege!' said Edith. 'That is what we want of people, that sacrifice should be for their own good and not for other people's, when it is simply the other way round.'

'Aunt Hetta has not made so much sacrifice,' said Clare. 'She has not had so much to give up. She has behaved naturally, not nobly.'

'And we grow to the life we lead,' said John. 'We are moulded to it and by it. It becomes our own.'

'What is all the talk?' said Hetta, coming in with her eyes going straight to her brother.

'We were talking about sacrifice,' said Victor. 'I don't know how we got on to it.'

'I do not know either. It is not a thing that has ever come your way. It must be quite an academic subject. What conclusions have you reached?'

'That it is a bad thing for the person who makes it, and tends to be regretted.'

'It may be a bad thing for her, but it is not regretted, I hope. It must bring its own inner satisfaction.'

'It is very inner,' said Clare. 'Self-sacrificing people do not incline to spirits.'

'You have met very few people, hardly enough to generalise.'

'Very few, and perhaps a self-sacrificing person has not been included among them.'

'You would not recognise one, if you saw her.'

'So the satisfaction is as inner as all that.'

Six

'It is kind of you to welcome us both,' said Miss Marcon, crossing the Ponsonbys' drawing-room, with her eyes on the chandelier which hung just above her head. 'I know I am always welcome, but Stephen is different. It may be my sisterly attitude, but I am afraid it is Stephen. Of course, I love him better for his failings, but I see you do not. And it is trying to have social and other relations with the same person; I don't think people used to know people with whom they had other relations. But Stephen does all he can to avoid them. I am glad to see you well again: it would be embarrassing if he did not cure you. And he keeps the rest of you well, doesn't he? That is the best thing doctors do, I think. And as it is done for nothing, even Stephen cannot mind it. It is better than presiding over deathbeds, which ought to be nothing to do with a doctor. He does seem to have failed, if things come to that. But people think it is his natural work; it is so confused and fatalistic.'

'To every man upon this earth death cometh soon or late,' quoted Chaucer.

'Yes. It is simply no use to be a doctor. No wonder Stephen does not like it. I wonder doctors exist.'

'Because of man's inability to face the truth,' said her brother. 'He must pretend there is some way out.'

'Well, he can hardly be expected to adapt himself to it,' said France. 'It is too much, coming to an end.'

'Death is coming to me late, thanks to Dr. Marcon,' said Sabine, whose respect for Stephen was not affected by his dislike for herself, which feeling she saw as a wayward force beating against the fundamental and essential.

'Yes. You really owe everything to Stephen, don't you?'

'You know Miss Hallam, I think, Chaucer?' said John.

'I have made her acquaintance, and I may be the more readily admitted to her friendship, that I have the honour of knowing her predecessors.'

'I don't think that is an honour,' said Edith to the sisters. 'That part of my position seems definitely dishonourable.'

'Miss Bunyan is Dr. Chaucer's niece!' said Muriel, hastening to Edith and speaking in an audible whisper.

'You have the honour of knowing Miss Hallam now,' said Sabine with a smile.

'You have good news of Miss Bunyan for us?' said Chilton.

'I think I may say so, Chilton. I feel she is happy and useful in my house, and few of us can ask for more.'

'Indeed few of us expect to be both,' said France.

'But I think my niece is of those few. Indeed, she hardly regards herself as of a nature to warrant her being one without the other.'

'She is in many ways very sensible,' said Sabine.

'Well, here I am with my twofold escort!' said Jane. 'It is good of you to allow me to arrive thus doubly supported. Though why I am any worse than you are, Hetta, I am at a loss to see. I cannot imagine you without John.'

'It would be a flight of imagination indeed,' said Chaucer.

'Or Charity without Stephen. I only err in the sense of having two followers instead of one!'

'We are all dependent on each other,' said Rowland.

'That is so in this house indeed,' said Chaucer. 'I always feel that the old patriarchal system is nobly exemplified in it.' He paused and laughed before his next words. 'Or shall we say matriarchal?'

'We will say that,' said Chilton.

'Morbid growths are often the strongest,' said Clare.

'An undertone of complaint is never absent from Clare's speech,' said Hetta to her brother. 'It would be decent to drop it when we have guests.' John did not answer, and she raised her voice and turned to her friends. 'It will be easier for me to keep my eye on everything, when I do not alternate between one place and another. Even I cannot be in two places at once.'

'No, Miss Ponsonby. Even to you, as you say, that problem must be insoluble,' said Chaucer. 'Though I venture to think that something of your spirit detached itself and held your place.'

'How did he know?' said Victor.

'He did not,' said Clare. 'There was complete relief when Aunt Hetta was away. She is a person who takes the whole of her spirit with her.'

'Miss Hallam,' said Chaucer, with a little laugh to give his speech its place, 'what do you make of this family?'

'More than of any other. I should already be sorry to leave it.'

'Miss Hallam, I think I may say,' said Chaucer, with an expression of some pain, 'that there is no danger of such a contingence. I am not entitled to speak for the family, but I venture to say that something comes through, which points the lie of the land, if I can so express myself.'

'He should not express himself on the matter,' said Clare.

'I should think he may do so with authority,' said France.

'Miss Clare,' said Chaucer, overhearing and turning at once, 'I should not. I am rightly pulled up, and hope I may profit.'

'I hope Clare will profit anyhow,' said Sabine. 'Do not stand on top of me, you two great boys. Don't you hear me? Don't hover over me: I cannot bear it.'

'Victor, keep away from Grandma,' said Chilton. 'She finds your proximity intolerable, as she explains.'

'Will you take my mother in to dinner, Stephen?' said John.

'If she can bear it, or pretend she can. I must insist upon a certain appearance.'

'I am too used to great men about me, to have any objection to it,' said Jane. 'I don't know what my life would be, if I had.'

'It will soon not be possible to have guests to the house,' said Clare. 'Not that we do it often enough to count.'

'I don't feel I could be embarrassed outside this house,' said France.

'Or anything but embarrassed in it,' said Victor. 'Grandma ought to know better. She will go too far.'

'She could not, if she has not already. She has gone the full length many times and nothing has happened. Miss Bunyan could only leave the house, and we can only stay in it, and both things are agreeable to Grandma.'

'Where is Alfred?' said Miss Marcon. 'I hope he has not been dismissed. He is not wandering about, afraid to come home? Perhaps I ought not to ask. It shows how awkward it is to know the tutor's family.'

'Here I am, Aunt Charity! I am not afraid to come home. You are right that this house is becoming that to me.'

'I am so glad, dear, as ours has never done so.'

'What do you do to make my nephew feel at home?' said Stephen to Sabine. 'You have succeeded in a few weeks when we failed in as many years.'

'I expect they succeeded in a few weeks,' said France. 'Things do not stand the test of years, certainly not homes.'

'Miss Marcon likes you better than any of us,' said Evelyn to Edith. 'How did you get her affection?'

'Perhaps on the basis of the few weeks.'

'No, her feeling does stand the test of years.'

'I see why a portrait of a family group is called a Conversation Piece,' said Rowland, coming to escort Miss Marcon. 'They don't generally have such good names for things.'

'Not such dreadful ones. I daren't look at those pictures, because of what I might read into them. It is really too morbid to paint family groups, with a father and a mother and children, and no attempt to leave out anything. After all, why dwell on these things? It does not alter them.'

'I had no fault to find with my family life, until my wife died.'

'No, but you would not have made a picture. There would have been nothing to read in. People say, the better a picture is, the more it suggests. I don't think they even ought to talk like that. Emphasising it does no good.'

John had been aloof and silent, and now led Jane to her seat, and stood while his other guests settled in theirs, as if barely holding himself from his words.

'Now I am going to disregard the laws of civility and talk of myself. I can't help being the host. My personal life does not stop for that, and it happens to have been going on. I know that shame is due to me, but something else is due to me as well.' He took a letter from his coat, and remained standing to read it, holding it spread between his hands. ' "Will you accept this tribute from a grateful reader, who can sign himself in no other way?" Just that. And what do you think it is? A cheque for a thousand pounds! My time is not past for giving pleasure to people. It is measured by what they will give, like other things. We are not down to the bottom. People still have their feeling for me, and will show it in the way that counts. For this is the way, say what you will.'

'What should we say?' said Rowland. 'Of course it is the way.'

'What a thunderous piece of news!' said Victor.

'Well, it is a unique moment in the lives of us all,' said his brother.

'I have never heard of its raining pounds before,' said Clare. 'Cats and dogs, compliments, insults, anything, but never pounds.'

'And it never rains but it pours,' said France. 'What a good thing that is!'

'I admit it is a fairy tale moment for me. I have not had too many of late; I have not had many in my life at all. But here is a real one.'

'You have not had many?' said Evelyn. 'Do you mean you have had a certain number? How little we know of other lives!'

'Will Father be rich now?' said Muriel.

'No, of course he will not,' said her aunt. 'It is because he is poor that this is given to him. But it is a wonderful thing to happen, and you ought to be very proud.'

'It is about time they gave him something for all he has done,' said Sabine.

'So they have seized the moment,' said Stephen.

'Yes, why not after all?' said John. 'Why not show their feeling? I have lived my life for them.'

'Of course they ought to pay you a thousand pounds,' said Miss Marcon. 'We all ought. I hope you will take the will for the deed? I never understood that phrase before; I thought it was unreasonable. But now I don't know what I should do without it. You will give me a little of the gratitude? I feel I should not like to have none.'

'Seymour is the only one of us who could afford such a sum,' said Alfred.

'It was not me,' said Rowland, quickly and seriously.

'And when you could have afforded it, Father!' said his son.

'I do not flatter myself that he is my grateful reader,' said John, laughing.

'I will be honest and say I should never have thought of such a thing!' said Jane. 'Even if I could have afforded it. People do like to share credit, but I think we are so much more interesting, if we allow our real selves to be seen.'

'Well, you ought to be in spirits now, John,' said Hetta.

'We are all in spirits,' said Sabine, 'and most of all his old mother.'

'What is the signature to the cheque?' said Victor.

'Robert Seaton,' said his father. 'A genuine name, I hazard, but we respect the virtual anonymity. The donor has a right to it. And I respect it in another sense. It has been a good way to do it.'

'It has indeed,' said Miss Marcon. 'It saves you the effort of gratitude. You really don't have to make any return. Fancy not wanting credit for giving a thousand pounds! I can hardly believe it, when I almost wanted it for not giving anything.'

'It does make one feel one would like to be admired for such a thing,' said Alfred.

'This person does honestly forgo his admiration,' said Stephen. 'He is one by himself: I should like to meet him.'

'Fancy Stephen wanting to meet someone!' said Miss Marcon.

'No, no, that is forbidden ground,' said John. 'We will not venture on it.'

'Miss Hallam, how are you and I to express our feelings?' said Chaucer. 'You may be sharing with me a sense of being somewhat inadequate. But on this point we may follow Miss Marcon, and ask to have the will taken for the deed.'

Chaucer was inclined at this time to fancy that women shared his feelings. The experience of having his niece in his home had suggested a state of the same comfort and more suitable companionship, and he had come to a mind for marriage.

'I hoped my silence was eloquent, and, as I am not one of the family, perhaps golden as well.'

'Well, I know you all rejoice with your father,' said John. 'Is your silence golden too? You have not Miss Hallam's reason of not being one of the family, though I would hardly grant it to her. It is not every day that reward comes on this scale. It may never come to any of you.'

'These things are unfortunately not hereditary,' said France.

'Who knows, Miss France? Your feet are in the same steps,' said Chaucer.

'They are not hereditary,' said John, 'but they can be shared. It is a good form for a tribute. I am not one of those who feel that the form of money takes from a gift. What gives a gift its value, is the feeling which prompts it, not the form it takes. If that is chosen in understanding, it only adds to it. I can take it simply, in simple gratitude. If I could not, I were a meaner man.'

'It would be dreadful if you felt you could not accept it,' said Miss Marcon. 'We should all be ashamed. It would be so petty not to take a thousand pounds.'

'And the fellow wants you to take it; he wants to give it,' said Rowland. 'He sends a cheque and not notes, so that you can have your choice. You need not put the cheque through; he will not force your hand. But he wants his way; you will let the fellow have his way.'

'Now I will not have him continually referred to as a fellow!' said Jane. 'He must be such a very good type.'

'To refuse would be to repudiate a man's generosity,' said John, 'to show a hesitation in taking the lower place. That is a lesson we all have to learn.'

'It is not one that comes in very usefully,' said Clare.

'What a good thing it is you have learnt it, Ponsonby!' said Evelyn.

'Why are we so sure the giver is a man?' said Stephen. 'The signature on the cheque simply shows that use has been made of a man's banking account.'

'We are not sure,' said John, 'but I somehow think it is. There is the terseness of the letter, the lack of the personal touch, the sacrifice of the acknowledgement; and few women would have as much to give.'

'And women would spend it on people nearer to themselves,' said Rowland, in a tone of understanding.

'It is fortunate that you have come together!' said Jane.

'We have not done that. We shall not do it. I accept the conditions of the benefit. In no other way have I a right to it.'

'I should have thought a woman was as likely to give it,' said Hetta, 'though, as you say, less likely to have it to give.'

'I am with you, Miss Ponsonby,' said Chaucer. 'I should have thought indeed that the whole idea, the unobtrusive manner of its carrying out, were feminine. I should not claim for my own sex such selflessness and power of taking another's place.'

'I should not claim it either for that sex,' said Jane, bending her head and looking up from under it. 'Though one hardly likes to claim it for the other, as it is one's own.'

'Well, man or woman, it is a great spur to my effort. There is not so much zest in going on, year in and year out, for things to be taken as a matter of course and judged as a due. But this is a sign of another spirit at work, for many must feel what one has been able to acknowledge and reward.'

'Many indeed must feel it, for one who pays a thousand pounds for it,' said France.

'Many indeed,' said John in a quiet tone. 'That is worth more to me than the thousand pounds.'

'It must be worth a good deal,' said Evelyn.

'Evelyn, don't be foolish,' said his aunt. 'Things cannot always be expressed in terms of money.'

'They very seldom are. That is what is remarkable about this,' said Stephen.

'We ought to pay for what we have,' said Rowland. 'I am

afraid we often don't. We get it for nothing if we can, and forget someone has to give it.'

'I don't know how we should have managed without the money,' said Hetta to her mother. 'That so often seems to be the case with anything that falls in.'

'We will leave that until we are alone, my dear.'

'No, we will not,' said Hetta, sharply. 'It raises an interesting point. Is the giver of the money someone who knows us?'

'We must not find the point interesting,' said John. 'The words were "a grateful reader." That is the given point of connection, and we must be content. We have given him his due in the way he chose it, and in the measure he should have it. He does not have less because it cannot be given to his face.'

'Yes, yes, he must get his way,' said Rowland.

'He does not have it at all. That is the best part of it,' said France. 'We don't have to feel we have paid, and paid too much.'

'No, he has paid,' said Rowland.

'People cannot really give at all,' said Edith. 'They can only exchange. This case is an exception.'

'They feel the agony of giving,' said Chilton. 'And they want their agony soothed. This man does not seem to feel any agony.'

'Exchange is no robbery,' said Miss Marcon. 'We have some dreadful sayings. I have always wondered how the custom of gifts grew up. And now I see there is no such custom. There is just this man by himself.'

'My boy, it is good indeed,' said Sabine, putting out her hand to invite her son's and also to hold him at a distance. 'I feel it, and so would your father. But I am an old woman.' Her tone changed and lost its almost conscious quaver, 'I suppose we could trace the cheque?'

Rowland laughed.

'My dear mother, we could or we could not. We do not know. We shall not know. Miss Hallam, you are silent. You find this unusual incident perplexing?'

'Ponsonby,' interposed Chaucer, leaning forward and raising his hand, 'you have found me also silent. But I would speak for Miss Hallam and myself, and protest that in some cases silence may convey as much as speech.'

Rowland laughed again and continued to do so.

'I am full of discontent that I have not given the money,' said Alfred, 'that I have not received it, that I have not played any part in the matter at all.'

'I have not said what part I have played,' said Evelyn. 'And so I do not say what my silence has conveyed.'

'Evelyn, even that kind of joking suggestion is not straightforward,' said Jane.

'Well, well, it has given me a moment's happiness,' said John. 'There is that to be said for it.'

'Are you allowing reaction to set in?' said Evelyn. 'And so soon? I am disappointed.'

'So happiness can be bought,' said Miss Marcon, 'though they say it cannot. But if a moment costs a thousand pounds, it is too dear to be afforded. It would be bought too seldom to count.'

'I don't know how much would come from a thousand pounds,' said Alfred, 'but a number of thousands would bring a lifetime.'

'My poor thousand pounds!' said John.

'Poor thousand pounds!' said Edith. 'What a word for such a sum!'

'This is disheartening for the giver,' said Evelyn.

'Evelyn, Evelyn!' said his aunt.

Sabine smiled and rose from the table, and the women went to the drawing-room. Some rugs and cushions had been laid about which would be removed in the morning. Sabine adjusted the cushions with a careless touch, but put one aside where it would not be handled.

'This is a great encouragement for John!' said Jane. 'And I have an idea somehow that he wanted it. A writer's life is not all success and triumph.'

'A certain amount of it is,' said Sabine.

'Of course money is dross,' said Miss Marcon. 'And yet it is accepted in exchange for everything.'

'Why is it called dross and filthy lucre and sordid gain?' said Edith.

'Filthy is really an unnecessary word, when we have to be in constant contact with it. It is said to soil our hands, and I suppose it must. It is deceitful too; the deceitfulness of riches.'

'I cannot understand anybody's really liking money,' said Jane, 'except for the things it brings. I should never like it for itself.'

'I should think not, when it is filthy and sordid and deceitful. And John has a thousand pounds of it. I hope it is all right.'

'I don't know why Muriel stayed up to dinner, Mater,' said Hetta. 'She has not opened her mouth except to eat. Her father's success has not drawn one syllable from her.'

'It seems to be clear why she stayed up,' said France.

'Muriel, speak to your father about his present, directly he comes in,' said Sabine.

'Yes, Grandma.'

'What are you going to say to him?'

'I don't know, Grandma.'

'Then how can you say it?'

Muriel did not explain.

'She cannot say it, it is clear,' said Miss Marcon.

'So let it be recognised,' said Clare.

'She must not be allowed to be too boorish, for her own sake,' said Hetta.

'For other people's, surely,' said Edith. 'We should all be boorish for our own.'

'What are you going to say, Muriel?' said Hetta more firmly.

'If we don't tell her what to say, we shall seem to be in the same position as she is.'

'Muriel, you may say to Father that you are so pleased about his present, and that you think he more than deserves it.'

'I don't want to, Aunt Hetta.'

'Why not?'

'Because I don't say things like that.'

'That is no reason why you should not begin.'

'Of course it is,' said France. 'She does not want to present herself as a stranger to her parent.'

'She can ask him what he is going to do with the money,' said Miss Marcon. 'I am sure she wants to know that.'

'She does know it,' said Hetta. 'He will have to spend it on the household.'

'Does she really know that? How sad at her age! What can we do to make up to her?'

Muriel felt the tension less, and leaned against a cushion, and Sabine stretched forward and drew it from her back.

'Sit up straight, child,' she said in explanation.

'Well, what are you going to say to Father?' said Hetta. 'Whatever are you crying for?'

'Because of the hopelessness of the situation,' said France. 'Despair is the natural thing.'

'What are you crying for, Muriel?'

'Leave her alone, Aunt Hetta,' said Clare. 'What good does it do to torment her?'

'Are you the mistress of the house?'

'Yes, I am, when you and Grandma fail in the part. I come next. Muriel, you can go to bed, and you need not say good night.'

Muriel threw her sister a look of relieved acceptance of the account she gave of herself, and disappeared.

'You think that is kindness to the child?' said Hetta.

'I know it is.'

'You are not generally so concerned about her.'

'There is generally no need to be concerned about her at all. She has the easiest position in the house.'

'That is what she should have, at her age,' said Hetta, with a note of reproof. 'We should not grudge it to her.'

'Now adapt your talk to simple, masculine ears,' said John at the door. 'To tell the truth, I am excited to-night, and want my family as well as my friends.'

'A disposition which leads to advantages for us all,' said Chaucer.

'We saw Muriel mounting the stairs in tears,' said Chilton.

'Had anything untoward taken place?'

'Grandma has been finding imperfections in the poor young girl,' said Victor. 'To Grandma childhood is not innocent, only age.'

'Mrs. Ponsonby is doing her best to get us all perfect,' said Alfred. 'I shall love being perfect: I have always enjoyed imagining myself a perfect person.'

'He has got more enjoyment out of being one,' said Victor.

'Victor, was there a flavour of ill nature in your speech?' said his brother.

'Victor,' said Chaucer with a hesitant air, 'you will allow me my word? You will remember your grandmother is a very old lady, and, as such, is entitled to your chivalry as she is dependent upon it. We show honour to the weaker vessel.'

'We do not show honour to Grandma in that character,' said Clare. 'Hers is the honour paid to power. And it is a better kind of honour.'

'But, Victor, are you listening to Dr. Chaucer?' said Chilton.

'Miss Hallam, I am glad to see it is not incumbent upon you—that you are not desirous of following your pupil,' said Chaucer.

'It does seem that I ought to be more tied to her.'

'It does not seem so to me,' said Chaucer, drawing up a chair to Edith's, so that they sat apart from the rest. 'It would indeed seem to me unfit for you to be in any way dependent upon the movements of others.'

'We must all be that, but I think I have more liberty than anyone else in the house.'

'Miss Hallam,' said Chaucer, leaning forward impulsively, 'I had almost said, "What liberty?" Liberty of a kind, yes. Kindness in a measure. But what is such kindness, liberty—courtesy —to anyone strung up to every tone, as you must be?'

'They are everything to her, surely. It is to people like that, they make so much difference. And they are generally given to them.'

'Ah, you prove your mettle; but you do not tell me you would rather be a stranger in the house than a member of it.'

'I would much rather: I could not bear to be a member. You don't know what it is like.'

'You may say it, but the heart knoweth its own bitterness. What is a little impatience, hastiness—tyranny, if it must be said, compared with a real isolation and loneliness?'

'I am afraid it must be said, and they are a great deal worse.'

'You do not think it,' said Chaucer, almost tenderly, with his eyes on her face. 'How different a thing is a woman's courage from a man's! How could a man dare the woman's lot, the little pinpricks and pettinesses, the grinding, pitiless monotony?'

'It is not the stranger who endures the worst of those. I think your niece must have been made more one of the family than I am.'

'May I come to what is in my mind?'

'I think you had better not. There is a story about someone who saw into people's minds, and it was impossible for him. And what is the good of not being able to see into them, if you are told about it?'

'You would have to be told. You can have no inkling. It would transcend your furthest dreams. And if you could guess it, your tongue would be barred.' Chaucer spoke with a great gentleness of a woman's further compulsions. 'I will go slowly. You shall have time.'

'What can it be? I thought you were going to propose to me. But that has nothing to do with my dreams. Have I not seen into your mind after all?'

Chaucer looked at her in silence.

'You forgot a woman's intuition, when you enumerated the things about her. And you forgot her tongue. It is not so often barred. It is not really supposed to be. Is it going to be yours that is barred?'

'Did you want me to say it in words?' said Chaucer, struck by a thought.

'No, no, your way of saying it was much better. Your tongue was so nicely barred. I hope it will continue to be. You see how mistaken you were in me. Suppose I were to accept you now?'

'I should be honoured.'

'You would be, I suppose, more than you would have been. But it is no good to marry a dependant, if she is not grateful. You might as well marry someone who had no need to be.'

'Am I to understand you do not wish for what I offer?'

'Well, don't you understand it? My tongue has not been barred. I hope yours is not going to break its bars.'

'It is not,' said Chaucer, bowing. 'I hope I know how to conduct myself under a refusal. I have not much to offer a woman, but some might have found it acceptable.'

'It was to transcend my furthest dreams. So no wonder you thought I should find it so. I quite understand it.'

There was a pause, and then Chaucer spoke.

'Well, perhaps you know what is best for us: I will take your decision as the right one.'

'Will you really? I did not expect you to do that. I did not know that men who were refused, took the decision as the right one. I think it is I who have been refused. It has to be made to appear that it is the man. Perhaps it is really I who have proposed?'

'No, it is I who have done that,' said Chaucer, with grave gallantry. 'I do not go back on it. It remains, and will remain. Now should we join the rest, lest our remaining together occasion comment?'

'Yes. It would never do, if it was thought that anything has passed between us.'

'What is your wish with regard to our letting the truth become known? I wish to deal in nothing but the truth.'

'Then we will have a secret between us for ever.'

'What have you two been discussing so earnestly?' said Jane.

'A woman's lot,' said Edith. 'The pinpricks and pettiness of it.'

'Well, I have not much to learn about it, though I have not come in contact with the pettiness. Being always outnumbered by men may tend to prevent it. Women generally find themselves in the majority. I think either sex becomes petty, if left without the other.'

'Well, Father,' said Victor, 'you look round on admiring faces. We are unreasonable enough to think more of you for your piece of fortune.'

'It is not unreasonable, my boy. We all have our market value as well as others, and it does not mean nothing.'

'You are not like Stephen, ashamed of taking payment,' said Miss Marcon. 'Personally I should love to be paid with a thousand pounds, but then I daresay so would he. Perhaps he is naturally ashamed of what he is paid.'

'I love it indeed,' said John. 'To have given pleasure to that extent! That is the thing. And now let us forget me and talk of other people.'

'No, don't let us,' said Evelyn. 'Let us talk of this. We don't often get such a subject. Why should we not talk of it?'

'Whenever we have an absorbing topic,' said France, 'the person most involved says we must leave it and turn to others. There are no others. Nothing has happened to anyone else.'

'I think it is so nice of Ponsonby not to say it is not the gift he values, but the thought,' said Evelyn. 'People might anyhow value both, when they accept them.'

'He only nearly said it,' said Stephen.

'Even when they refuse, they explain that it does not alter the thought,' said Edith. 'But it does alter it. It makes it unnecessary. And unnecessary is the worst thing for a noble action to be.'

'I don't know what we should have done, if John had refused,' said Miss Marcon.

'Ponsonby,' said Chaucer, leaning towards him, 'the ability to accept simply is a great gift. You teach us all a lesson.'

'Some people have too many gifts,' said Alfred.

'No one accepts simply,' said Stephen, on a high note, though half to himself. 'It takes the whole of human effort to accept.'

'Well, you have not said much to congratulate your father,' said Hetta. 'Don't you take more pleasure than this in his success? It is a greater one than you will ever have.'

'Are we to take pleasure in that?' said France.

'We can't have any fellow-feeling,' said Chilton, 'as you explain.'

'You can judge our feelings by your own,' said Clare.

'I don't know that I can. You don't seem to me to have the same feelings.'

'Well, you are only Father's sister, and we are his children.'

Victor gave a faint laugh and received a quick frown from John.

'It is belonging to the same generation that makes the difference,' said Hetta, in an easy tone.

'Or belonging to the generation before,' said Sabine. 'That is the only way to be his mother.'

'You are unkind to boast of your generation, Mrs. Ponsonby,' said Alfred, sitting on the arm of her chair. 'There are enough matters in which we cannot compete with you, without your finding another, which is no credit to you at all.'

'I do not ask congratulations,' said John. 'I have had too many, and given too many to myself. I have only been the object of an individual's comprehension and generosity. I have had no true success.'

'It is well not to ask congratulations now that they have ceased,' said Chilton.

'The other kind of success is better,' said France. 'True success seems to be effort and achievement without any reward. It is as bad as true kindness or honest advice or anything else of that kind.'

'Being cruel to be kind is just ordinary cruelty with an excuse made for it,' said Evelyn. 'And it is right that it should be more resented, as it is.'

'You have had kindness without any touch of cruelty at all, John,' said Miss Marcon. 'I don't think I have ever seen any of that kind before. The bitterness of success is a dreadful phrase to have arisen.'

'You do not take part in the badinage, Miss Ponsonby?' said Chaucer.

'No, I feel it would hardly become me. My brother's success is so much my own, and so much involved with me, that to make too much of it would not do. I must be quiet, as people are when they are receiving applause.'

'You are indeed receiving it,' said Chaucer in a lower tone. 'You indeed are your brother's truest success.'

'Oh well, yes: I don't think he is in any doubt about that.'

'I should not have thought this was the family to have this kind of success,' said Evelyn. 'I am astonished that one of them has it: I can hardly believe it.'

'Now I think we have really felt a friend's success as if it were our own,' said Stephen to his sister.

'Miss Marcon, you write biographies,' said Chaucer. 'Why not consider writing one of John Ponsonby?'

'I only write them of people whose biographies have been written, so that they can be in the British Museum.'

'You cannot give up your erudite tastes even for the sake of a friend?'

'I have thought of writing an autobiography,' said John. 'But I think I have not yet reached the age. A life of anyone has to be all looking back.'

'It cannot be looking forward,' said Victor. 'Even from a biographer the future is hidden.'

'That is what your father said,' said his aunt.

'But not entirely from an autobiographer,' said Evelyn.

'Evelyn, do not be foolish,' said Jane.

'Well, well, biography has to be looking back, or it may have to be keeping back, anyhow an autobiography.'

'We will go home at once, if you are going to talk on that level,' said Jane, opening her workbag.

'Consider how much Father's would be the second,' said Chilton to Edith.

'Not more than people's must be. He would write his own life well enough. He may be the only one who knows it. You all underestimate your father.'

'I do not,' said France.

'I think we only estimate him,' said Chilton.

'It may be the same thing in a man's children.'

'Jane, must you knit when we are out to dinner?' said Rowland. 'So that was the bag I carried.'

'The irony of things,' said Victor.

'Well, well,' said Jane, clicking her needles together, rolling the knitting round them, and leaning back with her hands falling to her lap. 'Is that better?'

'It is much better; it is quite perfect; thank you.'

'You are one of those men who believe that a woman exists purely for ornament,' said Jane, sitting up to adjust her hair and her dress, before settling down to fulfil this function.

Her brother turned on her eyes of automatic appreciation.

'Are they never going?' said Sabine, suddenly from her chair, where she sat with her hands on its arms and her head bent forward.

Her guests threw her a glance and rose to their feet, Rowland with concern, Stephen with comprehension, Evelyn with interest and a sparkle in his eyes, and Miss Marcon in a manner of looking down on a phenomenon from a height, as indeed she was doing. Jane snatched up her belongings in the way of one caught by a wave on the shore, and stood as if poised for flight.

'Must you all go?' said Sabine in apparent unconsciousness.

'It appeared that we must,' said Stephen.

'It is early to break up the party.'

'True,' murmured Evelyn. 'But we do not set our opinions against those of older people.'

'We must go indeed,' said Rowland, advancing to Sabine. 'We have been here too long.'

'It shows we have enjoyed it!' said his sister.

'My mother has surpassed herself,' said John. 'We must plead her years.'

'She is a remarkable hostess for her age,' said Jane.

'A remarkable hostess is a good term for her,' said Victor.

'We are always saying she has gone the full length,' said Clare, 'but there is always a further. Shall we reach the end?'

'Yes, very soon now,' said Stephen to his sister. 'And it will be the end of a good deal.'

'We must cultivate the courage of despair,' said Victor. 'I feel I am getting it.'

'Why do you keep talking about yourselves?' said Hetta. 'The point of the matter is that your grandmother is tired.'

'The matter has involved us,' said her nephew. 'Personally I feel I cannot hold up my head.'

'Victor,' said Chaucer, walking to him and bending his eyes on his face, 'there is no need for you to feel embarrassment over the little contretemps. I can assure you that we view it with complete understanding, and with a respect for our hostess that is undiminished.'

'There is no need to view it in any way at all,' said Rowland. 'Mrs. Ponsonby is overtired and has told her friends. She knew it would be a cloud in our evening, if she allowed us to see it earlier.'

'I will go to bed,' said Sabine, seeming to struggle in her chair, 'and you can go on with everything without me.'

'The only solution, if we insist on staying,' said Stephen.

'We cannot go on with everything without you,' said Alfred, stooping to the chair, 'as everything centres round you.'

'That is Grandma's trouble,' said France.

'Why do we not go?' said Jane. 'It is the most absurd thing we can do to stay.'

'And hardly a lovable absurdity,' said Miss Marcon.

'I don't wonder you are paralysed,' said Chilton. 'You must be rooted to the ground by shock.'

'No, no, Chilton, there is no need to take that view,' said Chaucer, shaking his head and taking a step towards him.

'We have so enjoyed the evening,' said Miss Marcon, shaking hands with Hetta. 'We are so very sorry we came. It was absurd of us to feel we were really wanted. Of course we are a burden and not a pleasure. And your mother had to tell us, as we could not see it for ourselves. It was like her not to shirk an unpleasant task. Ah, Charity, rightly named!'

'We must say goodbye to Mrs. Ponsonby,' said Jane, pushing forward.

Her brother put out his hand and guided her to the door, and the gesture somehow swept the other guests in her wake.

'Where is the letter you had?' said Sabine, in a sharp, clear tone to her son.

John gave it to her, and she read it through her glasses, dwelling on every word.

'Nothing to take hold of.'

'Nothing.'

'To bed, to bed, all of you!' said Hetta, waving her arms. 'We don't want another word. Unless you would like to say one of congratulation to your father?'

'We have said our word. You are the one of us who has not,' said Clare. 'We will leave you to say it.'

'Of course mine waits until we are alone. You might know

that by this time. So to bed, one and all, if Miss Hallam and Alfred will excuse my including them with the rest.'

'I don't see why they should excuse it.'

'Good night, Grandma,' said Chilton.

Sabine made a simple, repulsing gesture, which included all her grandchildren, and dropped her eyes to the letter.

'I shall not be ruined by success,' said John, when he was alone with his mother and sister. 'Rather shall I be ruined by the lack of more of it. A thousand pounds does not take me the whole way. It needs twice the amount for that. But what is the good of such talk, unless one of you is my unknown benefactor? I shall certainly be ruined by success, if I begin it.'

'The same person might do it a second time,' said Sabine.

'It is clear you are not the benefactor.'

'It was clear before,' said Hetta. 'If Mater could do it, there would be no need of it. I can do more by cutting off every farthing in the house.'

'Money is not spent in farthings, although it is saved in them,' said John.

Seven

'This Edith Hallam has nothing to do with you, Miss Hallam?' said Hetta, glancing over the paper at breakfast and catching sight of an advertisement. 'This Edith Hallam who has won this great prize for a book?'

'No, nothing at all, I am sorry to say. I wish she were my very self.'

'She is no relation of yours?' said John. 'Simply a namesake? It is just a coincidence?'

'Simply that. She is not the remotest cousin.'

'What is the prize,' said Sabine.

'Two thousand pounds,' said Edith. 'At least, I think that is the sum. I remember noticing my namesake's success. I am not sure about it.'

'You have letters from a publisher yourself sometimes,' said Sabine. 'I have noticed them when I have sorted the letters.'

'I am sure you have, Grandma,' said Victor, 'and everything else about every other letter which has come under your eye.'

'It is not the same publisher, I expect,' said Hetta. 'Mater is making something out of nothing.'

'And if it were,' said Edith, 'he would not be concerned with the coincidence. He would hope for no profit from it.'

'Who is your publisher, Miss Hallam?' said John.

'I have not such a connection. Corresponding with one does not mean he is mine. You may have been too fortunate to realise that.'

'Anything you cannot help seeing, Grandma, you should at once forget,' said Chilton.

'She would not forget much on that basis,' said Clare.

'Don't be silly,' said Sabine. 'I have not surprised any dark secret of Miss Hallam's.'

'Indeed you have,' said Edith. 'People's first dealings with publishers are always secret and very dark. Especially when they come to nothing.'

'Ah, it is a rough road, Miss Hallam,' said John. 'If I have climbed a little higher on it, I can only know it better.'

'It seems to be strewn with roses sometimes,' said Victor.

'If only Grandma's sight would fail a little more!' murmured Chilton. 'Just enough to prevent her from sorting the post.'

'You are wishing her to become blind,' said France. 'We hesitate to put a curse on her.'

'What are you muttering about?' said Sabine. 'Are you afraid of being heard?'

'They seem to be ashamed of everything they say,' said Hetta.

'What are you going to put on to me?'

'A double curse is the only thing,' said France. 'Grandma must be deaf as well as blind.'

'I am neither deaf nor blind,' said Sabine. 'Both my sight and my hearing are good for my age.'

'True,' said Victor.

'I never know why you mention your age, Mrs. Ponsonby,' said Alfred. 'Its only result is a greater experience than other people's.'

'That is not true,' said Chilton in the same low tone. 'The

results are piling up. Grandma does not need any curse put upon her. The curse of years is enough.'

'She must become gradually less of a problem,' said Victor.

'She will have fits of being herself,' said France. 'This is the dangerous stage.'

'Her fits of being herself seem prolonged and frequent,' said Clare.

Sabine rose to her feet.

'I will not stay at the table: I will not be left out of things in my own house. I will not have talk going on all round me, and be invited to take no part. You may consider the reason why I am leaving my own board.'

She paused at the door, waiting for it to be opened. Alfred was the first to reach it, and having ushered her out, picked up her stick and followed her.

'If Grandma has her stick carried for her, it is not much good to her,' said Victor.

'Its being carried for her is of general good,' said France.

'Well, I hope you are all satisfied with the beginning of your day,' said Hetta, looking at them coldly.

'We are dumbfounded,' said Chilton. 'To think there are three other meals at which we have to meet Grandma!'

'Who will presumably be again at the table,' said Victor. 'May words be put into our mouths.'

'We had better put some into Muriel's,' said France, 'as the office is not performed for her. We must take matters into our own hands.'

'Muriel, let me hear you observe: "Grandma, you and I may now engage in a little chat." '

Muriel broke into mirth.

'Don't be too foolish,' said Hetta. 'It is no good to assume you are ill-used, and make jokes on that basis, when you have simply been ill-behaved and dealt with accordingly. It does not go without saying that you are always right.'

'I am bound to say I agree with your aunt,' said John, looking up. 'I can't have two opinions about the way to treat my mother.'

Sabine took advantage during the day of the mood to which she had reduced her grandchildren. The hours passed without further mishap. When the second post came in the afternoon, it was taken, as usual, to the drawing-room. She looked through the letters, laid them in a pile, and rang for some tea.

'I am tired, Gertrude,' she said in a quavering, aged tone. 'It is the sudden cold weather. It seems to sap my strength.'

'You ought always to have your own tea earlier, ma'am. It is late when Mr. Marcon has finished with the young gentlemen.'

'I am afraid I spend too much of my life in adapting myself to others.'

The maid was silent over this extension of the position.

Sabine waited until she was alone, poured out some tea, poured part of it away, took a letter from the pile and laid it on the jug. When she read the letter, her eyes lighted with a sort of leap, as if she were pouncing on an expected prey.

'DEAR MISS HALLAM,

'Thank you for your acknowledgement of the cheque for £1,000, which we sent to Robert Seaton Esq., 54, Melton Square, London, according to your directions. We are retaining the balance of £1,000, pending your further pleasure. We are paying great attention to the advertisement of your book. With our renewed congratulations——'

There followed the name of the publishers whose advertisement Hetta had seen, and whose printed name Sabine had seen on Edith's envelopes. The name of the man was that on the cheque which had come to John. Sabine sat on, fingering the letter, sinking into the sudden lethargy of her age. When Hetta entered, she gave a start and controlled it in the same movement, and sat looking at the letter almost dreamily, as if her mood had not been broken.

'Tea at this time, Mater? Are you not well?'

'I was cold and tired,' said Sabine, laying her hand on the open jug and looking in to gauge the depth of the water.

Something in the action struck her daughter, and she glanced at the letter and the open envelope.

Sabine took up the envelope, held it deliberately open to avoid the damp glue, and reinserted the letter.

'I am going to forward this: it was something I had to read. There was no need to waste a stamp and a fresh envelope.'

Hetta knew nothing of her mother's correspondence, or did not know how much she knew, and some feeling rooted in childhood, held her from further speech.

'Ring for another cup, my dear, and we will have some tea together.' Sabine's tone of propitiation puzzled Hetta, as it could not be referred to the present scene, for which she would tender no apology. 'You and I must remember how to be companions.'

Sabine continued in her cordial mood, joined her family at tea in an equal spirit, deferred to the men, petted Muriel, and drew Alfred and Edith into the talk on the same terms as her son and daughter.

After tea she went away by herself, and, coming on her son without appearance of contrivance, appointed an hour for a talk without laying any stress on it, so that he should not speak of it to his sister. Then she went about some household affair with a brisk, light air, sometimes almost singing to herself.

'Your notion that Grandma was failing had not much in it, Chilton,' said Clare. 'She has definitely renewed her youth.'

'It may be the last spasm of energy before the system runs down,' said Victor.

'Victor, you speak beyond your age, as you intended,' said Chilton.

'And he also does his best for the idea,' said France. 'I wonder he is not struck dead or turned to salt or stone.'

'Is it worse to say things about Grandma than about other people?' said Muriel to Edith.

'Much worse, except perhaps about your Aunt Hetta.'

Muriel accepted this account as likely and reasonable.

'I am glad you did not give Father the whole of your money, France,' said Clare. 'There has been even more economy since he had it. We must beware of sending the second thousand pounds after the first, if it is to have no result.'

'I suppose debts are being paid. And anyhow he had the first excitement. It has not done nothing.'

'Father's brief pleasure was bought high,' said Chilton. 'Would you not say so, Miss Hallam?'

'It does not follow that it is not worth the price.'

'I thought it was going simply to come out at breakfast.'

'It is a good thing I am not one of those people who cannot tell a lie.'

'You did not tell any lies,' said Muriel. 'Everything you said was true.'

'If we talk about it, it is bound to come out,' said Clare. 'We had better keep our rule that it is not to be mentioned.'

'I think it had better come out soon,' said Chilton and Edith at the same moment.

'No, no, not yet,' said France. 'I am not prepared. I could not face it yet.'

'You are in trouble, France,' said Chilton. 'You have done Father a kindness and deserve his gratitude, and that is bad. And he will have to relinquish his idea of the grateful reader, and substitute one of a successful daughter, and that is worse. And it caused him to rejoice in public, and that is worst of all. But the sooner it comes to light, the less will be the result.'

'No, I don't agree,' said France. 'When it falls back into the past, it will loom less large.'

'She may be right,' said Edith, 'and it is for her to decide. And your father's difficulties will be real and not of his own making.'

'He is not to be made a butt because he has been deceived,' said France. 'Why give a wrong impression, if you are not going to maintain it? I decide that the thing shall be kept a secret for ever. And if I want to give him the other thousand pounds, I shall do it.'

'What words are these that escape the door of your lips?' said Chilton.

'Bring forth men-children only!' said his brother.

'She had better bring forth brain-children. It will be better for the family,' said Clare.

'Can people decide what kind of children they bring forth—have?' said Muriel. 'I thought they couldn't.'

'You are the one who is right,' said Edith.

Muriel looked gratified, but hardly surprised that such information was not general.

Sabine went to the library to keep her appointment with her son. She waited without sign of impatience, sitting in the especial chair which was hers in every room, and moving her lips as if rehearsing something to herself. When he came, she motioned him to a seat, and, leaning towards him, spoke with deliberate certainty, bringing one hand down on another to point her words. She allowed herself neither to become argumentative nor to be deflected from her course; and when she had finished heard his side with an air of weighing what he said, and resumed with simple confidence that she would gain her end.

'How did you come on the letter?' said John at last.

'I opened it by accident, when I was sorting the post, and read it before I realised. It was typed and very clear.'

'I suppose you should have kept what you read, to yourself.'

'You suppose, do you? I suppose we should sell what we

have and give to the poor; I suppose we should forgive unto seventy times seven; I suppose I should not be telling you this; I suppose you should not be listening; I suppose we should return the thousand pounds and say we could not take it. Oh, suppose, suppose!'

Sabine had reached the end of her tether and John was silent.

His mother was not for long.

'You said that another sum like this would tide you over and give you a chance. You said it because you meant it, because it was true. We can go on living from hand to mouth, but we cannot do more. We have to put our hands to our mouths. Edith would cost no more as your wife, than she does now. And there is money coming to her later. And think what her feeling for you must be, to bring her to this!'

Her son showed that the stroke had gone home.

'What will Hetta say?'

'What she must say. And it will hurt neither herself nor anyone else. Hard words break no bones, and anyhow Hetta's don't.' Sabine gave an almost tender laugh, but John was silent, knowing that his sister's words broke more than her mother knew.

'I am not putting her to one side,' said Sabine, mistaking his thoughts. 'Why should I think of her as second to you? Hetta is the first person in all our hearts. But it is better for you both that things should be changed. She has had too much trouble from other people's lives. They are not her own; and her making them so is to her credit, not to her advantage.'

'She will feel she is being put to one side, and you know it.'

'Of course I know it. I should not be blind to it, should I? Who but me is her mother? And should I look forward to it? But it cannot last. Edith will settle into any place: she will not want to manage the house. She only wants to be your wife.'

'You are sure she does want it?'

'My dear boy, I have told you the truth. I have watched her, as one woman watches another.' Sabine felt no scruple in putting the case to her mind, as she had no idea she was not on certain ground. 'She gives all the signs, though she hides them in a way that does her credit. No one has noticed them but me.'

John was too used to his mother's supremacy to wonder

why this was the case. He smiled to himself before he knew it. This conception of a woman's feelings was soothing to a man, who had long given his family more than it gave. He rose and walked about the room, with his head bent and an aspect of rather conscious thought.

Sabine put on her glasses and began to read, almost openly implying that her end was won.

'I am not to tell her of the letter, of course?'

'Of course not. You are to tell her you want her for herself. She will tell you the rest in her own good time.'

John was still in the moods of exaltation and reaction, which had resulted from his gift, and was ready to embrace any hazard which postponed his daily routine.

Edith was not unwelcome in the place he had given his unknown friend. He put her intelligence high, and her proved admiration of his work put it higher. It was a further help to know that the end he sought was assured. He took an early chance of finding her alone.

'Am I welcome in your private domain? May I ask to share what is yours? We are safe from the young ones, are we? I have never wanted them less. You will understand when you know my purpose.'

Edith already knew. John's manner and his mother's had told her, and she was glad the climax had come. The response she was ready to make, would have amazed her a year ago. Her sympathy with John in the constraint and isolation of his life and the threat of his future, his rather wistful friendship, her own susceptible age had resulted in a feeling which she had believed was foreign to herself. Sabine's watch for signs of that feeling had been to a point repaid.

'Are we to enter into a conspiracy?' she said.

'I hope we are. It must be almost that in this house. But you know the house. You know its three generations. Could you bring yourself to belong to it?'

'I already belong to it, don't I? Your mother is always telling me I do.'

'My dear old mother! It is not the least thing you have done, to win her heart. It is not given to many. I am less honour to win, as a lesser person; but I have given myself to just as few. Do you see into my mind?'

'No. But you tell me what is in it, so I suppose I know.'

'And what have you to say?'

'Ought you not to say a little more?'

'I ought and I will,' said John. 'I want you to marry me and be a mother to my children. Do you see your way to it?'

'I will try to do it, but I don't really see the way. What about your sister?'

'I am not afraid of her in any sense.'

'I think you must be. Anyhow I am. And one sense is enough.'

'She is not her brother's keeper.'

'That is a foolish thing to say. Of course she is. What is she, if she is not that?'

'Let us not think of her, except to be grateful to her for the past.'

'That is a contradiction in terms. If gratitude for the past has no effect on the present, in what way are you grateful?'

'She will always have her place in my heart and in my house.'

'Of course she will. So what place shall I have? I mean in the house: places in the heart are easier.'

'Do you want to undertake its management?'

'No, not at all: I have no idea how it is done. But I must be somewhere. If I am your wife, I can't be got rid of. Your sister has always wanted to get rid of me, and for a governess it was usual and reasonable. But now it will have to stop, and I hardly think it will. Did you have the same problem with your first wife?'

'I saw less of my sister as a younger man. But when my wife died, she did her utmost to fill her place. I hope I shall never forget it.'

'It is the remembering of it that we are arranging. She will manage the house, but I shall have to be a member of it. It can't be avoided.'

'It will not be avoided,' said John. 'And you must learn to call her Hetta.'

'And will that make me a member? Yes, I suppose it will. Of course it will, if you think. Well, then, that is an end.'

'You will want to give your time to your writing. We must not take you from that.'

'Oh, I write very little. Really hardly at all. It is not worth considering.'

'We shall alter that. Indeed we shall consider it. My mother was reminding me of it to-day.'

'Shall we pass from your sister to your mother? Does either know the truth?'

'My mother knows it, knows my feelings. She is waiting to hear if I have met with success.'

'And your sister does not know?'

'My mother may be preparing her. Neither can know my fate.'

'Your mother must guess it, if she is preparing your sister. It would not occur to her that the governess could refuse her son. And she is quite right. In all the books she accepts him. Does your mother mind?'

'She has lost her heart to you, as you know. She is waiting to welcome you as her daughter.'

'You see she has guessed. But she already has a daughter. And I am sure she has not forgotten it.'

'Come, come, my sister will be simply glad to welcome you. She wants nothing but what is good for me.'

'She is a very odd person then, and I don't see her as so odd. She must want what is good for herself, like anyone else.'

'She has made a sacrifice of herself. I shall be glad to see her freed.'

'If you felt like that, you could have freed her. I really think you should have.'

'Well, better late than never.'

'That is an untrue saying. Things are often no good when they are late.'

'My poor sister! But I feel I can trust her. Let us go and put her to the test.'

'Tests are meant to find out weak places, and we all have them. Let us put it off. Your mother can think you are not winning me too easily. She had better not believe I jumped at you, and jumping at anyone would only take a moment. Shall I go on teaching Muriel?'

'No. She will have another governess. You will have the choosing of her.'

'I am the last person to do it. It seems impossible to people to find anyone to fill their own place. And it was your mother who chose me, and I must not interfere with other people's duties. People resent being deprived of their duties more than anything else. They must feel that work is the way to happiness.'

'I shall always be grateful to my mother.'

'I was much the best of the people who applied. She had only to read my letter to see that: I think she said so.'

'Would you call it a reasonably nice place for a governess?'

'No, I should not: it is quite impossible. Only I could have filled it.'

'We are not thinking of filling your place. Only Miss Bunyan's.'

'Well, only Miss Bunyan could fill that. I was talking of my place. For Miss Bunyan I hardly like to say what it was. I will certainly leave the duty to your mother.'

'We must see that the post is better.'

'Well, no one would recommend a post, who knew it as only the person who has filled it, can know it. People never let servants who have left, know the new ones. The new governess and I really should not meet, but I don't see how it can be managed. I will behave as if I knew nothing. And now we will go and break it to your mother and sister. They say that things get worse, the longer you put them off, and I find it is getting worse.'

They went to the drawing-room, where Sabine and Hetta were together. There was no hint of disturbance about them. The mother had meant to prepare the daughter, but had not dared.

'Well, Mater, here I am, a triumphant man and feeling unworthy of my triumph in the approved way! The sense of unworth common to the accepted does not interfere with their spirits. That seems to be allowed.'

'My son, I am glad. My dear, I am so indeed,' said Sabine, rising to embrace Edith, and keeping her back to her daughter until the truth should be revealed. 'We could not have parted with you, and it is good that any risk of it is past.'

Hetta had sat with her eyes on the group and her brows impatiently contracting.

'What is it? What is it all? Can't you make it clear? What is all this acting?'

'It is what you see: I have two of you instead of one,' said her brother, taking her hand and drawing her to Edith.

'What do you mean? What is it?' said Hetta in a sharper tone.

'Hetta, I am to be even less alone than I have been. You, who have been enough for me, will rejoice that I am to have more than enough. You, who have saved me, will rejoice that I am doubly safe.'

'What do you mean?' said Hetta, looking into his face.

'I mean that Edith and I are to take each other for better, for worse, for richer, for poorer, in sickness and in health, according to the pessimistic outlook of the marriage service. May we escape what is there laid out, and may you have a sister, who will be less trouble to you than your brother has been.'

'You are not thinking of doing anything foolish? You are not really thinking of marrying?'

'I have put it plainly, Hetta,' said John, with a gravity which brought home the truth to his sister, and angered her with its acceptance of the different outcome to her and herself.

'But why do you want to marry?' she said in a perplexed, impatient tone. 'You have nothing in common. You have no great feeling for each other. What is in your minds?'

'Let us say we are the victims of the attraction of opposites.'

'Well, mind you don't do anything foolish and regret it too late,' said Hetta, turning away and taking up something from the table.

'Hetta, we were relying on your sympathy and understanding.'

'Well, what do you want me to do about it?' said his sister, jotting something down, and then turning and continuing in a manner which showed that she spoke from a sudden thought. 'You must remember you had my sympathy and understanding in an event so different, that it does throw a strange light on this one.'

'Hetta, that is the last thing which should be said. I should not have believed the words could pass your lips.'

'Why should they not pass them? Why should I force back my natural words? Is that what you are doing? You can't think the thought will not occur to everyone. But is it a thing to be so much ashamed of? Your trouble was genuine at the time.'

'We must observe the customs of the civilised.'

'Marrying more than one wife never does seem to me so very civilised. But why should not people have their own ideas? I suppose I should marry more than one husband, if I wanted to. Perhaps I am over civilised.'

Sabine, who had listened with a look of simple pain, sank into a chair, as if feeling how long she had stood.

'We should grudge you to even one husband,' said John,

forcing his tone. 'We need you in your present place. Edith does not want to take over the house.'

'Take over the house?' said Hetta, drawing her brows together. 'Well, of course she does not. How could she? She would not be able to. People can't suddenly do another person's work. I suppose she is not going to write your books?'

'She is not going to do either your work or mine. She is going to do her own.'

'Well, teaching is useful and I should think difficult work. I would not claim to be equal to it. We are all made for different things.'

'I meant her own writing work. She will not go on teaching Muriel.'

'Won't she?' said Hetta, raising her eyes. 'Why, who will do it, then?'

'Now it is my work to manage that,' said Sabine. 'My work need not be disturbed, any more than anyone else's. Hetta, you are going to congratulate them, my darling.'

The endearment, rare in Sabine, forced Hetta's response.

'Oh, congratulate them! Oh, yes, one does, doesn't one? I give them all the congratulations possible, but it does seem so odd. But I do everything expected of me.'

'We are giving you a sister to look after,' said John; 'but we know you are equal to that.'

'I have looked after Miss Hallam for some time. That won't make any difference.'

'You must learn to call her Edith.'

'Must I? Well, that is easily done. One can easily say a name.'

'Hetta, you do not feel I am not dealing fairly with you?'

'Dealing fairly with me! You are not dealing with me at all, are you? It is Miss Hallam you are dealing with—Edith, I mean. There, I have got it out! That is progress, isn't it?'

'Now Edith must do the same by you,' said Sabine.

Her soothing tone caused her daughter to turn and walk from the room, and to leave the door open in apparent absence of mind, but, as her mother knew, in an actual instinct to force the group apart.

Hetta went to her room and stood with clasped hands and her eyes fixed, and began to walk up and down without relaxing either. Then almost without transition she went downstairs, impelled by a vague feeling that something might have changed. She found the three as she had left them, and a great wave of resentment swept over her at their indifferent blindness.

'Well, when do you want me to arrange the wedding?' she said, tapping her foot and looking out of the window.

'I suppose that is my family's duty,' said Edith.

'You have no family, have you?'

John gave an open frown.

'I have an uncle who will act as my family, who is my whole family, in fact.'

'Is that the uncle whose wife—is your uncle married?' said Sabine.

'He is a widower. He is my uncle by marriage. He married my aunt.'

'Is that the aunt—I think you told me you had lost an aunt.'

'Yes, she died some years ago. I missed her very much.'

'Then you will just be married, and come home and go on as usual?' said Hetta.

'Edith's uncle may have his ideas,' said John. 'It is his affair. But we hope, whatever the marriage will be, that you will come to it, Hetta.'

This coupling himself with Edith and placing her apart wrought his sister to a further pitch.

'You won't find the uncle difficult to get over,' she said with amused confidence. 'It can't be that sort of uncle, who has let Edith earn her living, and never wanted her in his home; not the old-fashioned kind who would think her one of the family. He will let you have any kind of marriage you like.'

'Then we will be married at once by licence, and have no one there but ourselves,' said John in another tone. 'That will be the best way to get our path clear.'

'Well, do you know, I thought that would be best from the first. I do think it best for a second marriage. The feeling of having lived a thing before, is trying when it is a delusion; but when it is accounted for by actual fact'—Hetta gave a laugh—'it must indeed be difficult. And we shall not have to get new clothes for Mater'—She hurried on in face of her brother's silence—'or new clothes for me, or new clothes for Edith and the girls; and that will be a great saving of expense at a time when it seems to me that our expenses will be increasing. There is the new governess, if nothing else. Edith should not cost more than she does now, must not cost more, in fact.'

Sabine rose with the open purpose of ending the scene.

'Let us go and tell the children the news.'

'No, I can't have that,' said Edith, glad to get on to open ground. 'I could not face it. Let me go away to-morrow and have nothing said, and come back when it is over. It is to be quite soon: John does not want to wait.'

'I should think not,' said Sabine. 'It would be odd if he did. Well, as you will, my dear. There is nothing against it.'

'You will remember not to speak of it, Hetta?' said Edith.

'Me? I shall not think of it,' said Hetta, standing with her finger-tips touching a table, and turning in a vague manner. 'What did you call me? Hetta? Yes, so you did.'

'Of course she did: you are to be sisters,' said Sabine, putting her hand on Edith's shoulder. 'What else should she call you? You were clever in calling her Edith.'

'Was I? I suppose I was,' said Hetta, almost dreamily. 'Yes, I see I gave her permission. And I can go on doing it: there is nothing in saying a name. It is easier than Miss Hallam.'

'It is also better. Miss Hallam is already strange. You will go to your uncle, my dear?'

'Yes, I will go to-morrow, if I may. Then I shall be out of danger.'

'Your uncle is in London, isn't he? Have we heard his name?'

'It is Seaton,' said Edith, driven off her guard, and afraid the next moment that the name would recall the cheque.

It recalled it to Sabine, who was equal to giving no sign, and to her son, who saw it as proof of his mother's case. Hetta was maintaining her dreamy pose and did not hear.

Edith left the next morning, ostensibly on a sudden visit, John later in the day on a similar pretext; but it was not until the evening that Sabine chose to break the news.

'Muriel may come to dinner to-night. I have something to say to you all.'

'What have we been doing?' said Victor. 'It can't be much, if Muriel is involved. I hope Grandma is not going to offend one of these little ones.'

'I hope it is not the other way round,' said Clare.

'You have been doing nothing,' said Sabine. 'It is other people who have been doing this time. You are to hear what it is, and to forget about yourselves.'

'Our very innocence is turned against us.'

'Don't raise their hopes, Mater,' said Hetta, looking up from some needlework, which she had had in her hands all day, though she seldom sewed. 'They will be expecting some great excitement, instead of something which is to leave their lives just as they are.'

'We certainly expect nothing which will not do that,' said Clare.

'I think I can guess,' said Alfred.

'Now I daresay you can,' said Sabine, in the tone which she began to reserve for Alfred. 'I am not suggesting that you need things explained like my grandchildren. But you will be quiet, if you please, and leave me to tell my dull witted ones in my own way.'

'I would not miss that,' said Alfred.

'We would none of us miss it, indeed,' said France.

'I am a dull witted one: I have no idea,' said Chilton.

'Mater, you are making a mistake,' said Hetta, almost laughing.

'Must we really wait until dinner?' said Victor. 'Will not Grandma put us out of our misery?'

'You will wait, and, what is more, you will wait in silence,' said Sabine, who was feeling the strain of what was behind.

'Muriel is the only one who can obey without effort,' said France.

'I said you would wait in silence, and you will do so.'

They did so, and did not wait beyond the hour.

'Now are you all listening?' said Sabine at the table. 'Muriel, you are not woolgathering? I am not going to tell the news, and then tell it again because of some gaping inattentiveness. You are giving me your mind?'

'Yes, Grandma.'

'I am on thorns,' said Victor.

'My breath comes short and fast,' said Clare.

'There, Mater, I knew you were doing that,' said Hetta, with serious expostulation. 'You are lifting their hopes to the skies, and then down they will come with a crash. Well, I can't help it: I have done my best.'

'Now, you know that your father and Miss Hallam have gone away,' said Sabine, not turning her eyes from the young faces. 'They went away separately, and they will come back together, and you will have to learn to think of them together. Now do you know what I mean?'

'No,' said Muriel.

'So I was right,' said Alfred.

'We know what you should mean,' said Chilton; 'but do you mean it?'

'Put it into words, Mater,' said Hetta, laughing. 'There is nothing obscene about it, or nothing supposed to be obscene. Marriage is the commonest thing in the world, after birth or death. Why should we make a mystery of it, as if it were indecent or illegal? It is not the last anyhow, whatever some people would say about a second marriage's being the first. There is no reason why it should not be put simply.'

'I chose to put it as I did. Now what do you say to it? Is it a pleasant surprise?'

'It is a surprise indeed,' said Clare. 'We had no inkling. They have not even been much together.'

'You don't know yet how these things come about. Your turn may come in time.'

'Perhaps not twice,' said Hetta. 'It is the second marriage side of things that is puzzling them. It is something they have not met.'

'And it is pleasant as well,' said Victor. 'Edith cannot leave us, and Father will have companionship.'

Hetta gave another laugh, a little louder.

'He has always had that,' said Sabine, 'but there are other things. Now haven't the rest of you anything to say?'

'We shall have a member of the family who is not really a member,' said Clare. 'That should render things less intimate and shameless.'

'Trust Clare to get in something that gives an awkward twist to it all!' said Hetta, almost gaily.

'I feel a failure in that I have not become a member,' said Alfred. 'I knew Miss Hallam was destined to make me look small beside her.'

'Don't talk nonsense,' said Sabine.

'It is not nonsense, Mrs. Ponsonby. You know quite well you would not accept me, and people always follow your lead.'

'Is Miss Hallam going to be Father's wife?' said Muriel.

'Yes, she is,' said Sabine; 'and you will be very fond of her and do everything she tells you.'

'Muriel will not think it is to make much difference,' said Hetta.

'Will she and Father have any children?'

'No, they will not; Edith is not young enough,' said Sabine, who observed a certain directness with the young, the result of her pre-Victorian youth.

'Will Miss Hallam still be my governess?'

'She will be neither Miss Hallam nor your governess. Now that is enough.'

'The news has unloosed Muriel's tongue,' said France.

'It has not done the same for yours, my dear.'

'We have not observed the right methods with her. People have said that Father ought to marry.'

'Won't she go on teaching me?' said Muriel.

'No, she will not,' said her grandmother. 'She will be Father's wife, as you said. You will have another governess.'

'More and more expense!' said Hetta. 'And I thought at first that the change would be an economy, that it was almost intended for one. It will be less than no good.'

'Marriages are not often intended as an economy,' said Clare, 'whatever else they are expected to achieve.'

'I was talking about this marriage.'

'Miss Hallam will not have to be paid, if she is not my governess,' said Muriel. 'Oh, but, of course, the new governess will have to be.'

'Muriel, that is very rude,' said Sabine. 'Children never talk about grown up people's affairs. I shall have to forbid you to speak.'

'A change in tactics indicated on more than one ground,' said Victor.

'Let us not interfere with Muriel's utterance,' said Chilton. 'It's natural lack of development may be meant.'

'Well, have you not anything to say to the news? Are you not interested in your father's life? You took his present of a thousand pounds with great calm, and now you seem as little affected by a more important event. You need not criticise Muriel's utterance: give your attention to your own.'

'Mater, you make too much of it for them,' said Hetta, looking with amused indulgence at her nephews and nieces. 'What can it seem to them, but an event which will leave things much the same? I can't see what change it will make myself.'

'I can see what change it might make,' said Clare.

'I said "will make,"' said her aunt with sighing resignation.

'Miss Hallam is always here,' said Muriel.

'There, of course!' said Hetta.

'Muriel, if you want to talk, you may make a suitable speech,' said Sabine. 'Now we will wait to hear it.'

Muriel did not show the discomfiture which was her relative's expectation for her.

'What shall I call Miss Hallam, Grandma? She can't be Miss, if she is married.'

'You will have to wait and ask her. And I did not tell you to ask a question.'

Muriel seemed to feel she had now received this injunction.

'What will she be called by other people?'

'Mrs. Ponsonby,' said Clare.

'The same as Grandma?' said Muriel, astonished.

'It does seem unfit,' said Alfred. 'I feel with Muriel.'

'Mrs. John Ponsonby,' Hetta instructed her niece. 'Grandma is Mrs. Ponsonby; I am Miss Ponsonby; and she will be Mrs. John.'

'Which is the best, Miss Ponsonby or Mrs. John?'

'Well, Miss Ponsonby shows you belonged to the original family,' said Hetta, half laughing. 'Now that is the last question.'

This was not to be the case.

'Which is the highest in the house? I mean the next to Grandma?'

'Did you hear what your aunt said?' said Sabine, in a tone which stayed the tongue it had urged to action.

After dinner Hetta went to her room; Sabine lay back in her chair, exhausted and at comparative peace; and her grandchildren talked in hushed tones to each other.

'I suppose we are stunned by the news,' said France. 'That is why we failed to do ourselves justice. I certainly failed.'

'I was uncertain what was expected of us,' said Clare.

'Is stunned the same as surprised?' said Muriel.

'An interest in the use of words!' said Chilton. 'There are strange results from shock.'

'We might have been required to show distress at Father's replacing Mother,' said Victor.

'He replaced her by Aunt Hetta long ago,' said Clare. 'And Grandma has never been affected by the blank.'

'Was it nice for Aunt Hetta, when Mother died and she had the place?' said Muriel.

'Muriel, your ability for silence has been proved,' said France. 'It is your real gift and should be cultivated.'

'I don't think Aunt Hetta had the place at once,' said Clare. 'She gradually worked her way into it.'

'Oughtn't she to have had it?' said Muriel.

'What are you saying?' said Sabine, rising to her feet and looking fiercely over her stick. 'Your Aunt Hetta is a very gifted and remarkable person, in her way the most important person in the house; and you should regard her with great respect and affection, and with deep gratitude for all she has done for you. If you do not, you are coarse and ungrateful people, and quite unworthy of intercourse on her level. I can't understand your feelings; they show how far you are beneath her; and in you great boys they are unmanly and unchivalrous, and would make your father blush with shame. Now understand that the first person who speaks of her again in that manner, may leave this house and not return. Understand it! Do not understand?'

Sabine rapped her stick on the ground and spoke in a harsh, hoarse voice.

'Yes, Grandma.'

'Who are you, who do you think you are, to be able to speak in such a way of anyone so far above you? What do you think you are? You are raw and ignorant girls and boys, of no use to anyone but yourselves, dependent on others for a roof above your heads, food to put into your mouths, teaching to enable you to associate with the civilised——'

'We have no means of our own,' muttered Chilton. 'But why thus expand the phrase?'

'And your aunt is a gifted, experienced woman, with her own powers, her own poise, her own place in your father's life, from which nothing will dislodge her!' Sabine's voice rose and became shrill and strained. 'Her own place in the esteem of others and many other things you will never have——'

'Whenever people's advantages are enumerated, we are told they will never be ours,' said France. 'Why should nothing fall to us? A place in our father's life might be natural, and people are even supposed to love their weak and erring offspring best.'

'You ought to understand how to treat your aunt, without my having to teach and train you,' said Sabine, seeming not to hear her grandchildren, and possibly not doing so, as precaution was taken to prevent it; 'without my having to browbeat and bully you as if you were idiots or savages——'

'Grandma's views of the suitable treatment of the simple and afflicted invite criticism,' said France.

'I am glad to see you are crying, Muriel. It shows you understand what I say.'

Muriel, relieved by this view of her tears, raised a lightened face and ceased to shed them.

Sabine's voice failed and she fell back into her chair, her stick rising into the air and striking Victor. She clutched it to her with a movement of exasperation that he should be in her way, and watched him from under her brows to assure herself he gave no sign. Alfred, who had witnessed the scene in silence, stooped gravely and placed it at her hand.

'Will you see Dr. Chaucer, ma'am?' said Gertrude at the door.

Sabine leant back in her chair and did not speak.

'The mistress is tired,' said Clare. 'Show Dr. Chaucer into the library, and we will come to him there.'

'Show him in here,' said Sabine, not lifting her head to dispose of her granddaughters as hostesses. 'And tell Miss Hetta.'

Chaucer bent lower than usual over Sabine, having indeed no choice but to do so, and something about him suggested that her condition caused him no surprise.

'I have come, Mrs. Ponsonby, to make my enquiries concerning what I hear has befallen. I am told that Miss Hallam has left your house, and that your son has followed her'—He looked at nothing in particular with fixed eyes—'and am anxious to be assured that nothing untoward is indicated. It occurs to me that she has had some family trouble, and that he is giving her his escort to her home.

'That could not have occured to him, as they left at different times,' said Chilton to France.

'Well, he could not say what did occur to him.'

Sabine did not lift her head, but signed to Chilton to explain, and on a second thought transferred the sign to Alfred.

Chaucer turned to the latter with some hesitation, as if he would have preferred to hear a member of the family. Alfred saw it and turned the hint to his purpose.

'No, you must do your duty, Mrs. Ponsonby. What would happen if you began to shift it?'

'Mater, don't keep poor Dr. Chaucer out of our family excitement,' said Hetta at the door. 'We are egotistic enough to think it is of general interest. And I am sure it is of interest to him, as our old friend. Yes, my brother and Miss Hallam have both left the house, Dr. Chaucer. Think of some way in which they may return together.'

Chaucer looked at her in silence.

'Can anyone put it into words?' said Victor. 'Muriel, use your new-found gift.'

'I can put it into words,' said Hetta. 'I wonder what the rest of you are jibbing at. My brother is fulfilling my long prophecy, Dr. Chaucer, and taking unto himself a wife; and most happily taking Miss Hallam, who has her niche in the house, so that the change will not ruffle its surface. That is a piece of news, isn't it? We shall soon think of them as on their honeymoon.'

'And is none of you to be present at the ceremony?'

'Oh, well, no; it is a second marriage, and has that atmosphere which rather unfairly characterises such events, which are innocent enough, if not romantic. They wanted it over quickly and nothing said. Then we shall receive them back, as if unawares, and shall be as if nothing has happened.'

'But, Miss Ponsonby, something will have happened,' said Chaucer in a low tone. 'There will be a great change.'

'No, that is what we are avoiding in having Miss Hallam. Though we should not take the credit to ourselves: it is my brother who deserves it. He has been very wise in looking all round the situation, and acting with thought for us all. I only hope he has considered himself as well. Have you not anything to say to our news?'

'Nothing, if you have nothing,' said Chaucer, moving away and somehow taking Hetta with him. 'But what sort of requital is this, for the years you have given your brother?'

'It is nothing to do with that: I don't think John means to requite me, or thinks he could. He has explained that I shall not even have the reward of more freedom. He is thinking of increasing his debt rather than repaying it.'

'He must indeed think of his debt at this time.'

'I believe he said he would carry the thought with him, or something of the kind. It was instead of me, I suppose. I can't go with him on his honeymoon, as I had to explain to him.'

'But, Miss Hetta, when he comes back, there will be the great adjustment,' said Chaucer, who had never addressed Hetta except as Miss Ponsonby.

'Oh, I have almost everything arranged,' said Hetta, in a

tone of simple explanation. 'I am used to the change and growth of a family. I have always had to organise it.'

Chaucer stood, almost imperceptibly shaking his head.

'The first flush of feeling renders people strangely blind to the claims of others.'

'These are not in such a flush of feeling: that is a hardly fair description. They are good, considerate, matter-of-fact, altruistic people. We must not talk of them as if they were lovers in a selfish sense.'

'The future must stretch before you with many problems.'

'There must be a certain number. I wish it had happened before the girls were grown and set. I often spoke to John about it. I shall have to arrange all the shifting and adapting. He will have nothing to do with it.'

'Miss Hetta, it is you who will have to do the great adapting.'

'No, it is I who will not have to do it. I am the free and unaffected person. It makes me feel quite apart and selfish, an unusual feeling for me. I shall have my old ways with my brother, the ways which make his life; and his wife will fill in the spaces between, which will be very useful, as I have long wanted them filled. It is really Clare's place which she is taking, or the place which should have been Clare's. I don't commend Clare enough in it, to be too sorry about her being supplanted; but I wish, as I said, that this had happened while she was younger.'

'She is still at an age when adaptation should be easy,' said Chaucer, not free from his idea of adaptation performed at another stage.

Hetta turned to the others, and Sabine's voice was heard.

'Now, Muriel, say something pretty and suitable to Dr. Chaucer. He has hardly heard you speak.'

Chaucer advanced with a smile, perhaps of anticipation.

'I think I am going to call Miss Hallam, Edith.'

'Are you? That is a great advance for one so young. Your aunt sees fit to permit it?'

'Well, yes,' said Hetta, who heard it for the first time. 'Edith has no other name but Hallam, and that she is giving up, and Ponsonby is worked hard enough. And I don't think she wants to take any stand-offish position with the young. She has lived with them, and is prepared to go on in the same way. That is the settled plan.'

'But she is not going to teach me any more.'

'Muriel, that is characteristic of youth,' said Chaucer, shaking in disproportionate mirth. 'To see the changes in people's lives in their bearing upon your own! That will put even more upon your aunt.'

'I am the official engager of the governess,' said Sabine. 'I have made one discovery, and now I must make a second.'

Chaucer looked towards the window at this precise enumeration.

'Yes, the choice is my mother's duty,' said Hetta. 'We are making no change at all.'

Chaucer still looked dubious over this account.

'My thoughts turn to Clare,' went on Hetta. 'Edith will in effect take her place and leave her free.'

'I have no place to be taken. And Edith will have a place of her own, which has not been occupied since Mother died.'

'Dear, dear, this bale and ban on second marriages!' said Hetta, raising and dropping her arms. 'It does seem rather unfair. All this sentiment and memory! Well, it can't be helped. They drag up a past which should be just a past, and I suppose must go on doing so. Secondary things are not meant to be copies of the first, and might be left to do their own work in their own way. But I suppose it is not to be. Of course it is not. Well, well!'

'Is secondary the same as second?' said Muriel.

'Never mind,' said France.

'Dr Chaucer is staring more than ever at Aunt Hetta, isn't he?'

'Well, she can hardly object to his following her with his eyes.'

'Perhaps he feels she would only accept a doglike devotion,' said Chilton.

'Most of us accept any devotion which is given us,' said France.

Eight

'So you are out already, Charity; you are out by yourself,' said Rowland, meeting Miss Marcon on the road leading past the Ponsonbys' gates. 'You are not going into the house?'

'Yes, of course I am going in. But we can't arrive in a body to ask questions.'

'No, no, not in a body, no. But we want to ask some questions; yes, I think we do.'

'To find out about the marriage we have seen in the papers. How else are we to know about it? It is a wonderful and startling thing and fraught with bitterness for others. It may make one's own lot better by comparison.'

'Then it will really help,' said Evelyn. 'But if we ask no questions, we have no lies told us. I have subtler methods of finding out the truth.'

'You mean you have subtler ways of asking questions. If you ask no questions, you have no truth told you either. It is surprising how much truth people tell: I would not, if I were they. And you can get a lot of truth from the falsehoods they tell, when you ask them questions. I admire them so much for telling them so awkwardly: I have a great respect for people. I can't think what people mean when they say disparaging things about human nature. Poor, weak, erring human nature! Ah, Charity, rightly named! I think it is absurd.'

'Won't you go home and let us go in?' said Evelyn. 'Father did not like the errand for Aunt Jane. She is sitting at home, waiting to hear everything.'

'Stephen insisted on it for me. He is doing the same, so he had to insist on it. We are always afraid he will lose his self-control with Mrs. Ponsonby, when he is a man and she is an aged woman. It is always the fault of men that the other people in the world are women. But he does want to know the family secrets; he has a morbid curiosity about them. Though I don't know why curiosity is so often morbid; I expect this is ordinary curiosity. Now what exactly do you want to know? If you wait here, I will come and tell you. Things are not so good at second hand, but they are better than nothing, so much better.'

'We want to know the whole thing,' said Evelyn. 'Our

curiosity is neither morbid nor ordinary. It is the kind known as devouring. We want you to be completely satisfying. It is awful not to be satisfied.'

'A good battery of direct questions,' said his father with a smile. 'That is the way. People are obliged to tell you something.'

'I think they are obliged to tell you everything,' said Miss Marcon. 'They always seem to be.'

'When people do not wish to talk of a matter,' said Evelyn, 'we do not refer to it again. I told you I had subtler methods.'

'But they do not refer to it again either. They just do what they wish. They have methods too. But generally they do wish to talk of it. Think how dreadful it is not to talk of things! That is why we must not let them bottle them up. It is really not allowed. We have to show we think nothing of them. And I really do not think much of this. Miss Hallam's marrying John is not so much after all.'

'Indeed your voice trails away in reaction and disappointment.'

'No, the son's marrying the governess might have been much more,' said Rowland, with a note of regret.

'I don't know. Might it?' said his son. 'There is the deposition of Hetta. Could anything be more?'

'No, no, no. That isn't coming. No.'

'It is too much,' said Miss Marcon. 'It could not be. I want to know how it is to be avoided, and if you wait here, you shall know too. It is well worth your while.'

'Indeed,' said Rowland, settling himself against a tree.

'I am glad Jane did not come; it is going to rain,' said Miss Marcon, turning towards the house. 'It does not matter about me; I am as strong as a horse. It is always a horse's strength that human beings have, and it would make them indifferent to weather.'

'Why should we always give way to women?' said Evelyn. 'Savages do not.'

'People always talk as if we should base ourselves upon savages,' said Miss Marcon, looking back, 'when we have been all these centuries getting away from them. Savages do a good many things besides not giving way to women. And we are all based upon them at heart. That is the explanation of your hankering after them. The term, "noble savage," is a great disgrace to us. Personally I am very highly civilised; I hardly give a thought to the savage; I am not giving a thought to him now.'

Miss Marcon went on to the house, asked if Mrs. Ponsonby or her daughter was at home, and on being told that the maid would see, followed her to the drawing-room and found the women of the family.

'I knew you would want to see me. It is a time when you would only want to see old friends. I have not brought Stephen, for fear you have not looked on him for long as a friend.'

'Have you come to congratulate us?' said Hetta. 'On the new addition to our family?'

'Yes, that is what I have come for: to congratulate you, and to hear how it happened, how you arranged it. You have had to arrange it before for John. I have never had to for Stephen. He does make less work.'

'Oh, I had no hand at all in John's first marriage. As far as this one is concerned, I managed by impressing upon him, early and late, that we could only do with someone we were used to in the household.'

'And the only person was Miss Hallam. You certainly had a hand in this marriage. How about the wedding?' Miss Marcon knew that no one had attended. 'Did you think it worth while to go?'

'Oh, well, no, not for this kind of marriage,' said Hetta, leaning back and putting her hands behind her head. 'We should have found it an echo of the first; and why drag up the past, when you are turning an interested gaze towards the future?'

'The children could not have found it that. They did not exist before the first.'

'And would that help them to keep their thoughts from it?' said Hetta with a laugh. 'They must see it the reason of their existence. And some of them remember their mother.'

'My dear, how shallow I am! It is because the deep experiences of life have passed me by. Do go on telling me about the second marriage. It is the only one I can understand.'

'Well, it has happened, and I am to have Edith as a permanent member of my household. What do you think of that?'

'Edith will have Aunt Hetta as a member of hers,' said Clare to France. 'That is the truth.'

'You have just heard it is not. And I hardly think it is.'

'I am going to call Miss Hallam, Edith,' said Muriel, addressing the guest betimes.

'Muriel, you should wait to be spoken to,' said Sabine. 'Children should be seen and not heard.'

'Muriel must learn early to reckon with life's inconsistencies,' said France.

'What a dear child she is!' said Miss Marcon. 'I am sure I should have wanted to marry her father and her governess and everyone to do with her.'

'I am going to have a new governess.'

'The weak point of the new arrangement,' said Hetta. 'More expense, even if not much. And we hoped there would be no more.'

'Your father can't marry her this time, Muriel. And he generally doesn't, does he? You often have a new one; I remember you had Miss Bunyan. I can't think why people say it is difficult to talk to children. They so often have a governess. Edith will be able to train the future governesses.'

'Yes, that is a great thing,' said Hetta in a serious tone, turning aside with her friend. 'I shall put all that on to her, as Mater gets past it. I have no knack for that side of things, and John does not want me occupied with it. He gets so fidgeted, when I insist upon talking about children and education and the rest of it.'

'Well, do not insist on it, dear. John has married Miss Hallam to prevent it, and it would not be reasonable. What would be the good of his doing it? Has he married her for any other reason, do you think? I know he tells you everything, so please betray his confidence. That does not matter between one woman and another. It can't, or it would matter too much to be possible, and it is always found to be possible.'

'Well, we thought it over and threshed it out and came to the conclusion that the reasons were enough. We had an uncertain time, and he wanted his mind made up for him'—Hetta gave a laugh—'but we got things to a head at last. Yes, it is behind us now.'

'And Edith was glad you decided on her, that you did not prefer to talk about education? You might have had a liking for it: I suppose she has.'

'Oh come, don't put it all on to one line like that; and mind you don't betray me. I think John is really attached to her, and welcomes her as an addition to the house. And you like her yourself, don't you? I have heard you say you do.'

'Yes, but I preferred her to be a spinster. I do prefer clever women to be spinsters; I have some thought of myself. And Stephen is never annoyed by her, as he is by most people. I ought to have arranged for him to marry her: I should have thought about it, as you did. You are a much better sister. People are always asking me why I do not make my brother marry. They seem to see it as my duty. They are really asking me why I do not break up my life, and of course they see that as my duty. I could not choose his wife, and have her for a member of my household, as you can; and I suppose they see I could not. You have made your brother marry without giving people any secret satisfaction, and that is a great success.'

'I believe John is never annoyed by her either,' said Hetta, as if this dawned on her mind. 'And that is such a good foundation. I really don't think things will break up. If they do, I will never undertake any responsibility again: I will not; I have made up my mind.' She ended lightly and turned to the others.

'Now what do you all think about it?' said Miss Marcon. 'Muriel is the only one who has talked of it, and she does not usually speak for you all.'

'I welcome an addition to the family,' said Clare. 'We were getting too set and sordid among ourselves.'

'And it is nice to have things different, isn't it?' said Muriel.

'Change should be for the better,' said France, 'when reasonable people make it.'

'It would tend in that direction here,' said Clare.

'I don't think you are at all set among yourselves,' said Miss Marcon.

'Oh, that is Clare's note,' said Hetta. 'We take no notice of it.'

'We are glad Father is to have Edith's companionship,' said Clare, looking at her aunt.

'Now that is better,' said Hetta, with a laugh of understanding. 'I was wondering if any of you would have a reason apart from yourselves. Muriel, what do you think about it? You have not really told us.'

Muriel found her disability reassert itself.

'You must know why you are glad Father is marrying Miss Hallam, if you are glad. Now don't say you are going to call her Edith, or going to have a new governess. We know that.'

'When Muriel speaks, she drives her words home,' said Clare.

'She must be one of those people of few words, whose words are always remembered,' said France.

Muriel stood at a loss, as her advance in conversation was nullified.

'You must have some reasons. You have only to state them,' said Hetta. 'Perhaps you are not glad, are you?'

'No, Aunt Hetta.'

'If you have not any reasons for being glad, of course you cannot state them. Perhaps you have some reasons for being sorry, but we will not ask you to state those.'

'I must go now,' said Miss Marcon. 'I see Rowland and Evelyn standing in the rain. Perhaps they saw me come in and waited for me.'

'I saw them with you outside the gates,' said Muriel.

'Then of course they saw me come in, dear.'

'You can tell them we are all glad of the situation but Muriel,' said Hetta. 'Children are conservative.'

'I don't think anything can make them glad,' said Miss Marcon. 'They always despise their surroundings and dislike innovation. I don't see what can be done.'

'Here is a letter from the new governess,' said Sabine. 'Blake seems to be her name; I thought it was Bloke. I did not think to open it; I thought it was nothing. Governesses write so many letters before they come. And she is coming to-day by the early train. Does it matter, Hetta, my dear?'

'No, not so much. She has to come soon or late, and she may as well settle down before our truants return.'

'May I stay and see her come?' said Miss Marcon. 'I enjoy that, and I am good at it, a great help.'

'I think it is a thing for the family,' said Sabine, leaning back and using a weak tone.

'I am sure it is,' said Clare. 'And I doubt if any of the things for the family are fit for other eyes.'

'Ours are dark dealings with governesses,' said France. 'There is a skeleton in every cupboard. Grandma is right not to bring it out. What is the use of the cupboard?'

'A skeleton is none the better for being ridiculous,' said Clare.

'It may be better, but it is more embarrassing. It should be guilty and tragic.'

'Are you talking quickly to cover my embarrassment?' said Miss Marcon. 'I think Muriel might have spoken. I do see why you teach her to speak. This is when people wish the floor would open and swallow them. I wonder if I am carrying it off: I shall tell Stephen I did so. I behaved as if I were one of yourselves, when I am a mere acquaintance. If I am a friend, I presumed on the friendship. If I am an old friend, I am one of those who think they can do and say anything. That was worst of all. No, I behaved as if my particular touch justified anything; that was worst. I hope I do not seem at all ill at ease; I hope I seem sorrier for all of you than for myself.'

'No one is ill at ease,' said Clare. 'We are all hardened.'

'Well, goodbye. I will go away quietly, without having my wish gratified.'

'Must you go?' said Sabine, offering her hand.

'I wanted to stay, to welcome the new governess, to help you to receive her. I thought I was more one of the family than I was: I don't know why people are ever one of the family.' Miss Marcon moved across the room, talking as she went, and Hetta went to have a word with her in the hall.

'How old will Miss Blake be?' said Muriel.

'She is about thirty-eight,' said Sabine. 'Now that is enough.'

'Enough is as good as a feast,' said Clare. 'We do seem to savour Muriel's words.'

'Let me see the letter, Mater,' said Hetta, returning in a lighter mood.

'It is an unnecessary letter. Changing her day, giving inconvenience, arriving just after luncheon, when she will have had luncheon, or not had it, and we shall not know whether she has had it or not! Well, she will not have it. Our time will be past and it cannot be altered.'

'The letter is certainly unnecessary,' said France.

'We need not know whether she has had it or not,' said Clare.

'We had better not know,' said her sister.

'I desire to hear no more from any one of you, until she arrives.'

'This is how Muriel's weakness grows upon her,' said France.

Miss Blake arrived while luncheon was in progress, stood inside the door with a shy, bright air, and then came forward and greeted Sabine with more than the usual deference for her age. She was a dark, small woman, with a swift, short step, a bright, kind glance of which she seemed to be aware, clothes which seemed independent of any principle of choice, and an air of respect for herself and others, which she held to be her main attribute, and held to be so justly, as she attended to its being the case.

'Now do not get up; I could not have it,' she said in low, quick, staccato tones, holding Sabine's hand a moment longer than was usual. 'I am disturbing your family luncheon, which is better for me than for you.'

She gave a deep little laugh, and Muriel was already enough in sympathy with her to echo it.

'Muriel, you may go out of the room,' said Sabine.

'No, Mrs. Ponsonby, I ask for my first favour that she may stay,' said Miss Blake, looking at her pupil with a charitable, interested gaze.

'Then you must understand me, Muriel.'

Muriel understood her grandmother, and knew that Miss Blake was placed between Miss Hallam and Miss Bunyan, and surveyed her making a luncheon without emotion.

'I am not Muriel's first governess?'

'No, she has had several. The last one has become more to us, and is on her honeymoon with my son, Muriel's father. They will be returning in a week.'

'Now I shall have no chance of getting as far as that,' said Miss Blake, laughing and continuing to laugh. 'The ground is cut away from under my feet. I do not start fair at all.'

'I must remember to get John's papers sorted and ready for him,' said Hetta, indicating her position with her brother. 'He will want to get back to work at once.'

Miss Blake turned her eyes on Hetta, allowing them to recognise her looks.

'So I am not the only person who does necessary work. I have to admit another to my level.'

'You do. My brother keeps me firmly to it. I am seldom allowed to step down.'

'I claim to be on a level with you both,' said Alfred. 'I do not allow that my labours are less, or that my pupils' education is less important than Muriel's. I recognise the pre-eminence of women, but in the matter of education their most earnest advocate only demands for them equality.'

'We work on a level indeed,' said Miss Blake in a low, deep tone.

'Have you spoken to Miss Blake, Muriel?' said Sabine.

Muriel did not reply.

'The youngest child of a large family is often backward,' said Victor.

'Speak to Miss Blake when I tell you, Muriel.'

'I can't think of anything to say, Grandma.'

'It is astonishing how a backward child will suddenly say a whole sentence at once,' said Chilton.

'There was never any real need for anxiety,' said his brother.

'How old are you, dear?' said Miss Blake, not seeming to change the subject as entirely as she intended.

'Twelve,' said Muriel with tears in her voice.

'Yes, it is sad,' said Chilton, 'a very sad case. I think such a thing is sadder when the subject realises it.'

'It is better when there is a merciful lack of comprehension.'

'Do not talk nonsense,' said Sabine. 'You are making Muriel as silly as yourselves. As you cannot talk in a reasonable way, we will have silence. I was never less proud of any of you.'

'An extreme occasion, as you suggest,' said Clare.

'When were we least proud of Grandma?' said Victor.

'Muriel, are you coming to help me unpack?' said Miss Blake.

'There is one branch of Muriel's education not neglected,' said France, as Miss Blake left the room.

'Miss Blake does not want a child who cannot speak,' said Sabine. 'Such a child might not be able to understand what she said.'

'Several kinds of deficiency do often go together,' said Victor.

'I said we would have silence,' said Sabine almost on a shriek.

'We will have it, Mrs. Ponsonby,' said Alfred, coming to help her from her chair. 'If we cannot have silence, we will go where silence is.'

'It is silly to put out your grandmother on the day when Miss Blake comes,' said Hetta. 'We shall be having Miss Bunyan over again, if you do not take care.'

'We have had some of her,' said France. 'I don't think we shall have it all. Grandma has exact perceptions.'

'Miss Blake is better than Miss Bunyan, isn't she?' said Muriel.

'You go too far in talking about your elders. I ought to make a change, before your father comes home and takes my time.'

'Will he want your time now?' said Muriel.

'Why should he not?'

'Well, he will have Miss Hallam.'

'That will make no difference. He has explained that he will want my time as he always has, and I must be prepared to give it to him. He has been quite clear.'

'Why does he want you both? Why did he marry Miss Hallam?'

'Muriel's power of speech!' muttered Chilton. 'Grandma, Grandma, you little know what you have done.'

'Because you were all getting fond of her,' said Hetta, in an instructive tone, 'and she was getting fond of us, and Father was becoming fond of her too; and it seemed best to put things on a regular footing. Father and I both thought it was best. Now how can you all spend so much time standing about? Do you feel it is an occupation? I could not.'

'We do not feel it is that,' said Clare. 'That is the point of it.'

'We are having some conversation,' said Chilton.

'You are certainly not doing that. Your little schoolroom brightnesses are not anything approaching to it.'

'Do you mean to give us pain, Aunt Hetta?'

'I mean to say the simple truth. That will not hurt you. You are too fond of shutting yourselves up in your own little world and tossing about your own little speeches.'

'You are wrong, Aunt Hetta. The truth has hurt us.'

'Has habit bred affection unawares?' said Clare.

'Dr. Chaucer is coming to dinner, and you will behave as if you were civilised. Miss Blake will be thinking you are savages. I should be sorry to hear her opinion of you.'

'I should like to hear her opinion of Grandma,' said Clare, 'or rather, should also be sorry to hear it.'

'Muriel, would you like to come down to dinner, as it is Miss Blake's first night?'

'No, thank you, Aunt Hetta.'

'You had better come down. Then there need be no school-room tea. You can think of some things to say. And remember questions will not do.'

Chaucer arrived at the appointed hour, looked at Miss Blake with covert curiosity, and prepared to devote himself to Sabine, as a preliminary to transferring his attention.

'Miss Blake came by a different train, Grandma,' said Muriel at the table, breaking into precautionary speech. 'That one is a more punctual train. The other was late when Miss Hallam came, and late when Miss Bunyan came. It was only when Aunt Hetta came by it, that it was in time.'

'It evidently draws a distinction between governesses and members of the family,' said Miss Blake, laughing. 'The former's is a history of an oppressed race.'

'Miss Blake, you are surely thinking of the time when their position was different,' said Chaucer, leaning forward.

'People are inevitably oppressed in some positions, are they?'

'Mrs. Ponsonby,' said Chaucer, 'do you make it a stipulation, when you engage a—when you seek an instructress for your grandchild, that she should evince powers of repartee?'

'I bear witness that no such stipulation was made,' said Alfred. 'As an instructor of the grandchildren, I was accepted without it.'

'I was thinking of the sex which is more noted than ours for quickness with the tongue.'

'I can hardly do that,' said Sabine, 'but it is an advantage to the grandchild.'

'Grandma has her own conception of Muriel,' said France. 'It may be the explanation of her demands.'

'To the grandchild, I make no doubt,' said Chaucer; 'but what of the guest, who happens to be at your table?'

'The guest must need fewer weapons, when all is said and done,' said Miss Blake, laughing again.

'Mrs. Ponsonby, I ask you!' said Chaucer, making a gesture.

'I don't think anyone needs any weapons in my house.'

'No, indeed, and that is a view which Miss Blake will second, when she has had the experience.'

'I suppose Chaucer has forgotten Miss Bunyan now,' said Chilton. 'He always made light of her.'

'Mater, this chattering in mutters!' said Hetta. 'It is incredible at their ages.'

'Age is not a thing to taunt, but to respect,' said Chilton.

'It is a thing to taunt when its obligations are not observed,' said Alfred. 'It is generally taunted then.'

'Old people do return to the habits of childhood,' said Clare.

'You have not returned to them. You have never left them,' said Hetta. 'There should be a stage in between.'

'Is Aunt Hetta in it?' whispered Muriel.

'Muttering again! Did you hear what I said?'

'Yes,' said Chilton, 'but we only have at our disposal the feeble accents of age.'

'Did you hear what I said, Victor?'

'Well, Aunt Hetta, my hearing is hardly what it was.'

'Smartness and pertness! I get so sick of it,' said Hetta, as if to herself.

'Miss Hetta, you can hardly expect the young people to live and move and have their being on your level,' said Chaucer, with a note of earnestness. 'If you want an equal on your own ground, I should recommend Miss Blake, as the most likely to come up to your standard.'

Hetta turned, as if reminded, to talk to the newcomer, and the meal drew to its close.

In the drawing-room the boys put chairs for the women, and Chaucer took a chair and carried it with some urgency to Miss Blake, as though to ensure that she was not left out of the attention.

'Thank you,' she said in low, deep tones, glancing at him as she took it.

'Miss Blake,' said Chaucer, sitting down beside her, 'it must be a great adventure to come to a new household, and confront the little human interchanges which make up the relation of a family. It must need, if I may say so, a brave spirit.'

'It has its demands,' said Miss Blake, speaking very low and then changing her tone. 'I do sometimes feel it rather a heroic position. It would be natural to cry myself to sleep, and I never do.'

Chaucer shook his head at the truth thus lightly expressed.

'I hope you will find a home here. I vouch for it that there is a real welcome.'

'I hope I shall: I have to find a home.'

Chaucer gave this admission the tribute of a moment's silence.

'I had the acquaintance of your predecessor. You will also become acquainted with her, as she is now a member of the family.'

'She has found a home here,' said Miss Blake, laughing. 'It is held a success for the governess to marry the widower. But I would rather hold to my own position; it is the one I chose.'

'You are wise not to relinquish your chosen work until an alternative really recommends itself,' said Chaucer, thinking of one which should do this, and of supporting the recommendation at a later date.

Nine

'They are coming,' said Miss Marcon, standing in the Ponsonbys' hall. 'Let us move to the back. Our being asked to dinner does not mean we are to be continually to the fore. Stand here with me, Alfred, in case we seem to be in evidence. The tutor and his aunt are not the family, because no difference is made. If they were, people would not have to trouble about the difference. Miss Blake is not even here; she is showing true dignity; but I always wonder if the true kinds of dignity, the dignity of toil and simplicity and frugal independence, are as good as the other kinds. Edith seems to like the ordinary dignity of being married to John: I have noticed how well ordinary dignity sits on people. Now we turn our eyes on a simple, family scene. I don't know why simple is so often coupled with family. Simple family affection, simple family life; yes, it is wrong. We ought to surprise a tear in Stephen's eye; disillusioned people are so often surprised in that way.'

'Well, my three generations!' said John, embracing in turn his mother, sister, and daughters. 'Well, my two fellow men! So we return to play our part in our complicated family.'

'Complicated! There, I knew it,' said Miss Marcon.

'Not so complicated,' said Hetta, coming to the fore. 'Only one more than it has always been. And I am used to the complication. Now I have put dinner early, in case you need it, and Charity and Stephen are here to welcome you. You need not at once confront the domestic round.'

'It is the best welcome in the world,' said John. 'It is one of the better thoughts that strike my sister.'

'I have not managed for you all these years without knowing what you like. We need not behave as if this were a working day. Now I have put you and Edith in the adjoining rooms which have been the spare rooms, and I am using your bedroom and dressing-room as spare rooms instead. You want to start afresh and not repeat past history.'

'History repeats itself,' murmured Clare.

'We are starting afresh anyhow. Rooms make no difference,' said John; 'but it is as well to have them well chosen.'

'Then what is the difference between his view and Aunt Hetta's?' said France.

'Rooms which have been the spare rooms!' said Clare. 'It is an office easily filled.'

'Away with you all!' said Hetta. 'Away to your own places. We do not want groups of you about. We want to have air to breathe.'

'What of you and Alfred and me, Stephen?' said Miss Marcon. 'There is clearly a group of us; and when you are told to come early, it is difficult not to breathe the air. When dinner begins, we shall feel more natural and justified.'

Dinner soon began. It seemed as if Hetta had foreseen the hour of strain. Sabine and her daughter took their ends of the table. The Marcons had their recognised seats. John went to his place by his mother, and was turning to summon his wife, when Hetta smilingly motioned her to his side, and signed to the others to adjust their seats, making this the only change. Miss Blake unobtrusively entered and approached her place with short, quick, noiseless steps. John had a friendly manner to his wife, as if they had found their relation. Hetta watched the servants and seemed to manage the meal, giving more directions than were needed.

'Have you all met Miss Blake?' said Sabine.

'No, but we know her by name,' said Miss Marcon. 'We do so hope she will stay. People put a new pupil back to the beginning, and it is time for Muriel to advance.'

'I am glad she is here too,' said Edith. 'I should not have known how to come by her. I only know the other side of the process.'

'You would not have had to trouble about it,' said Hetta. 'Mater and I are not shirking our responsibilities. We shall not bother you with all our workaday arrangements.'

'Did the station master admire you for being married to John?' said Miss Marcon to Edith. 'He does not admire me for going to the British Museum. He thinks I may be earning my living. I would tell him how far it is from being the case, if I were not ashamed of it. It is known to be odd, what different things people think shameful.'

'Considering his views, his manner to me has done him credit,' said Miss Blake with a laugh.

'He always admires me for being the head of things,' said Hetta.

'I am that,' said Sabine.

'Oh, well, the actual and ultimate head. It makes no difference to him.'

'It makes a difference to me, my dear, whether I am alive or dead.'

'Won't Miss Hallam be the head of things next to Grandma now?' said Muriel.

'She will be busy with her own work,' said Hetta, turning round. 'She should not have wasted her time in teaching you. That is not her province.'

'Wasted her time! Come, come!' said Miss Blake.

'Do you like the beginning, dear?' said Miss Marcon.

'Muriel, look a little brighter and answer Miss Marcon.'

Muriel modified her expression.

'I suppose Muriel's face is speaking,' said France. 'Indeed we see it doing so.'

'You need not make a grimace,' said the grandmother.

'She has no choice,' said Stephen. 'It is what she was told to do.'

'Father's train was late, Grandma,' said Muriel.

'We must teach Muriel another speech,' said France, 'one of more general application.'

'It is surprising how this has come in,' said Clare, 'considering the extent to which we are addicted to travel.'

'You observe, Miss Blake,' said Victor, 'that Muriel is the exception among my sisters in the matter of a tongue.'

'Well, women have the reputation of a tongue. We will not have the discredit and not the licence.'

'We will continue this meal in silence,' quavered Sabine.

'Indeed we will not,' said her son. 'We will continue it in the social intercourse which celebrates my return.'

They continued the meal in a condition between the two,

and were relieved when it ended and the women left the men.

'May I come and sit with you presently, Miss Blake?' said Edith. 'Then I shall not look as if I did not know what to do on my first night, and as if I were lost in my own home.'

'It would be better to disguise it,' said Miss Marcon.

'Indeed you may,' said Miss Blake, very low.

'All your problems were mine, so if mine have to be yours, it is only fair.'

'They shall be mine indeed.'

'I do like to hear you talk like this,' said Miss Marcon. 'I have not held a post in the house, but being the tutor's aunt is not very different. It makes all the problems mine. So what is the first?'

Miss Blake turned obviously away to talk to someone else.

'I think you know it,' said Edith.

'Yes, that is why I want to deal with it.'

'I have heard of wives who did not tolerate the husband's sister in his home, but not of a sister who did not tolerate the wife.'

'It is a unique problem,' said Miss Marcon. 'I am glad it is mine.'

'If I come second to Hetta in everything, will it solve it?'

'Well, that is what they all do, and you are one of them now. And it seems to be a solution.'

'Father ought to like Miss Hallam best now,' said Muriel's voice. 'Isn't a wife better than a sister?'

'I will have this problem for mine,' said Miss Marcon.

'I think I will go and sit upstairs,' said Miss Blake, with a movement to rise.

'You need not go,' said Miss Marcon in an encouraging manner. 'It is one of those things when a threat is enough.'

Miss Blake looked at her and sat down.

'You see a threat was enough.'

Miss Blake laughed freely at herself.

'Mrs. Ponsonby will settle all the problems,' said Miss Marcon. 'I suppose they are not really mine.'

'I am sorry for the poor old lady,' said Miss Blake, in a tone of stating a view which would not be general.

'Well, it is a tragic house. But I think it attains to the dignity of tragedy. I think we are allowed to pity. Anyhow you were allowed to.'

'I meant nothing disparaging.'

'Well, pity does mean you don't find things satisfactory,' said Edith.

'Well, well!' said Miss Blake.

'Do you like teaching Muriel?' said Miss Marcon. 'Is she good at the beginning?'

'Not very,' said Miss Blake with a smile. 'Perhaps she is tired of it. She seems to have reason to be.'

'I am sure you meant nothing disparaging. How she despised Miss Bunyan, dear child! She did mean something disparaging.'

'What became of Miss Bunyan?'

'Nothing became of her,' said Edith. 'She is Dr. Chaucer's niece. That is her tragedy.'

'What are you all laughing at?' said Sabine.

'We have so much in common,' said Miss Marcon, 'we women who go forth from the home.'

'I am sure you know a great deal the rest of us do not. I wish I had had more opportunity. I should have made the most of it.'

'Is Grandma not satisfied with herself as she is?' said Victor. 'This is a new idea.'

'I have seen her so under the most unlikely circumstances,' said Clare.

'More opportunity!' said Chilton. 'More!'

'You must all forgive my sister and me for talking apart,' said John. 'Our reunion brings us many problems.'

'So many, that we question the wisdom of having been apart,' said Hetta.

'The chief is so pressing that we question the wisdom of facing it.'

'Then do not face it,' said France. 'Facing things is the least likely way to elude them.'

'I don't know,' said Miss Marcon. 'When people have faced things like risk and danger and death, they always have eluded them.'

'Well, we may elude this,' said John, 'but I don't see how. To-morrow we will face it and trust to the efficacy of the method. To-night we will forget.'

'It is money, I suppose,' said Victor. 'If Father was going to forget it, I wish he had done so.'

'I suppose France's money has come to an end,' said Clare.

'I had better send the rest,' said her sister in an offhand manner. 'Shall I send it all at once or in thrifty instalments?'

'Oh, at once. You may as well save postage, when you are going to the expense of a thousand pounds.'

'Thrift does not come into the matter,' said Chilton.

'It may do more good all at once,' said France. 'Every little may help, but it cannot help much. "Take care of the pence" is a foolish saying. Pence do not come to pounds.'

'And pounds certainly do not take care of themselves,' said Chilton, 'even a thousand together.'

'A pound is two hundred and forty pence,' said Muriel.

'Muriel knows the beginning,' said Miss Marcon, drawing nearer. 'She can go on now.'

'A pound is surely not so many pence,' said John. 'If it were, it would have to do more.'

'Father is going too far in dragging forward his poverty,' said Victor. 'It seems that France may do more harm than good. He will have to adapt himself to his position.'

'People very seldom do harm, when they try to do good,' said France. 'Even temporary benefit is benefit while it lasts. People want some reason for not doing good. Or they would have to do it, as I have to.'

'The difference will have to come,' said Victor. 'Is it any better a few months later?'

'It is a little better, and anyhow it is later.'

'Death comes to us all soon or late,' said Chilton. 'Yes, that shows us. Things are better late.'

'Now, Muriel, you may run to bed,' said Sabine. 'You have been up much too long.'

Miss Blake rose also, but with hesitation, from her seat.

'I will go with Muriel,' she said in a low, quick tone, glancing round without raising her eyes.

Sabine made no demur; Muriel performed her good nights; Miss Blake stood for a moment and then murmured, 'Good night,' and rapidly followed her.

'Ought Alfred to go too?' said Miss Marcon to her brother.

'Alfred's charge is still here. Mrs. Ponsonby is not going to bed.' Stephen changed his tone as Hetta drew near. 'So John and his wife will be a pair of writers together.'

'Not together,' said Hetta, lightly. 'You do not know the ways and needs of writers. Strictly apart, and neither of them pushing in upon the other! That is how it will be, or I shall hear about it. But I am used to it. John has made me an indulgent assistant, I am afraid.'

'You will be attached to John, and Edith will manage by herself?'

'Yes. Women are much more independent than men. I always say so.'

'It would seem so, as France also manages by herself.'

'Of making many books there is no end,' said John. 'Does anyone not try to make them?'

'I do not,' said Alfred. 'I am a reader of them, and fulfil a humble but essential part.'

'Humble!' said John. 'You are the paymasters, the employers, you people who read. We are your hired servants.'

'Does Alfred think he is living a human life?' said Stephen to his sister.

'I don't think so. He feels he is avoiding one, as he meant to.'

'What does it lead to?'

'To being dismissed, when Chilton and Victor are grown up. It does not seem true that the whole of life is education.'

'The boys are twice the man he is.'

'I am sure he would insist on that. In his way he is conscientious.'

'He seems content with himself and his position.'

'Everyone is content with himself, which is odd, when you think he knows all the hidden, petty evil in him.'

'But everyone is not content with his position.'

'No one but Alfred. Do you suppose the hidden, petty evil in everyone is the same?'

'I should think it is a little different in different people.'

'I should think it is. You can tell that by Mrs. Ponsonby, who does not hide the petty evil in her. It is such a good thing it is petty. I never know why people think pettiness makes evil worse instead of better. Let us say goodbye, before she shows she wants us to say it. We will go while that petty evil is hidden. Goodbye, Mrs. Ponsonby. We have enjoyed it so much. We have taken everything and given nothing, which must be enjoyable. Goodbye, my dears. Thank you for making Alfred at home. Stephen and I behaved so much like his uncle and aunt, that he could not forget it; and now we regret it, when it is too late. But I never heard of anyone who regretted anything in time.'

Miss Marcon vanished, followed by her brother, and as the door closed, it seemed to the family that this was the real moment of John's return.

The next days passed in a tentative following of the old routine. John depended on his sister, sought his wife, and seemed uneasy and uncertain of his course. Hetta spent her former hours with him, indicated to Edith when she should take her place, and organised the life of the household from morning till night. She had even taken the sorting of the letters from Sabine, who seemed to acquiesce in the gradual yielding of her place. Alfred spent more time with Sabine, and it became an accepted companionship.

It was a few days later when John received his second gift. He opened the letter at breakfast, and, except to those aware of his experience, gave no sign. When all had left the table but the three older women, he rose to his feet and paused.

'I have a great reason for thankfulness. And I am thankful. It is what I can do on my side.'

'What is it?' said his mother.

John handed her the letter and cheque.

'This has happened again, and as it happened before. It seems almost too much. There is a word saying it must be the last time, and I am glad indeed it must. This is all I can take in simple gratitude. But I can take this and be grateful.'

Sabine looked up at the letter and cheque without putting out her hand for them.

'Yes, yes,' she said, nodding her head; 'yes, so it has come. Yes, it is a wonderful thing. Who would have thought it would happen twice? It is a wonderful surprise, wonderful. But it is blessed to give.'

She sat murmuring and nodding to herself, and her son handed the letter across his wife to his sister, unconsciously acting on his hidden knowledge.

'It is wonderful indeed! What a thing to take so calmly!' said Hetta. 'You will be missing it when it does not come, if you get used to it. It cuts a great many knots, but if the labourer is worthy of his hire, we have deserved it. I am glad someone holds that opinion.'

She passed the letter to Edith, accustomed to her own precedence, and the latter read it and did her part.

'It is blessed to give,' repeated Sabine.

'It seems so,' said Edith, 'as the person has done it twice.'

'The person!' said Sabine in a tender tone, taking up the paper.

'I never knew people so calm over such an event,' said Hetta, looking from one to another.

'They say it is easy to get used to pleasant things,' said Edith, 'and a thousand pounds is so very pleasant.'

'It is, my dear, it is,' said Sabine, looking up over her glasses. 'But it is blessed to give.'

'It is blessed to receive as much as this,' said John, with his forced liveliness. 'It is blessed to see the obstacles rolling away and the future clear.'

'Yes, yes, we know, my son,' said Sabine. 'There is no need to say it. We know, all of us who need to.' She rose to leave the room, and on passing Edith, laid a hand on her shoulder and at once withdrew it. 'We do not need to be told.'

Hetta observed the instinctive action, and saw a sudden wave of comprehension surge over Edith's face. She waited for her brother and his wife to leave her, and sat alone with her thoughts. She saw that light had come to Edith on the matter of the gifts to her husband; she thought of the words and action which had shed the light. She had not sorted the letters without doing so as her mother's daughter, though Hetta never broke the accepted code. She knew that Edith heard from a publisher, and, struck by a thought, she rose and found a paper. She saw by an advertisement that the same firm had issued the book by Edith's namesake, which had won the prize. The amount of the prize was that of the sums which had come to her brother. Many things rose up before her and fell into place. The scene when she surprised her mother tampering with the letters; her mother's subsequent willingness that Edith should marry her son; Edith's willingness to marry him; her mother's feeling to Edith—it all stood in relation and made a whole.

Later in the day she drove to the town on some regular errand, and obtained the book by Edith's namesake, or, as she now believed, by Edith. She read it in her room, assigning it to her brother's wife, but found that the book was based on the play which France had written and which they all had seen. Her mind was swift, and the lines of the truth were clear. She saw her mother's mistake, the cover which her niece had taken, Edith's belief that John had married her without ulterior motive; saw how her own life was altered by the blind and blindly crossing forces.

When she met her family, she felt an urge to probe the hidden danger.

'I have mapped out the uses for the thousand pounds. It has been even easier the second time. The point of the sum seems to be that it should fall in regularly.'

'Twice is the right number of times,' said Chilton. 'It would not do to form the habit. Our benefactor has naturally broken it.'

'What is the good of postponing what will be the worse for the postponement?'

'You have found what good it is,' said Clare, 'and found it, as you say, easily, and would choose to continue to do so.'

'You seem up in arms for the benefactor, as you call him,' said Hetta, smiling.

'It is natural to be prejudiced in his favour.'

'If you mean things like economies and discomforts,' said Chilton, 'they are far from being worse for postponement.'

'I hope you will find that is so,' said Sabine. 'We must remember your view. It is the right one, but you must hold to it.'

'Postponement of something may mean avoidance of it,' said John. 'And it must mean the hope of it, and hope is sweet.'

'What do you think, France?' said Hetta. 'You are not often so silent.'

'I think with Father and Grandma and Clare and Chilton. It hardly needed saying again.'

'I wonder if we shall discover the benefactor. I should like to pry and probe and bring him to light.'

'Surely you would not,' said Chilton, 'when you have used the money, and the condition of doing so was ignorance.'

'What a proper young man!' laughed his aunt. 'I have not used the money for myself. It would make no difference to me, if it was forfeited.'

'Your aunt said she would like to discover, Chilton,' said Alfred. 'She did not say she thought of doing so. We are all in her place.'

'They cannot understand anything that is said to them,' said Hetta. 'It must be heavy work to teach them. I would rather do everything else, as I do.'

'People have to do what they can, Miss Ponsonby. I could

not do everything else.'

'Well, let us return to the subject. Has anyone any suspicion? Have you, Edith?'

'No, do not let us return to it,' said Clare. 'Let us by all means avoid it. We see the result of not doing so.'

'Our suspicions could only be of the pleasantest,' said John, 'but we are not allowed to have them.'

'The subject seems to trouble you all,' said Hetta. 'Surely Edith has something to say?'

'It does not trouble me,' said John. 'It fills me with relief and thankfulness. I do not wish for more congenial feelings.'

'Let Edith speak,' said Hetta.

But someone else wished to do this.

'Can I speak to you, Mrs. Ponsonby?' said Miss Blake at the door.

'Why, yes, of course, Miss Blake. I hope nothing is amiss. Is it Muriel?'

'No, indeed it is not. It is something else, someone else. I would rather not speak of it; I hardly know what I can do.'

'I hardly know either,' murmured Chilton.

'I have no choice but to say something. I must ask to leave at once. I do not know how I sound.'

'We do not know either, Miss Blake,' said Hetta. 'Can you not be a little clearer?'

'I cannot; I must ask indulgence; I do ask it. There is not only myself involved.'

'You cannot go like that, when we have come to know you,' said John. 'Neither of the boys has annoyed you?'

'No, indeed not. I really cannot explain.'

'It was gallant to attempt the impossible,' said France. 'So Muriel is again at the beginning.'

'Has anyone been in the house but ourselves?' said Sabine, with weary shrewdness.

'I am glad Victor is here,' said Chilton, 'or suspicion might have fallen on him.'

'The man came about the roof,' said Hetta, 'and I saw him myself, as usual. The woman came about the carpets, and I saw her. Dr. Chaucer was coming to bring some books, and I suppose I shall see him. I know no more.'

'And you now see Victor,' said Chilton. 'My brother is cleared—cleared!'

'Let me go and talk to Miss Blake,' said Edith. 'I must have the most understanding of her problems.'

'That is no good,' said Hetta, looking after them. 'I had better have gone on managing the matter, as I manage everything. It is the only thing that works.'

'But you were not managing it,' said John. 'It was baffling you, as it was baffling us all.'

'Do you suppose Edith is doing any more?'

'She cannot be doing less, and Miss Blake seemed willing to go with her.'

'Well, if Miss Blake does leave, either Clare or France will teach Muriel. I will not have another stranger in the house; I have made up my mind.'

'It seems she is leaving,' said Chilton. 'That did emerge.'

Edith and Miss Blake had reached the schoolroom.

'Is it Dr. Chaucer?' said Edith.

Miss Blake stared at her in silence.

'Did he do anything worse than propose? That is said to be the greatest honour a man can do a woman, so you should not resent it too much.'

'He came up here——'

'Of course. That was the place to find you. But did he do worse than propose?'

'No—yes—well, yes, he did worse. He went too far, considering I had not accepted him, that he did not wait——'

'Of course he should have waited. It was worse than proposing, not to wait. It must have been trying.'

'Yes, it was trying,' said Miss Blake with her normal terseness.

'How did he do when you refused him?'

'He did fairly well,' said Miss Blake in a low, quick tone, dropping her eyes. 'And he had offered me all he had; I must remember it; I will remember it.'

'I should forget it. It is what he would like, and I see you want to consider him. It is not as good as it sounds, to be offered all a person has.'

'Did he ever propose to you?' said Miss Blake.

'It is odd it should be so awkward to admit that someone has offered you everything. It doesn't sound anything to be ashamed of.'

'One feels ashamed,' said Miss Blake very low. 'One wonders if one has done anything—but no.'

'It is odd too that it should be awkward to tell anyone he is not all the world to you. It is really a great deal to expect.'

'Does he always propose to the governess?' said Miss Blake in a lightened spirit. 'Does it throw light on the changes?'

'I have only met Miss Bunyan, and she is his niece and can be his housekeeper anyhow.'

'Well, I shall not supplant her.'

'It would be unfair to her to accept him. It is a pity we did not think of that reason.'

'I have only had one proposal in the house. You fared twice as badly. I have nothing to make a fuss about; I am ashamed of making a fuss. But I think I must go; I should have to meet him; I feel I have given him away; and your telling me what you have, does not make it better.'

'No. One's being the one woman in the world to him would have been his excuse. And it was not his excuse. I wonder where we come on the list. I hope we were fairly high.'

'You are one in advance of me. But it was hardly fair, your being here first.'

'If he gets so much worse every time, think what our successors will suffer! You won't stay for their sakes?'

'No,' said Miss Blake, in her normal low, terse tones, 'I could not do it. Perhaps a better woman could; I cannot. I am doing the second-rate thing and running away. Perhaps I could not be behaving worse.'

'It sounds as if you could be easily replaced, but you know it is not the case.'

'And there are other reasons; I did not tell Mrs. Ponsonby.'

'Oh, of course, the post is not possible. I did not know you saw it as it was. If your eyes are open, of course you cannot stay. I don't see how Muriel can have any education. What reason shall I give for your going? Is Dr. Chaucer to have his due?'

'He may have his due,' said Miss Blake after a moment, shaking Edith's hand and going with an air of knowing what she did, out of the room and out of her life.

Edith went down to the family.

'Miss Blake is going as suddenly as Miss Bunyan. But Dr. Chaucer is playing a different part. He offered her a home before she decided to go, and not after.'

There was a pause.

'Proposed to her?' said Clare.

'Yes, and she did not like the manner of his doing it, and

will not be where she may meet him.'

'Proposed!' said Sabine, her voice dying away after its first sharpness, as if the scene were coming before her eyes.

'What utter nonsense!' said Hetta, who was standing against the chimneypiece, looking cold and aloof. 'What silly trumpery! You did not believe it? Why does she not say she wants to leave, without putting it on to a false, romantic footing? I would soon have had some truth out of her, if I had dealt with it.'

'You would,' said Edith. 'The truth soon came out.'

'Surely truth is what we have from Miss Blake,' said Victor.

'I am going to have this from her, truth or not,' said Chilton. 'I am enchanted by the scene which is brought before my eyes.'

'Is it brought before your eyes?' said France. 'You are fortunate. I cannot imagine it.'

'How absurd of her!' said Sabine, who saw the whole thing as it was, and impatiently excused Chaucer and more impatiently condemned Miss Blake. 'Refusing one provision for herself is not a reason for giving up another.'

'Oh, enough of it,' said Hetta. 'She has her reasons for leaving, and if anyone wants to know them, I will find them out. But it is not worth while; I do not wish her to stay; I don't want fibbings and falseness in my house. It is not fair to our friends to have cock-and-bull stories made about them out of nothing. She must be a woman who thinks a man is proposing to her, if he is polite in passing on the stairs.'

'I hardly think it happened on the stairs,' said Clare.

'It quite well may have. Dr. Chaucer was bringing some books, and would not have met her anywhere else. But why be so literal? If you would be less so, and Miss Blake more, I should have an easier house.'

'You seem in an odd mood, Hetta,' said John. 'Don't you feel yourself?'

'Of course I feel myself. If I did not, things would soon show it. But I do not know how I can manage, if I am to be confronted by things done behind my back. I did not want Miss Blake to go at the moment; I am not prepared for another stranger.'

'It is no good to have someone who is unsettled.'

'She would not have been unsettled, if I had dealt with her.'

'She was clearly unsettled when she appeared at the door,' said Victor. 'It is the word for her state.'

'Oh, my dear boy, if you don't know what I mean, you don't. I won't try to teach you.'

'You could have interviewed Miss Blake yourself,' said John. 'You did not suggest it.'

'How could I suggest it, when there was not a moment? The two of them disappeared'—Hetta gave a laugh, as if recalling the scene—'before anyone could get in a word. Not that Edith did not mean to help; she did not understand the workings of the house; that is all. A house is a complicated organism and needs understanding.'

' I don't know why our house is so much more complicated than other houses.'

'Think of it, and you will know.'

'Why not go after Miss Blake and see what you can do now?'

'Oh, Edith has surely not done her work with as little thoroughness as that!'

'Perhaps the work I could do with most success,' said Edith, 'would be to take Muriel beyond the beginning.'

'That would be a real help,' said Hetta. 'It is something no one else could do. I should be sorry to attempt it.'

'Edith may be sorry to attempt it too,' said Clare.

'It would be kind of you, my dear,' said Sabine.

'Now why so kind?' said Hetta. 'Am I so kind to organise everything for everyone, and do the thousand and one things which come to my hand every day?'

'I hardly think you are,' said her brother, in the cool, drawling tone which marked his rare loss of temper. 'You want recognition to an extent which constitutes a reward.'

'Why should I not have reward?' said Hetta, in an easy tone with another note underneath. 'Why should you want people to work without it? You want reward yourself for what you do; I never knew anyone want more: and you will go to any length to get it too.' Her tone became ruminative and she gave a slow smile. 'I don't know nothing about you. Why should your sister be so different? Why should you want her to be?'

'Edith and Clare and France will take your duties off you, if you wish. It would be nothing for the three.'

'Nothing for the three!' said Hetta with almost a scream in her voice, though she hardly raised it. 'Nothing for the three! Of course it would be nothing. How could it be anything, when it is generally done by one? You show what you think of it.

That is not the way to prove it does not count. Though why you should want to prove it, I do not know. I have never tried to prove that your work does not count, or done anything but help you with it.'

She ended with tears in her voice, and Sabine kept her eyes from her face, as if she could not bear the sight.

'I do not want a third part of Aunt Hetta's duty,' said France. 'It would not be nothing to me. I did not know duty was ever nothing, and a third is a large proportion.'

Sabine turned on France a look almost of gratitude.

'You know a woman's work is the highest in the world, Father,' said Chilton. 'You have said it in your books, in the hope that it may be immortal. You must not be too different in your books from your life.'

'He thinks the work should be divided by three, anyhow,' said Hetta. 'That is a better summing up of it than any in his books, I think.' She drew in her brows, as if recalling the passages.

The door opened and Miss Blake stood just within it, and spoke swiftly, deep and low.

'I have come to say goodbye. To thank you for your kindness. For your friendship. To ask you to let me hear of Muriel. I thank you for that and all other kindness; I say goodbye and thank you.'

The door closed.

'Will she want the trap?' said Sabine, breaking the tension and showing she had not suffered from it.

'Grandma has freed our tongues,' said Chilton. 'It is a pity she did not do it a minute earlier.'

'I hope the silence was eloquent,' said France. 'I should think it was.'

'Ought we to send Muriel to help her to pack?' said Clare. 'It seems an accomplishment which comes in useful.'

'It is only unpacking she has been taught,' said Chilton. 'When the time comes to pack, things have become strangely different.'

'Muriel, here is a chance to learn to pack,' said Victor. 'It is a rarer opportunity.'

'And Grandma would wish you to make the most of Miss Blake until the last,' said Clare.

'Would you like to go and help Miss Blake, Muriel?'

'No, thank you, Grandma.'

'Are you sorry she is going?'

'I don't mind, Grandma.'

'She has been very kind to you, hasn't she?'

'Yes, Grandma.'

'Do you feel you have learnt anything from her?'

'Yes, Grandma.'

'What have you learnt?'

Muriel paused, burst into laughter, and struggled into speech.

'The beginning, Grandma.'

Sabine smiled; the others did the same; and Muriel fell into the background, flushed by success but willing to abandon the question.

'Will Miss Blake want the trap?' said Sabine. 'Will someone answer me? I suppose she will.'

'I suppose so too,' said France. 'She cannot carry her luggage to the station.'

Muriel laughed anew at this picture of the person whose kindness she acknowledged.

'I had better go and see about it,' said Hetta in a sighing tone, seeming to drag herself from her chair.

'Ring and order it,' said John, going to the bell. 'We need not make work.'

'The work is there, isn't it?' said his sister, looking at him amusedly. 'If you call ordering a trap work; I do not myself. The work of running up and down stairs you are making yourself, and I do call that work.'

'You seemed so tired.'

'I am tired,' said Hetta, folding her hands above her head.

'Yes, ma'am?' said the maid to Sabine.

'Miss Blake will want the trap for her luggage for the next train. She has been called home. See that she has any help she needs, and that she gets off in time. The young gentlemen will see her off at the door. The rest of us have said goodbye. You understand?' Sabine ended in a rapid tone and turned away, as if putting Miss Blake completely from her mind, as indeed she was doing for ever.

'That is it, Mater,' said Hetta, in an amusedly approving tone, turning her eyes on her mother without moving her hands or her head. 'That is it. I could not have done it better.'

John sent his sister a cold, appraising glance, and Sabine did not move her eyes.

'No one helped me to unpack, Mrs. Ponsonby,' said Alfred.

'But Chilton and Victor shall both help me to pack. I shall be a pathetic figure. "Are you sorry to lose Alfred, boys?" "We don't mind, Grandma."'

'We won't talk about that time,' said Sabine. 'I hope it won't come in my lifetime. I think we must see it does not.'

'Are Alfred and I to see Miss Blake off, Grandma?' said Chilton.

'No, you and Victor. Why should Alfred trouble? It is time you learned to behave like gentlemen. You won't always be awkward boys.'

'So you still have hope of Victor, Grandma? He has not quite killed it?'

'I have hopes of you both,' said Sabine with rare indulgence.

'It is women's faith in men that brings out the best in them. Victor, I have felt you may have a better side, and now Grandma with the eyes of love has glimpsed it.'

'What has Grandma with the eyes of love glimpsed in Alfred?' said France. 'I suppose it is his better side. Anyhow it is much better. I wonder if she will ever find out how much better it is. But it would take some time and she is eighty-five.'

'You should not have given Dr. Chaucer away, Edith,' said Hetta, keeping her hands behind her head and turning smilingly to Edith, 'especially as you thought Miss Blake's story was true. We might have believed it. I believe some of us did.'

'I believe it,' said John. 'Why should she not give her reason for going?'

'There you see. What did I say?'

'You said what was nonsense and you knew to be nonsense.'

Hetta remained in her position, with her eyes fixed on space and her foot tapping it.

'Isn't it fatiguing to sit in that attitude?' said her brother. 'Why do you consider it your duty to keep to it?'

Hetta sat up, a little trill of laughter coming from her lips.

'Why is a proposal a reason for going?' said Clare. 'It is not an insult.'

'It seems to have been in this case,' said John.

'Chaucer forgot what was due to womanhood,' said Chilton. 'Victor, that is the last thing which should be said of a man.'

'I think a proposal is often an insult,' said Hetta in a dreamy tone, her hands again behind her head. 'I always wonder women do not see it. But they do not. And I daresay it is a good thing. The world has to go on.'

'Miss Blake's perceptions were above the average,' said Clare.

'And the world has received a check,' said Chilton. 'Muriel is again at the beginning.'

Muriel burst into laughter at the reminder of her late humour.

'I did not mean that kind of insult,' said Hetta, still dreamily.

'It is a good thing she is going,' said Sabine in an ordinary tone. 'Whatever Dr. Chaucer meant, it was less than she thought, and he is glad of his escape. It means he is in the mood for marriage and does not meet a woman to his mind.'

'The proposal was clearly an insult,' said France.

Ten

'Where is your aunt?' said Sabine, her word for her daughter and her tone of criticism directing the question to her grand-children.

'We do not know,' said Clare. 'It appears we are all in the same position.'

'Do not use silly phrases, girl.'

'She is not in her room,' said Victor. 'Her door was open when I passed.'

'Then will you offer to go and find her? You must know that her breakfast will be cold. You are all sitting there, eating yourselves.'

'What should we do with breakfast,' said Chilton, 'if not eat it?'

'It does seem a gross way of dealing with it,' said France.

'We shall never cease to feel guilty over the ordinary needs of life,' said Clare. 'We know that Aunt Hetta has organised the meal. Why did she do it, if there is something unfit about it?'

'What did you say, Clare?'

'I said Aunt Hetta has organised the meal, Grandma.'

'Then see that you realise it. There is no joke in what is true.'

'Aunt Hetta often misses prayers,' said Victor. 'Can she have miscalculated the time they take, after her long practice?'

'The gong should go after prayers and not before,' said France. 'What is it for, if not to mark the beginning of Aunt Hetta's day?'

'Go and find your aunt,' said Sabine. 'And the rest of you lay down your knives and forks until she appears.'

'Then life will go on from the moment it stopped, as if in the fairy tale,' said Clare.

'I go to lead the search,' said Chilton. 'Victor comes to work under me. Aunt Hetta should be here to organise it.'

'I will go and look in the library,' said Edith and Alfred at the same moment.

'No, I will go,' said John, feeling his mother's eyes.

'I will remain at the table,' said France. 'There must be someone to eat forgotten food with the old-fashioned forks, if Aunt Hetta does not appear for a hundred years.'

'Oh, a clever fancy,' said Sabine, who seemed wrought up beyond reason.

'Will Grandma be an interesting survival in a hundred years?' said Clare. 'Or does she appear in every generation? I hope Aunt Hetta will soon be here. We are managing badly without her.'

'I am glad you see that,' said Sabine, 'if only in your own selfish and silly spirit.'

John's voice was heard at the door, at once low and sharp, controlled and shaken.

'France, come here; I want you, France. Come to me alone; do not bring anyone. Come here at once.'

France went out and Sabine rose to her feet.

'What is it?' she said, the instant cry in her voice sending them forward into fear. 'What is it? Where is my daughter?'

John was standing in the hall with a letter in his hand. He drew France to the light and held it for her to read. He was pale and he watched the signs of her face.

'MY DEAR BROTHER,

'This is my one word of goodbye. You know I do not waste my words. My place in your life is filled. You know I have had no other place. I am not afraid of the final step. You know I am not a person who is afraid. I need not go on telling you what you know. You know we shall not meet again.

'Your loving sister,

'HETTA.'

'What does it mean, France? What does she say? Is it not what it seems? What is it? What can I say to my mother?'

France could never recall the feelings of the moment. She could remember a sense of relief that her father did not suffer first for himself. Sabine was at his side, but his question had no answer.

'What is it? What is it to do with France? Tell me, my son. Answer your mother!'

John signed to France to keep the letter in her hands. Sabine screamed aloud for her glasses, and Clare came out and gave them to her, unaware of the truth. Sabine put them on in a fumbling, aged way, seeming absorbed in the task, and then with an almost wily movement snatched the letter and held it to her eyes.

'What is it? What does she say, my Hetta? She is not gone from her mother! What has she done? What have we done to her between us? I did not know what I was doing. I ought to have known. I was her mother; I ought not to have let them hound and hurt her, people stronger and younger than she. I ought not to have let them; I ought not, I ought not.'

Sabine's voice failed and she staggered where she stood. John came to support her and found Alfred was before him. He gave him the letter, including him among themselves, and signed to him to show it to the others. The brothers heard the sounds and came downstairs, and Chilton read the letter aloud in a low tone. John moved aside and stood in thought, as if he were alone. France kept her eyes on his face. The sound of Chilton's voice with the words she knew, caused Sabine's voice again to rise.

'My Hetta, my daughter! Why do women think of men? Why do mothers think of sons, when they have their daughters? Men can think of themselves. She was a woman and helpless. She has been sacrificed to others, my daughter.'

Edith held out her hand for the letter. Sabine almost snatched it from her grandson and thrust it towards her, as if willing to force on her the worst. Chilton's eyes followed it, as if it was a living thing. Clare looked stricken; John had the same expression; Victor had a startled look and glanced at his sisters. If Hetta had returned, she would have seen what she had done. This thought came to Sabine and raised her voice again.

'I did not know; I did not know what I did. I did not see I seemed to think nothing of Hetta. She lived for us all, and we did nothing for her, nothing. She went on, year after year, never had change, never had pleasure, never wanted her years for herself, though she knew they would not come to her again. She will never know what her mother felt, how my heart ached and bled when I found I had done her harm. She thought I did not care, thought that of her mother. It is I who have done it. My son and I have driven Hetta to her death. They say the old do not feel like the young, but it is not true that he is feeling more than I. It is I who am grieving for Hetta, who am grieving alone for my girl.'

The thrust in her words went home, and John was free from his deepest pity and faced her.

'I cannot see it in that way. I cannot see that as the truth. Looking back on it all, I cannot see that it should have driven her to this. I do not take the blame on myself: I do not put it on to you.'

'Is Aunt Hetta dead?' said Muriel.

'No, no, we hope not,' said Alfred. 'We think she is not—yet——'

His voice failed on the word, but Sabine had heard.

'Not yet! Not yet! We are in time; we can do something. Go after her and find her. Go, all you young men, go!' She swept her son and grandsons together with a gesture which recalled her daughter, and seemed to point the truth that it was the mother who survived. 'Go and find her and bring her to her mother.'

She sank into a chair and sat as if almost content, waiting for her words to come true.

Edith stood apart, feeling the cause of the tragedy, shrinking from speech, knowing she must soon be heard, faltering into idle and empty words.

'Shall I take Muriel upstairs and keep her out of the way?'

'No, do not keep anyone out of the way,' said Sabine. 'All go and look for her together. Then you will find her; then you will come to her before she gets there, before she can reach the river. She can't do it if you are in time.'

The words came simply, evenly, as if the thought behind them were too strong for her strength, as if grasping it took all her power.

John came forward and spoke quickly and clearly, without any hint of seeing and hearing himself.

'We will go, as nothing should not be done. Victor and I will go in one direction, Alfred and Chilton in another; and clearly we will go at this moment. It is only a chance: there are other ways. There is enough in the house for the rest of you. There is what your aunt does; there is your grandmother.' He kept his voice swift and steady on all the words. 'There is nothing for you to have on your minds; there is no blame on anyone; I even feel there is none on me. People can act for themselves and by themselves. My sister never acted in any other way. When they do that, the action is their own.'

He left the room, followed by the three young men, stooping to his mother as he passed, forcing himself to meet her almost vacant eyes, sending a smile to his daughters, seeming to see his family as what it had been for so long. Then, remembering, he turned and came to his wife, and took a natural leave, as if showing others and himself that he was justified in what he did.

'What has Aunt Hetta done?' said Muriel, as the door closed.

'Nothing, we hope,' said Clare. 'You had better go upstairs.'

'You need not spare the child,' said Sabine. 'You did not spare my daughter. You did nothing for Hetta; you would not care if she was dead. You only think of the five of yourselves. You think you are the world.'

'Well, that is not unnatural, Grandma. We have had to be our own world. We have had no other.'

'Smartness, smartness,' said Sabine, so much in her daughter's voice that she might have been mimicking the words. 'I get so sick of it.'

A silence followed.

'You have taken what you want from her. You are too old to need her now. You have had her years, and now you will have your own. You are old enough to manage for yourselves, old enough to manage for Muriel. And nothing else matters; nothing else counts; Hetta does not matter; Hetta does not count; Hetta who is brave and gifted, who has not kept things for herself, who is so much more of a person than any of you;

you who would snatch it from her, the little she would have had, the little that would have kept her for her mother.'

Sabine rose and went out of the room, seeming to wander, seeming to feel some purpose she could not grasp with her mind.

'That is the trouble,' said France, 'not keeping things for yourself, not having what is your own. The lesson is driven home now.'

'What ought Aunt Hetta to have had?' said Muriel.

'I am the cause of it all,' said Edith. 'But how could I know? Why should I cause a tragedy by doing what other women do years before?'

'That is the tragedy,' said Clare, 'that it did not happen before.'

'The tragedy is giving up your life to someone who will not repay you with his own,' said France. 'Finding that he will not give you any part of his prime, in return for the whole of yours.'

'Not even the end of it,' said Clare.

'Father does not think of it as the end. We don't know yet how much of our life will be prime.' France hardly smiled, and turned and went to the window.

'They will not be back yet,' said Clare.

'What have they gone to do?' said Muriel.

'The horses will take them some way,' said Edith, 'and they took field glasses. It will not be so long. What about your grandmother?'

They could do nothing for Sabine. She did not seem to see them, did not speak when they spoke, wandered until she sank from weakness, remained in any seat until she had strength to rise. The time passed and the men returned. They had found nothing, and brought just this amount of hope. Sabine came to meet them with an air of simple welcome, and, seeing them without her daughter, fell into a wild mood, crying to herself, starting up at every sound, making it an effort to move and breathe in her hearing or sight.

The brothers came and sat down with their sisters, boyish and silent. They were tired and kept their seats, and seemed by this to have gone further with the truth.

'We can do nothing more,' said Chilton. 'We have done nothing.'

'Don't people sometimes drag rivers?' said Muriel.

'That would be no good,' said Alfred, seeming to answer them all. 'It would prevent nothing. It could only confirm it, and that would indeed be no good.'

The midday meal was not on the table, the first sign that Hetta was not in the house. The servants were so used to waiting for orders, that they had waited, giving themselves to their emotions. The young people almost wondered if such things would be held to count. But John gave a calm, firm order for the meal, the first sign that others would do what his sister had done. Sabine hardly ate and hardly stayed at the table, and resumed her wandering, now with a low wail.

The picture of their home without their aunt was in the young minds. In their thought the whole course of their day depended on her. It seemed that they could not eat or drink or sleep without her. Her effort through the hours of all their days grew to a mighty thing. Their life failed and fell away at every point. They seemed to lay down their separate natures and to be joined in one great feeling. Edith saw before her a life with her husband, clouded, burdened, shamed. Sabine wandered on, giving her unconscious cry. Muriel looked at the faces about her and wept. Clare did the same, less simply, feeling the rise of remorse. Victor tried to be admonishing and firm, and became childish and sharp. Chilton and France said a word to each other or were silent. Alfred swallowed some food and followed Sabine.

The day seemed to get itself to its end. Hetta was not there to guide it. The hours could only pass by themselves, dragging, failing, breaking down. The evening meal was on the table. It was met by a feeling of surprise and dim relief. Things could happen without Hetta. Other people could do what she had done; other people did what she had taught them to do.

In the evening Miss Marcon and Rowland came. The news had spread and they came from their families, sent to enquire and sympathise. Stephen might have done better than his sister. Miss Marcon's impression of humour was something she could not lay aside.

'We will not speak,' she said, standing with her opaque eyes seeming to strive for expression. 'Words are no good. We will just say nothing. We had to come to do what we could.'

Sabine had raised her eyes—she was unable to raise her head—and Rowland caught the look and came to her.

'It is too much; it is too much,' he said, kneeling by her

chair. 'You must not face it. Try to look aside. It may not be as it seems.'

'It ought to have been me,' said Miss Marcon in deep, solemn tones. 'It ought not to have been Hetta. I ought to have written a note and gone. Stephen and I both feel it ought to have been me.'

Muriel gave a tremble of laughter, and glanced about, guilty and startled by herself. The words seemed to bring the loss of Hetta into the range of the possible and permanent. Sabine raised her eyes again and her voice came, the voice of a woman older than eighty-five.

'You have not brought Hetta with you? If you have not, why have you come? Why have you come to her mother? We do not want what you can say. It is Hetta we want, not you.'

'It is Hetta we all want,' said Rowland.

'Of course you do not want what we can say,' said Miss Marcon. 'We knew words were no good. And of course it is Hetta you want and not us. We wish we could not be here. We wish we had gone with Hetta and done it with her. Then you would not have had us and not her: it would not have been the worst.'

'She was better than John,' said Sabine, looking at Miss Marcon with earnest eyes. 'She was better than all the rest. There was never anyone like her. Now everyone is the same.'

'She was indeed,' said John, using the past tense of his sister, as his mother had used it. 'We shall be without our head, without our leader. We shall go on as best we may.'

But they would go on; the word was said.

And from that moment they went on.

The friends said a few more words and left. Stephen was sent by his sister and Sabine was ordered to bed. She was helpless and only half alive, and was laid away out of sight.

The idea of rest had been put into their minds, and the hour was late. The day was over, this first day.

And the next day was different.

Sabine was not fit to rise and her son had his breakfast by her bed. The group downstairs seemed dimmed and weak with their leaders gone. Edith and Clare came to the head of the table. They smiled, gave way to each other, saw that Edith should fill the place; saw, as they did so, that things would settle themselves. And the new life was under way, and the place was filled.

'Edith had better sit there always, and say nothing to Grandma,' said Chilton. 'It is the only thing.'

'Is it difficult to do the things at that place?' said Muriel.

'It means you have to think all the time of other people,' said Edith, 'and that is difficult.'

'You don't mind doing it, do you?'

'I have only just begun. That means nothing.'

'Edith has had a hard training at the hands of people like you,' said Clare.

'Will there be luncheon to-day?'

'Yes, of course there will. It would do no good to starve. It only means talking to the cook; I can see about it.'

'Is that all—is that what Aunt Hetta did?'

'We don't know yet all that she did.'

The thought had come that they were beginning to know.

'Will anyone be able to help Father to-day?'

'He will not work much to-day,' said Edith. 'Later I shall do what I can. I shall not be able to do as much as your aunt.'

'Are we quite sure that Aunt Hetta won't come back?'

'I am afraid we are nearly sure.'

'I once heard Father say to Grandma that Aunt Hetta did more than he liked—more than he wanted her to do. So perhaps you won't have to do so very much.'

'He did not say it to you. And whatever there is to do, will be more than I have done.'

'You are talking more than usual, Muriel,' said France.

'Aunt Hetta used to tell me to talk.'

'Is Muriel now going to live her life as Aunt Hetta would wish?'

'She would like you to be quiet this morning,' said Edith.

'Someone will have to be with Grandma,' said Clare. 'Father can't give her all his time.'

'He won't be able to settle down to-day,' said Chilton. 'And that is a good thing, if keeping with Grandma is to be as it was yesterday.'

'You are talking like you did before—when Aunt Hetta was here,' said Muriel, looking at her with open eyes.

'I wish you would do the same, Muriel,' said France. 'You have a new way of talking.'

'You are talking like you used to talk too.'

'Well, we shall come to that. We shan't be able to claim that we are changed.'

'I think you have come to it now. And if Grandma dies soon, I don't think we shall be changed even then.'

'Is this Muriel's way of keeping green Aunt Hetta's memory?'

'Well, my girls and boys!' said John at the door. 'So we have to start again. We must go on the more steadily, that one of us has fallen out, show the more resolution, that we shall need more. That is what I can do for my sister, for my sister and the dearest and best of my friends.'

'Will Aunt Hetta know?' said Muriel in a lower tone.

'I heard your voices, and knew you had made your start. And I admired you for it. You had your father's sympathy.'

'Did he admire us?' said France to her brothers. 'Sympathy is not admiration. You do not sympathise over what you admire. And sympathy is what we had.'

'We did make the start rather soon,' said Clare.

'And it was a real, unconscious start.'

'Father, should anything be done?' said Chilton. 'Do we regard anything definite as having happened? Ought we to put it in the papers? Or do anything at all?'

'Ought we to go into black?' said Muriel. 'Everyone has black clothes, not only grown up people. Then perhaps the same clothes would do when Grandma dies, and that would save a lot of money.'

'Nothing at the moment, my son. We know nothing, though we feel we know. We can only wait, though our hearts may warn us we wait for nothing.' John had a look as of glancing back over a long past. 'I feel I can give you advice, as I have lost the most. I am asking no effort I am not prepared to make.'

'Then will things be so very different?' whispered Muriel. 'They will be the same, won't they, except for not having Aunt Hetta? And she did not like living with us very much, did she? I mean, she won't mind very much, if she does know?'

'She has chosen it herself, and that is our comfort or not,' said John to his elder children. 'We must take what we get from it, the comfort and the doubt, and carry them with us. I do not think our burden should be too great. My sister asked much from life; her demands were on the scale of herself.'

'And she did not like some things that Father does not mind,' whispered Muriel, 'and that Grandma does not mind either, now she is really old. I mean things won't really be so very bad. Because we only have to think of people who are alive. We can't help her being dead, can we?'

'My innocent child, you cannot help it,' said John.

'I don't call Muriel innocent,' said Chilton to France.

'Muriel has got over her first sorrow. Time, the healer, has done his work and done it in a day.'

'How is Grandma this morning?' said Victor.

'Sorrow has not done nothing for Victor,' said Chilton. 'It has brought out something that is not self.'

John laid his hand on Chilton's shoulder, with a smile as of understanding. The dor opened and Alfred entered, and stood holding it open, and it was realised that he had not appeared before that day.

'So you are all here,' said Sabine, in a weak, sharp voice, entering the room in a dishevelled state, which told of the loss of her daughter. 'I do not want to be shut up alone; I do not want that sort of comfort. That is a poor kind, though it is the kind we are given. So you have all had breakfast?' She paused by the table, leaning on her stick and looking over it. 'And a good breakfast too. Yes, you have had it as usual; you have made no difference. And my Hetta is where she does not need it. She will never eat again. And she has thought of it so often for all of you. She has taught you to think of it for yourselves. That is how you know. Yes, you know how to manage, don't you? You will say that Hetta was no good: I see it coming.'

'We did not do anything, Grandma,' said Muriel. 'The servants did it.'

'Yes, the servants did it. And they might always have done it, mightn't they? You say that Hetta was no good. Yes, I hear you say it.'

'We sent breakfast up to you and Father, Grandma,' said Victor. 'We are not the only people who had it.'

'That will do, Victor,' said John. 'This is not an ordinary day.'

'Yes, we are to talk like that now,' said Sabine. 'We are to blame each other for eating and drinking and being alive. And it seems wrong that we should do it. It seems it should not all go on, as if nothing had happened. But it cannot stop. We shall go on; I shall go on, though I am old and ill and alone, and I shall never see Hetta again.'

The door opened in a sudden manner, and stood open before its movement was explained.

'Well, have you all had a lesson?' said Hetta's voice.

There was the shock, the silence, the realisation, the rush of reaction.

'Well, have you all had a lesson?' said Hetta, coming forward with a strolling step and her eyes seeming to be fixed on nothing, as if her heart misgave her for what she had done.

The time to think sent all eyes to Sabine. The first shock had held the family still, and the instant of her seeing Hetta had passed. She was now sitting forward, as still as they had been, with her eyes drinking in her daughter, as if it was enough to gaze her fill.

'Hetta, this has been a gross piece of cruelty!' said John.

'So you have not liked it? I did not mean that you should. You will learn the more from it for that. I saw you needed a lesson.'

'We shall learn nothing. It is you who will learn. You will learn that you cannot resort to evil to work your way, to achieve any petty purpose. You cannot return after conscious wickedness, and be received as if nothing had happened, as if we were under some compulsion to bow to your despotic will, as if you were justified in any extreme to force us under it.'

'I do not want to be received as if nothing has happened; I do not intend to be. As for forcing you under my will, I hope I have done enough to ensure that, for it is a most necessary thing. I shall wait for the lesson to work its result.'

'You will see its result. You will not have to wait. You will not be welcomed back as if everything depended on you. Things depend on you no longer. You have taught us that your service to us is not worth the price we have paid.'

'You have not liked paying, have you? You had not meant ever to pay. But it was time you paid something for what you have taken, for what you call my service. You wanted to have it for nothing. That can go on for too long.'

John turned away, and Hetta went to the table, with her eyes ostensibly criticising the food. She did not say when she had eaten, did not say where she had lain. It was clear that she had not slept. The other things were never known.

Edith was still at the head of the table, forgetting where she was in watching the scene. Hetta came up to her and stood very close, waiting for her to withdraw. She had hardly risen, when her husband intercepted her and almost held her into the seat.

'Stay where you are. That is your place now. Hetta has

given it up. She made us believe she was dead, and dead people have no place. She has showed us how to do without her, and perhaps we have learned easily. Perhaps we were further with the lesson than we knew.'

Hetta stood still, with a smile on her lips, waiting for Edith to move. She stood so close that Edith had no choice; and, taking the seat, set to her meal, as if easily occupied with it. But she kept her eyes from her mother, as she had from the first.

Sabine watched her eat, as if she followed her every sensation, and then began to make signs from her chair, motioning the others back to the table. They saw what she meant and returned, and she leaned back in content, holding them together with a gesture and sometimes lifting her hand to repeat and enforce it.

'You have done great harm, Hetta,' said John. 'Mater may not recover from this. It is too much at her age.'

'It was about the right amount at yours. It was you I was thinking of. We can't always think of everyone. And I see I thought it out very well.'

Her brother turned his back, as if hopeless, and Hetta began to talk to the others, as if nothing had come between them. They had no choice but to respond, tied as they were to the table by Sabine's eyes; and by the time she fell asleep, they seemed on their ordinary footing. John, a man of rapid moods, and used to his sister's companionship, was drawn into the talk unawares, and no one coming on the family would have seen what was beneath the surface. One of them did not see it.

'Shall I have a holiday to-day?' said Muriel, in a voice that could just be heard.

'Why should you?' said Clare.

'Because Aunt Hetta has come back.'

'Yes, you can have one,' said Hetta, not moving her eyes.

'You had one when your aunt was away,' said John. 'You do not need another, unless Edith needs it.'

'That was not a holiday, Father.'

'Of course it was not,' said Hetta. 'It is quite clear what she means. She need not do anything to-day.'

'That is for Edith to decide. She has been teaching her.'

'Only in a casual spirit, hasn't she, as a temporary thing? If that is the case, it is for me to decide. Or has she gone back to being the governess?'

John did not answer, could not, was less ready with his words, found himself silent before his sister, silent before his future.

As they left the table, a pile of paper was shown at Edith's place.

'What is that?' said Hetta.

'I brought it down to copy something for John, the chapter which you had begun.'

'And you kept it on the breakfast table? You were not going to have it for breakfast.'

'We had just got up when you came in, and I had taken it from the desk.'

'Do not explain,' said John to his wife. 'We owe Hetta no explanation.' But he paused, dumb before the evidence that he had not broken his life for his sister's death, as his sister was dumb before it.

'That is not the paper we use,' said Hetta, taking a piece in her fingers. 'The ink will run on it, and show through on the other side.'

'The ink does not run on this,' said Edith, 'and we only use one side.'

Their custom was established, in one day.

Hetta gave her laugh and turned away, as if not concerned with her brother.

The brother did not work that day. He did not dare to ask Edith's help, did not dare to ask Hetta's, did not dare to work alone. Alfred and the boys sat at their books, Alfred alert for a summons from Sabine. Sabine followed Hetta about the house, standing with her eyes on her face, reproducing on her own face its every change, struggling with every step, leaning on anything that came to hand. Downstairs Edith and the sisters were left by themselves.

'Our glimpse of freedom was brief,' said France. 'Has it come to seem to be that?'

'We shall soon have another kind of freedom,' said Clare. 'Aunt Hetta has killed Grandma.'

'It is unfortunate to harm anyone of eighty-five. You are said to have killed her, when it is such a small part of the killing you have done. It is eighty-five years that have killed Grandma.'

'Aren't we glad that Aunt Hetta has come back?' said Muriel.

'Your aunt has defeated her own ends,' said Edith. 'We reached the stage of imagining life without her and not of realising it, and the second stage is the test. Her plan was sound, but she did not give it a chance.'

'She might have starved if she had stayed away any longer,' said Muriel.

'I think she had starved while she was away,' said Clare. 'She could not get food near, for fear of spreading the news. People don't want nourishment when they are going to their death.'

Muriel burst into laughter.

'Not—not for their after life,' she said, breaking off with her eyes on her elders.

'Is this our influence?' said Clare. 'Muriel, would you have been better if you had had another sister?'

'What had Father done to Aunt Hetta?' said Muriel.

'She thought he did not appreciate what she did for him.'

'What would have happened, if Aunt Hetta had stayed away longer and given the plan a chance?'

'Grandma would be dead, and we should all be in the power of Aunt Hetta.'

'She wanted the last,' said France, 'and she must have wanted it very much. And I don't know that it was too much to want in return for her life.'

'France is fonder of Aunt Hetta than other people are,' said Muriel. 'But Aunt Hetta is not so fond of France as other people are. We shall never forget this time, shall we?'

'We shall have to pretend to forget it,' said France. 'Aunt Hetta is going to be embarrassed by it. She is already embarrassed.'

This was the truth. The next days seemed to hover on the brink of something which threatened and gradually fell away. Hetta did her usual work, but gave it less time, betraying her sense that it had lost its mystery. Sabine recovered part of her strength, but seldom spoke, and never left Hetta in a room alone. John and his sister fell into their habit of talk, but never said an intimate word. John and Edith were openly husband and wife. The young people dealt with their aunt on easier terms. Their father worked alone, as he was to work for the rest of his life, and had more time for his family. The servants recognised Edith's authority as well as Hetta's. Hetta had not done what she meant to do, but she had not done nothing.

Eleven

'I think it is such a good idea to give a dinner, when you have been supposed to be dead,' said Miss Marcon to her brother, as they walked up the Ponsonbys' drive. 'It takes away the general sense of guilt. It is very awkward to feel you have driven someone to her death, and going to dinner with her is especially different.'

'It is Hetta who ought to have a sense of guilt. I hope she has it.'

'Everyone ought to have one. We did not deter her from her purpose.'

'You talk as if she meant to put an end to herself.'

'We shall never be sure she did not, that her heart did not fail her at the last. And the thought of us did not prevent her; it is a great disgrace to us. And now she is making our life brighter, when we had such a different effect on hers.'

'When the young ones see her entertaining her friends, the thought may come that they might have been entertaining theirs.'

'It is better not to talk about thoughts that may come. It would never do to begin it. It is odd that Hetta should be simple; you would think it would be her last quality.'

'I don't mind if it is her first, as it is most people's. I don't blame her for being simple. But she might have been the death of Sabine.'

'It is nice of you to blame her for that, Stephen. And if she had been, the young ones might have been entertaining their friends indeed. It is only fair to them to give a dinner. Better than their giving one themselves, in case they have not any friends. This is the Seymours' carriage. Let us stop and gossip on the steps. To share a friend who has almost been driven to her death, is a full excuse.'

'Well, this is good,' said Rowland. 'It will be good to be all together.'

'Yes, it is good that Hetta is not dead,' said Miss Marcon, 'or we couldn't have been all together. It is so nice to feel really glad about it. It is such a dreadful saying that it is an ill wind that blows nobody any good. It is shocking that it should not blow harm to everybody.'

'Yes, yes, it was an ill wind. It changed its course just in time.'

'It never had that course,' said Stephen.

'It must be awkward for them to meet us all!' said Jane. 'I don't think I could face it in their place. I suppose that is why we are asked together, to give the safety of numbers! Well, I hope we shall be equal to the demand on our tact.'

'People are always equal to demands on tact,' said Stephen.

'I shall just be myself,' said Evelyn, 'as that is the truest tact. And I think it must be more awkward for them to be alone. To give people a lesson and live with them afterwards must be very awkward. And to have had a lesson must be awkward too.'

'I hope they have not learned the lesson,' said Stephen. 'That is the great mistake.'

'It would never do to reward people for causing us discomfort,' said his sister, 'and that is what a lesson always is.'

'Suffering may be wholesome,' said Jane, 'but we should not cause it to each other.'

'Why is it wholesome?' said Stephen. 'And, if it is, why should we not cause it?'

'We generally do, so it is all right, dear,' said his sister.

'I have never known anyone improved by it,' said Rowland, as if with a thought of his own past.

'I have no capacity for suffering,' said Evelyn. 'That is why I shall never marry. I should be afraid to meet any deep experience: I don't want to prove how shallow I am. I do not like people in sickness and health, only in health.'

'Poor Alfred must have had a time!' said Jane. 'And not to be able to get away from it! To be tied there by duty!'

'Has anyone rung the bell?' said her brother.

'No, don't let us ring it,' said Evelyn. 'It is so nice here.'

'Here is Gertrude coming. She has seen us through the door.'

'I wish it did not say a great deal for people to keep their servants,' said Evelyn. 'I don't want a great deal to be said for the Ponsonbys. I want to think how shocking it has all been of them. And I suppose, if everything were so bad, Gertrude would have left.'

'Good evening, Gertrude,' said Jane. 'You have been through a sad time!'

'All's well that ends well,' said Rowland.

'I do hope all is not well,' whispered Evelyn. 'I do want to see just a little result. If there is not any, I shall stop blaming Hetta, and no one will like that. Then I shall feel I have somehow got my revenge.'

'Now this is good,' said John. 'This is what we want. It is a long time since we have been together, and a time we are going to forget.'

'Forget,' murmured Evelyn. 'That is too bad, and dishonest as well.'

'Oh, how do you do?' said Hetta, turning round as if she had just seen them, and coming forward with something in her hand which had occupied her. 'So the two families arrive together.'

'How are you both?' said Alfred to his uncle and aunt. 'I hardly feel I belong to your household now. I belong to this one.'

'Anyone would, who could just now,' said Evelyn. 'What a time you have had!'

'A bad time, Evelyn, and it is not over. We are anxious about Mrs. Ponsonby. It is hard to picture the house without her. You may make light of it, but she will leave a blank.'

'Of course I do not make light of it. It is a heavy matter. But why picture the house without her? Why not make the most of it, as it is? She is not leaving a blank yet.'

'Coming events cast their shadows before them.'

'I see they do; I see you are shadowed. But it is your duty to brighten her last days.'

'It is difficult to brighten days that are shadowed,' said Edith.

Sabine was sitting upright, talking with her first strength. Hetta leant easily against her chair. Chaucer came in and walked up to Hetta, and, standing with her hand in his, spoke very low.

'To say that I am glad to see you, Miss Hetta, would be a case of mere words indeed.'

'I hope we have not all said it,' said Miss Marcon. 'Stephen has not, because he has not said anything. He is very good about mere words. Dr. Chaucer could hardly speak, and Stephen could not speak at all. It is a triumph for Stephen.'

'Do pray look a little more cheerful, some of you,' said Sabine. 'You might be at a funeral instead of entertaining your friends.'

'We became rather used to feeling at a funeral,' said Chilton.

'As we have never become to the alternative,' said Clare.

'I have not made the effort, to be rewarded like this. I felt as if it would be the death of me; I feel it may be yet.'

'And you recommend us to be cheerful,' said Clare. 'You have lost yourself in the occasion.'

'We may in effect be at a funeral after all,' said France.

'It is hard for these poor children to live on the brink of so many graves,' said Miss Marcon.

'One, two, three, four, five, six, seven women!' said Sabine. 'And five of them in my family! And there would be eight, if Muriel were grown up. I hope I shall not live to see it.'

'She will not, if her death is to be this evening,' said France.

'As Grandma is seventy-three years older than Muriel, they may not long be women together,' said Victor.

'Shall we talk of something besides death?' said Edith.

'What a thing to say, Mater!' said Hetta. 'There are eight men. Victor cannot have a partner for dinner.'

'I was not counting Chilton and Victor. I do not reckon boys.'

'You are a woman yourself, and you have never thought less of yourself for it.'

'I have always thought less of myself, and so have other people. A woman takes the second place.'

'To whom has Grandma come second?' said Chilton. 'This new light on her is rather late.'

'So obviously to no one, that she is safe in saying what she did,' said Chaucer. 'I think women are generally safe in making such statements, or I make bold to believe they would not make them.'

'I came second to my husband, and was content to do so.'

'John, have you ever known Mater come second to anyone?'

'Never. And she is wise not to attempt it. She would not do it well.'

'I wish you would not all contradict me, and join together against me. I cannot stand against you all. My husband would not have let me stand alone against so many.' Sabine had begun to talk of her husband, as if there would not long be a barrier between them.

'People at the head of things are always alone,' said Rowland.

'Mater is not equal to being hostess to-night,' said John.

'No, I am not equal to it,' said Sabine. 'But I shall do it: I shall not give up. Edith would have to be hostess if I were not, and then what about your sister? I don't know what will happen to Hetta when I am gone; I don't know what will happen to my daughter.'

'Grandma has chosen a bad occasion for embarking upon her second childhood,' said Victor.

'She and Muriel are on a level before she expected,' said Clare. 'Only six women after all.'

'I should like it well enough if Edith were hostess,' said Hetta. 'It is she who would not. She does not take to the duties of the place.'

'Women are too fond of duties,' said Sabine. 'I have never let people think I would wait on them.'

'Never, Mrs. Ponsonby, never,' said Alfred, stooping to her chair. 'You have let them think the opposite and act on it, and very good it has been for them and for you.'

'The people are all here,' said Sabine, in a suddenly normal manner. 'Stand further apart. Do not all huddle together round my chair; I want nothing from you. Move about among your guests.'

'Grandma is restored,' said Victor, 'and in the nick of time.'

'Her authentic note,' said Clare, 'but does it fit her any better for a hostess?'

'It almost seems a pity there has to be a hostess,' said Edith.

'Did you feel on the brink of a volcano?' said Jane, rubbing her hands with the suggestion of a shiver. 'I did. I kept trembling lest it should erupt!'

'What did you do when it did erupt?' said Stephen.

'I don't dare to go near Mrs. Ponsonby,' said Evelyn, 'for fear she may tell me honestly what she thinks of me.'

'She may not think of you,' said Alfred.

'So I will not put the subject into her head.'

'I am to take her in to dinner,' said Rowland. 'I have to face the risk. Yes, it is a pleasure, an honour; it may be the last time. I hope I shall have the honour many times.'

'There is no risk for you, Father. You are the only one who would not mind anyone's looking into his hidden depths.'

'Isn't it wonderful that they are hidden?' said Miss Marcon. 'We really don't deserve it.'

'Why should Mrs. Ponsonby be able to see them?' said Jane.

'Especially as her powers are failing.'

'I think a great many people can see them,' said Evelyn. 'But Mrs. Ponsonby may speak of them. Her powers are failing in their own way.'

'Will you take my sister in to dinner, Chaucer?' said John.

'I take that as a rhetorical question, Ponsonby. It does not require an answer.'

Hetta had prepared the list of couples, and her brother was acting on it. He found Edith assigned to one of his sons; and as her due was a grown man and a guest, he made an adjustment and sent her in with Stephen. Hetta noticed the change as they sat down.

'John has muddled up the couples. And I made it all quite clear. Well, it can't be helped.'

'I am sure there is nothing that any man would have changed,' said Chaucer. 'I cannot speak for their partners.'

'Neither can I,' said Hetta, laughing and looking round. 'It was the women I was thinking of. Well, it is done now.'

'I have only made one change,' said her brother, 'and that is an improvement.'

'More than one couple are different.'

'One change involves others.'

'You should not have asked me to make the list.'

'I will not another time.'

'Of course Hetta pretended to be dead,' said Miss Marcon to Evelyn. 'A great many creatures do that when they are in danger.'

'It was an outrageous thing to do.'

'Well, revenge is outrageous. Or what would be the good of it?'

'Has this been any good? What would you do if Stephen married? You would not pretend to be dead?'

'No, no, I should pretend to be very alive and joyful at being free. That would be a better revenge on Stephen.'

'And it would not be outrageous.'

'Oh, yes, it would,' said Miss Marcon. 'It is dreadful to put any alloy into people's happiness. It must be because we do that, that happiness is never without alloy.'

'I wonder what Aunt Jane would do if Father married.'

'What?' said Jane, looking round. 'What should I do if Rowland married? I should not do anything; there would not be anything to do. He would not do anything if I married. And

I should still be myself: I think that is such a consolation in the vicissitudes of life, that one is always oneself! And I never feel that running my brother's house is such a great thing! It is necessary and useful and reasonably pleasant; that is what it is. And as for being a mother to Evelyn, I am nothing of the sort. I am his opinionated maiden aunt, rejoicing in her own cynical, open, perhaps regrettable personality!'

'Does not Muriel have a governess now?' said Evelyn, breaking off as he recalled that a governess in the house might not mean one at the table.

'Yes, she does in a way,' said Hetta, as Chaucer looked in front of him with eyes held stiffly open. 'Edith has gone back to her duty, and the problem is solved.'

'Only for the moment,' said John.

'Well, sufficient unto the day——'

'Edith cannot go on teaching the child. I shall make too much demand upon her time.'

'You will live very differently then.'

'Perhaps I am going to live differently.'

'Hetta will pretend to be dead,' said Miss Marcon. 'I am sure I would in her place.'

'What would my sister do in your place?' said Stephen to Edith.

'Perhaps she would really be dead. I am sure I could understand it. No one could live for long as I am living.'

'My dear children, don't keep talking to one another across other people,' said Hetta. 'What is the good of my training?'

'Training of that kind does not alter people,' said Clare.

'It hides them, shall we say?' said Hetta easily. 'So that it seems to alter them.'

'I don't want my children changed,' said John.

'They are changed,' said his sister, laughing. 'So how do you know what you want?'

'The real self looks through the disguise,' said Clare, 'when it is obtained like that.'

'Don't throw off the disguise, my dear,' said her aunt, 'or it really may look through.'

'My disguise is always complete and perfect,' said Evelyn. 'My real self is always hidden.'

'I believe my real self shows all the time,' said Alfred, in a plaintive tone, looking at Sabine. 'And I can think of so many nicer selves which I ought to cultivate. I believe most people simply choose a self and cultivate it.'

'I believe they do!' said Jane, pausing as if wishing to continue, but not finding her words.

'Wait until I am dead,' said Sabine to Alfred. 'I find no fault with your present self. I am too old for change.'

'My real self, Mrs. Ponsonby. That is very nice and kind. So I can be perfectly at ease before you.'

'I am glad it might have been kinder,' said Evelyn.

'He is also at ease before other people,' said Stephen. 'I can but admire him.'

'You evidently can't do that,' said Edith.

'I am afraid my real self is always exposed!' said Jane. 'I daresay it ought not to be, that I ought to make an effort to disguise its many individualities, but I fear so it is.'

'I suppose we go through the party, hearing they do not disguise themselves,' said Stephen.

'We have done several,' said his sister. 'I hope there are the easier ones left.'

'Evelyn does not have to be done,' said Rowland. 'He owns to a disguise.'

'Well, no one could be like me in himself,' said his son, 'always easy and amusing and considerate in all those small ways which make up life.'

'Other people are nearer to nature, are they?' said Alfred.

'Much nearer. They keep explaining that they have not left nature at all.'

'I do not know whether I am supposed to contribute my quota of self-description,' said Chaucer. 'But I am not conscious of assuming any disguise.'

'Another one done,' said Stephen. 'And an easy one.'

'I suppose the difference in people is really a difference in taking disguise,' said Chilton.

'Be careful,' said Stephen, 'or we shall go through the company again, hearing about their disguises, as we have heard about their freedom from them.'

'Hetta, must you keep looking round at the servants?' said John. 'They are not going to commit any crime. Do take your eyes off them. They are equal to what they have to do.'

'They are, if I do look round on them. If I did not, they would commit some crime. But I will take my eyes off them, if you wish. It is the easiest thing, and what the others do. In future I can do it.'

'If you would be as the others are, the home would be a different place.'

'It would,' said Hetta with her little laugh. 'It would cease to be a home.'

'I think we few of us realise,' said Chaucer, seeming to address no one in particular, 'how much our lives depend upon the constant and unseen effort of those who ask no recognition. If we did realise it, I think we should hardly dare to live and breathe and have our being.'

'If we did realise it, they would have recognition,' said France.

'We do hardly dare to,' said Clare, 'we who are made to realise it.'

'Is Chaucer thinking of Miss Bunyan?' said Chilton. 'No, he would not voice the thought. He is thinking of Aunt Hetta, and she is not a good example.'

'Why should she be?' said France. 'And we don't want that in addition to our other grounds for guilt. It would be a real ground for it.'

'You and I should not be sitting together, Hetta,' said John. 'Why did you make such an odd arrangement? Your plan of the table was not a success.'

'We both have partners. There is no reason why we should talk to each other. It is difficult to make arrangements for a family reinforced by the tutor and the governess. People don't like sitting by them, and there you are. It makes awkwardness.'

'What nonsense! And if that is the case, you and I should go in with them.'

'My dear, you could not go in with your wife, if you take exception to sitting by your sister. And you have two daughters and a mother at the table. It is not worth while to worry about separating you from your relations. What does it matter where you sit?'

'I am thankful we have Alfred with us. I don't know what Mater would have done without him.'

'And you are not thankful we have Edith? You could do without her? Well, I knew it would come to that.'

'I am thankful Mater has someone to take her thoughts off you, Hetta; and I should think you are too.'

'I have not thought about it. And I am not thankful about people's thoughts; I never see anything in them to be thankful about; and I am very good at reading them. That is why I try to put a disguise on your children. And it is a good thing I have done so. Seeing you without yours makes me see that. There is a great deal of you in all of them.'

'I wish you would resume your own, Hetta.'

Hetta gave a shrill laugh, which echoed down the table, and her brother spoke with his eyes on his guests.

'My sister is laughing me to scorn over something I said in all innocence.'

'Not in innocence,' said Miss Marcon to Evelyn. 'I heard; I listened.'

'I can't think how you dare to listen. You might hear anything.'

'I shall not dare any more; I did hear it. It is terrible, the lack of innocence.'

'We have to thank you, Ponsonby,' said Chaucer, 'for that peal of mirth which trilled across the room.'

'I do not thank him for it,' said Edith.

'There seems to be a threat in the air,' said France. 'Why did we have this dinner? With Grandma's death approaching, and Aunt Hetta's barely averted, it does not seem the moment in our family life, when so many have been passed over.'

'Aunt Hetta's death has not been averted any more than ours,' said Victor. 'I can't think how we believed in it. Perhaps the idea of freedom was father to the thought.'

'Aunt Hetta's letter was father to the thought,' said Chilton, 'and Aunt Hetta herself. There was no reason not to believe it.'

'Why are you three talking to each other?' said Hetta. 'You should be making the most of the company of your guests.'

'We are placed so that it hardly affects us,' said France. 'Our conversation is supposed to be only fit for each other.'

'And that is very true,' said Edith. 'It is hardly fit for that. They are much too young to hear it.'

'It is a mercy Stephen and I are separated,' said Miss Marcon. 'And to put Hetta and John by each other is a risk that may end anywhere. I think it is doing so. Customs are said to be based on something deep in human nature, and it is true.'

'You should not talk only to me, John,' said Hetta in a clear tone. 'You should think of your partner. She is being patient with you.'

'Oh, I have enjoyed listening!' said Jane. 'I think nothing is so amusing as family conversation! I have been regarding it as carried on for my express entertainment.'

'It has no doubt had that result,' said Victor.

'You should take your words to yourself, Hetta,' said John. 'Dr. Chaucer is being patient with you.'

'I, like Miss Jane, have enjoyed listening, Ponsonby.'

'This is dreadful,' said France. 'Of course they have enjoyed it. But if people must listen, they are the best people. Suppose it were Miss Marcon and Evelyn!'

'It is Miss Marcon and Evelyn,' said Edith. 'Look at the direction of their eyes. No, never mind. The direction has changed.'

'I shan't have many more opportunities of being with my friends like this,' said Sabine to Stephen.

'How awkward for Stephen!' said Miss Marcon. 'I suppose she will not. And it is for him to see that she does.'

'I feel each one may be my last.'

'So it may,' said Stephen to Edith on his other hand. 'Considering how rare these occasions are, it probably will.'

'I must not complain,' said Sabine. 'I have had my share.'

'Grandma is being heroic,' said Victor.

'Well, it is heroic to face death,' said France.

'Fearing it would make it seem to be true,' said Chilton. 'People don't think it is. I don't think it can be in this case.'

'I have got much older lately,' said Sabine.

'She means she has got much feebler,' said Victor. 'She has got a little older.'

'Time counts a lot at my age.'

'She is determined to have some praise,' said Miss Marcon. 'People always want it for youth and age. It would seem more sensible to have it for the prime of life, but nobody expects it for that.'

'They are ashamed of losing their youth,' said Alfred. 'I am getting to that stage. In some people it is shameful.'

'I am not talking about losing youth,' said Sabine.

'You are wonderful, Mrs. Ponsonby!' almost called Jane from the other end of the table.

'A very old woman is less wonderful than she has ever been,' said Sabine, bending forward in open weariness.

'Grandma has given her praise to herself, as no one else would do it,' said France.

'Shall you be sorry when Mrs. Ponsonby dies?' said Stephen

to Edith, too low for Sabine.

'Let me lean across the table,' said Miss Marcon. 'When people forget they are guests, I like to listen.'

'Yes, in a way. The house will be very different. And she has shown me only kindness.'

'I suppose I hardly know what I had half hoped to hear,' said Miss Marcon.

'Grandma is not less wonderful than she has ever been,' said Victor. 'She could not have done that once.'

'Been kind to the governess? I suppose she could not,' said Hetta with a casual laugh, hardly looking at her nephew. 'It was not in her line.'

'Let us talk about something which is not to do with ourselves,' said John.

'Let us have silence,' quavered his mother.

'Stay, Ponsonby,' said Chaucer, raising his hand, 'nothing else could so interest us.'

'I am sure that is true,' said Edith. 'We can only feel we deserve it.'

Rowland put his hand to his mouth and gave a slight yawn.

'Gapy-face,' murmured Sabine, moving her bent head to and fro.

'They need not be embarrassed,' said Miss Marcon to Evelyn. 'We did not hear. We all showed we did not.'

'Somehow I can't get used to it,' said France. 'You are supposed to get used to anything, but it is not the case.'

'Hetta has come home,' said Sabine, looking up, 'so there is no need for all this talk. We can be at peace.'

John sat up and spoke sharply.

'This cannot go on. Hetta, can't you do something?'

'Why should I? You behave as if I were in need of your criticism on every point, and then appeal to me in the first trouble. That does not work. Of course I will do nothing. You can ask Edith.'

'Edith, can't you do something?' said John at once.

'Could Alfred go and sit by your mother? He can do the most.'

'She is exhausted; that is all,' said Stephen.

'But that is dreadful surely,' said his sister. 'I do hope Alfred can alter it.'

'I will not be left out of things,' said Sabine, looking round almost with a scowl. 'This house is mine, and I will know everything in it. I will not have talk going on that I do not share.'

'Of course you will not,' said Alfred, coming to her side, while Rowland moved to his seat by Clare. 'You have always known everything and taught it to other people.'

'That was well thought of, Edith,' said John.

'It is a good idea, is it, to put it all on the outsiders?' said Hetta. 'Does it lessen the general embarrassment or add to it?'

'It lessens it,' said Chilton. 'We are at ease.'

'Or do we look more ridiculous?'

'That does not matter,' said her brother, 'if our guests are saved from discomfort.'

'But are they saved from it? Or do they feel more discomfort in being rescued from their hostess by Edith and Alfred, as if we employed a man and woman for the purpose?'

John gave his sister a look and turned away, and she suddenly rose and spoke in harsh, stumbling voice, in tense, stumbling sentences, which seemed to be torn from some depth within her below the level of speech.

'So Edith is everything, is she? Edith, whom you married because you thought she had given you money and would give you more! Edith, whom you married for the paltry sums you thought she would earn and go on giving you! You did not want her for herself! You did not want to earn for your wife! She was to earn for you. And the plan was an empty one after all. It is France who earned the money, France who gave it to you, France who wrote the book that won it! She hid behind Edith's name, because you were jealous of her, jealous of your daughter! She had to hide because she was afraid of your jealousy! Oh, I know it; I know it all. I know how Mater thought she found out; I saw her tamper with the letters; I saw her read the one addressed to Edith, which was meant for France. I know when she told you; I know when you talked about it; I know how you told each other that Edith would have other money in the end. And Edith knows why you married her. She found it out and did not dare to tell you. She did not dare to tell her husband that for the time she had only herself to give! She was afraid of the power of your feelings. Oh, people are afraid of you, though you think they are only afraid of me. It is not only of women that people are afraid.

What a welter of deceit I have found in my family! What a moral mess I have stumbled on unawares, stumbled on because it was everywhere. First Mater must deceive us all; then she deceived you; then you deceived Edith. Now Edith has begun to deceive you, though I admit she was afraid. France had already deceived you, though I admit she was afraid. Think of the feeling she had for you, when she wanted to save you the humiliation of not being able to earn; and did not dare to face your jealousy, and so took refuge behind that letter from a stranger! She knew what you wanted; she knew you. And I know you now; I know you. I am not going to do anything more; I am not going to serve you. I am going to live for myself, as you do. You have taught me how to do it, and I have learned. You tell me you have learned the lessons I have taught, and I can tell you the same. It is Edith who will have to serve you, because she cannot work, cannot earn the petty sums that mean so much to you. They are so paltry, these sums of money that mould your life.'

Hetta's words were more fluent as they went on, but her voice broke on its straining note, and the last words came without a sound. She seemed to stagger and looked round for her seat; and Chaucer rose and came towards her, holding out his arms, his face in a glow of pity, admiration, and rising hope. She turned towards him, half lifting her arms to his, and he put his arms about her, and, stooping over her, led her aside.

'We will take this meal in silence,' muttered Victor. 'Grandma need not say it.'

'If only we had had silence when she said!' said Miss Marcon.

Eyes did not turn to Sabine; they were still on her daughter; no one saw that she could not say it.

'We are supposed to be entertaining our friends,' said Clare. 'It is probably more the case than usual.'

France and Chilton turned to each other and broke into low, rapid talk. Victor leaned over them and joined. Stephen looked from face to face and relaxed, as if clear about the truth. Edith sat as if she were alone.

'We have had much to enjoy,' said Rowland, stumbling as he realised what might be read into his words. 'And our evening is not over. We know you have had some troubled days, and troubles must have their echoes. The circles in the water spread, but that helps them to fade away.'

'So this had to happen to bring the best out of Rowland,' said Miss Marcon. 'We can't be sorry about it.'

'We can't,' said Jane in a guilty aside. 'We should have known much less, if it had not happened. I don't quite grasp the truth even now. Even my rapacious mind cannot seize the whole of it.'

'Is anything justified which increases human knowledge?' said Evelyn.

'I don't think this was justified,' said Chilton.

'It had to come to it,' said Stephen. 'Where they are unfortunate, is that it happened in public.'

'Why did it,' said his sister, 'when they have had so many occasions by themselves?'

'That is the reason. When people shut themselves up, they cease to separate occasions.'

'Alfred, had you any private knowledge which sealed your lips?'

'None, Aunt Charity, and I have no knowledge now. I don't like too much knowledge. Life has to have its undercurrents, or it would not be life.'

'I think it is beautiful, the way people speak,' said Miss Marcon. 'So we shall see that something which is in every one, being brought out. It would be such a pity for it to be always hidden. But it is dreadful that life has to be life; I hardly knew it had to be until to-night, but I see it does have to.'

'I don't think undercurrent is the word for what has happened,' said France. 'I wish it were.'

'I hardly understand all of it,' said Evelyn. 'Do you all grasp as much as it seems?'

'You cannot possibly ask, my dear,' said Miss Marcon.

'No one can look anyone else in the face,' said Victor. 'So we are all equal.'

'Like all men,' said Evelyn. 'You can feel you are quite ordinary.'

'So France is exposed,' said Chilton in a clear tone. 'And it is time. She stands revealed as writer and family benefactor. And it is not a shameful position.'

'But people are always ashamed of their hidden kindnesses,' said Miss Marcon. 'If they are not, why do they hide them?'

'The risk of it is, that they might not always come out,' said Jane, in a just audible murmur.

John had sat with his eyes on each speaker in turn, holding to an appearance of simple desire for the truth. He now rose and looked at France, and held out his arms, and after their embrace went on to his wife and stood with his hand on her shoulder.

'If one good in my life helped me at all to another, I am the more grateful. If it put a truth into my mind, it was none the less the truth. And I am glad I am led to the full truth. The full truth is always good. My sister did not mean me to be grateful to her, but I can be grateful.'

'If there is a dry eye in the room,' said Evelyn, 'it is very unfeeling.'

'There can't be among the men,' said Miss Marcon. 'They are always found to be less hard than women.'

'I think only strong men,' said Alfred, 'and they are only less hard than good women.'

'I fear I am not a good woman!' said Jane. 'I have never conformed to the regulations! I fear I have no hard core of righteousness within me! I am simply my independent cynical self. But it may be less annoying for other people.'

'There is not a strong man in the room,' said Miss Marcon, 'though Victor may grow up into one. And Hetta is the only good woman.'

'They ought not to leave out strong women, ought they, Mrs. Ponsonby?' said Alfred, turning to Sabine, and breaking off suddenly, and sharply bending towards her. 'Mrs. Ponsonby is ill!' He stood up and faced his friends. 'I don't think she is conscious; I don't think she can hear what you say.'

Sabine was sunk into her chair, with her hands resting on its arms, and somehow having the same stillness as they, her head drooping forward and her face just hidden enough to hide that her eyes were also still.

Stephen went up to her and turned away, his lifted hand falling to his side.

'Look at Grandma!' said Victor, and did not look again.

There was a hush, a stir, the thought of what they had not seen.

Sabine had met Hetta's outbreak with a start which shook her frame, and then sat still, braced from head to foot to meet it, her face responding to every change on her daughter's. When Chaucer went to Hetta, she thrust her face forward with a sharp, uncertain light upon it, as if she looked on something which both seared and satisfied her soul, and then, with a sound almost of a satisfied sigh, relapsed with a single shudder and remained as she was seen.

Hetta never knew at which moment her mother had died, at which moment she had last looked on herself.

The guests made a movement to go, but were checked by John. They left the room, that Sabine might be carried away, carried from the room where she had been young and old, carried out of their life. It seemed that they had seen her for some time as at the point of her death. Her son and daughter, rising in their minds as her successors, seemed weak figures, dim and uncertain by Sabine. The house seemed to have a future, dim, flat, smooth, without extremes.

Stephen followed them, at ease, as usual, dealing with the death of an old woman come to her time to die, showing them for a moment their own deaths as natural and destined to be accepted thus. Hetta moved from one room to another as mistress of the house. She gave directions, easily, certainly, keeping her eyes from the rest, as if she felt that her self-exposure was lost in what had followed it. She went upstairs on some natural pretext, and did not at once return. Chaucer followed her, as if it was his right, John and Edith as if it was their duty.

The group in the drawing-room seemed without authority without the representatives of Sabine.

'We ought to congratulate France,' said Stephen.

'Congratulate?' said his sister. 'That is clever of you, Stephen. We might not have thought of congratulation.'

'Congratulate?' said Jane, raising her eyes and her voice. 'Why France more than anyone else? Oh, of course, because of her book! Oh, yes, of course.'

'We ought to congratulate Chaucer,' said Evelyn in a low tone. 'Who feels he can do it?'

'How do we know that France wrote the book?' said Stephen, keeping his mouth grave. 'Does she now acknowledge it?'

'France did write it,' said Chilton. 'I don't know how Aunt Hetta knew.'

'Ought we to talk about what Aunt Hetta knew?' said France. 'Where shall we end?'

'She knew a great deal,' said Jane to Miss Marcon, her head again bent; 'and we know it now.'

'Don't we forget what is spoken in haste? Isn't it as if it had not been said? I begin to think this can't have been said.'

'Then you are successful in following the rule. I am afraid my mind is too firm in its grasp of things to conform to it.'

'I think I shall recall it,' said Evelyn, 'when the first sharpness of memory is past.'

'Aunt Hetta may have spoken evil of the dead,' said Victor, with his father's consciousness. 'We don't know at what moment Grandma died.'

'We know she spoke of her as living,' said Rowland.

'I hope no one will say it is better for her,' said Miss Marcon. 'Of course it is not. It would have been better for her to renew her strength.'

'I feel sorry for Hetta,' said Jane, looking round to see if she had any following. 'I don't think she is necessarily a villainess. Feelings may become too much and break their bounds. Some people never have a real flood of feeling. Personally I must admit that I can imagine myself in her position.'

'We must not pity her,' said Miss Marcon. 'I am sure she would not accept pity. I don't know how people ever manage to give pity, when people never accept it.'

'Oh, how will you like Dr. Chaucer for an uncle?' said Jane to the young people.

'We have no experience of the relation,' said Chilton. 'We come to it unprejudiced.'

'Will you call him Uncle Herbert?'

'I cannot say; Aunt Hetta's wish will be law.'

'Aunt Hetta should be safe with him,' said France. 'He admired her most at her worst moment. It was not until then that his feelings overcame him.'

'Grandma foretold that this party would be the death of her,' said Clare.

'Old people are fortunate,' said Evelyn. 'Their speeches of that kind have so much chance of coming true; and it must be a pleasure to make them.'

'I think they are unfortunate,' said France. 'To think of making such a speech, and then feeling that perhaps you have spoken the truth!'

'It is Hetta's speech I am thinking of,' said Jane in an audible undertone.

'So are we all,' said France. 'If it had not caused Grandma's death, or rather been the last event in her life, what should we be doing about it?'

'Do look at Alfred,' said Miss Marcon to Stephen. 'He is standing aloof, pale, and grave. He thinks it is a solemn occasion: I do not know why it is not.'

Somehow it was not. The outbreak of Hetta overshadowed the death of someone known to be approaching death. The knowledge of all that was hidden in the house filled every mind. It was a relief when John and Chaucer returned, followed by the two women.

'Here are the three elder Ponsonbys, or rather the four,' said Evelyn, 'for Chaucer is a Ponsonby now.'

'We are free to spend an hour with our friends,' said John. 'You will forgive our going away. You see it had to be. It is a relief that my mother died without pain, and a regret that it has shocked and shadowed your time with us. I hold a strong brief for sudden death, and hope we may all do as well.'

'Shocked and shadowed our time with them,' said Miss Marcon. 'Of course it has. And Alfred knows it.'

'How did Hetta know that France had written the book?' said Stephen, in a simply interested tone. 'It was time we all knew it.'

'How did you know, Hetta?' said Chaucer, bending over Hetta and turning her face to the company.

'The book was based on the play, which France wrote and which we all saw acted,' said Hetta in a half exasperated tone, as if she thought everyone should have known it. 'Of course I did not believe in the other Edith Hallam; and I read the book, thinking Edith had written it, and was shy about it, as authors are. Though why they are shy, I don't know, for no one gives a thought to them. I can't think how people can be so incurious and uninterested. We ought to read the books which attract attention in our own time. The fact that a book is being widely read should be enough.' Hetta's voice had a rapid tonelessness, as if she did not wish to pause.

'Of course we ought,' said Miss Marcon at once. 'And I am the worst. I expect people to read my books, for, if not, why do I write them? And then I do not read theirs, though I can't have read them in other books, as they can have read mine. And so many of us have not read it. We are keeping down the sales. Hetta is much the best of us.'

'Much the best,' said Evelyn.

'We have not ever competed with her,' said his father.

'Do not praise her too much,' said Edith in a low tone, 'or you will defeat your own ends.'

'I suppose you are feeling Aunt Hetta is a noble figure, France?' said Victor.

'I am rather. She shows great spirit in coming back.'

'She knew the best thing for her reputation.'

'If we all lived up to that, we should do well,' said Edith.

'Are we all to congratulate Hetta on her speech?' said Jane, keeping her mouth open after her words.

'I think we have all done so,' said Stephen.

'I have not quite got to that,' said Jane, with a slight twist of her lips.

'Aunt Jane gave a wry smile,' said Evelyn.

'And I notice her brother has not.'

'He has done so behind the scenes,' said Stephen, 'or they would not have come back together.'

'It took their mother's death to reconcile them, did it?'

'Well, Mrs. Ponsonby would not have died in vain,' said Miss Marcon.

'A noble cause is the right thing,' said Evelyn.

'We all seem entirely satisfied with what has happened!' said Jane.

'Yes,' said Miss Marcon, 'I have spoken of that. It is only Alfred who knows about the shadow on us.'

'Do you think it was the shock of Hetta's speech, that killed Mrs. Ponsonby?' said Jane to Stephen, going to extremes.

'I do not know. It would only have taken a slight thing to kill her.'

'Then it was not Hetta's speech,' said Miss Marcon. 'That was not a slight thing.'

'It does not seem to have had any effect on anyone!' said Jane. 'I seem to be an exceptionally sensitive, shrinking creature. And we have not poured out enough congratulation on France. She is a most distinguished person for us to have in our midst.'

'We cannot pour it out,' said Chilton. 'It would be emphasising Aunt Hetta's speech. And Father would seem to be proving he was not jealous; Aunt Hetta would feel she might have done it before; and Grandma is dead.'

'Such good reasons,' said Miss Marcon.

'All our capacity for facing discomfiture has been used up by Grandma,' said Victor. 'We have none over for this final and extreme occasion.'

'Though we appear to be gifted in that line,' said Clare.

'I think you are managing wonderfully!' said Jane. 'I have been watching you with incredulous admiration.'

'We had better go,' said Rowland.

'In order that our gifts may not be put to too severe a test,' said Clare.

'My dear, they would not fail. It is the memory of them that will remain with us.'

'I like that way of putting it,' said Miss Marcon.

'But I was the one who thought of saying it,' said Jane. 'It is absurd to go on taking in the situation, and not thinking of what they are going through. It is so unimaginative! It is better to put it in any way one can, than not at all. That is just thinking of oneself instead of them.'

'But so many things are that,' said Miss Marcon. 'I think everything is; I think this is.' She ended too low to be heard and rose.

'It is time for us to go. We have had a lovely evening; I mean, we have enjoyed it all so much; I mean, we have been so glad to be at your side through everything. And of course there has been nothing. Except, of course, that Mrs. Ponsonby's death has been everything. Stephen, it is a time for you to speak. People of rare words always do the best. It is like rare smiles.'

'I am glad I was here,' said her brother.

'It was indeed a good thing,' said John.

'I do not think it sounded so much better, and it is the kind of word that ought to be rare.'

'I am sure you must be longing to see the last of us!' said Jane. 'Most people would hang about and think they were doing something, but we are clearer-sighted and do not deceive ourselves.'

'I think perhaps I will deceive myself,' said Miss Marcon, hesitating.

'You feel you can do something by your mere presence!' said Jane, turning her head in raillery, as she went to the door.

'I cannot say what I think I can do with my presence,' said Evelyn. 'I will just come back in the morning and do it.'

'So will I, if I am welcome,' said his father.

'I wonder what Alfred thinks he is doing with his presence,' said Stephen to his sister. 'He is doing nothing with anything else.'

'We must respect grief, dear, though it is known to be easy to be irritated by it.'

'I do not claim to do much by my presence,' said Chaucer, 'but I may make another claim. I claim the right to stay as a potential member of the family.'

'I wish some other man had found Aunt Hetta irresistible at that moment,' said Clare.

'Would any man have done for her?' said Victor.

'I suppose so, if Dr. Chaucer did.'

'We are fortunate that any man found her irresistible. It was really not likely.'

'He has always found her so,' said Edith. 'Her weak moment gave him confidence.'

'Something has evidently given it to him,' said France. 'The pity is, that he seems to keep it.'

'So you will be mistress here,' said Miss Marcon to Edith. 'You will have Mrs. Ponsonby's place and Hetta's: mistress will be the term. And you and I can have our life-long friendship. Do you remember that we began it on the day you came? I will even share Stephen with you, and I would do that for no one else.'

'You will forgive our seeming preoccupied,' said Hetta. 'You see it cannot be helped.'

'Plain dismissal,' said Stephen, 'and it had to be plain.'

'I see there is nothing Hetta cannot do,' said Miss Marcon. 'I admire her more than I ever did.'

'Ah, Charity, rightly named!' said Rowland, half to himself, as he disappeared.

'The tears have started to my eyes,' said Miss Marcon. 'I am weaker than you would think; it is absurd in a woman of my appearance. And really I am glad that Mrs. Ponsonby is taken and I am left.'

'I am glad I am left,' said France.

When the guests had gone, Hetta began at once to move about and give directions. She had a hurried, absent manner and avoided meeting people's eyes. There was enough to be done to maintain the appearance, and she held to it until they went to bed. Chaucer remained at her side, and she seemed to assume that her new situation counteracted the remembered scene.

The next day Muriel came downstairs, unaware of the changes in the house.

'Where is Grandma?' she said, when her father had read prayers, and Hetta had taken Sabine's seat.

'She is gone, my child,' said John, taking the line of simple directness. 'We shall not see her again.'

'Is she dead, Father? Is Grandma dead?'

'She died last night, with all of us round her, simply sitting in her chair. She had no pain and did not even know she was dying. It was the best way to die.'

The words, as they called up the scene, seemed to have no reason to call it up.

'Shan't we ever see her again?'

'No, we shall not. But she had lived longer than most people, and had more in her life. So we must not grieve.'

'But I want to see her, Father; I want to see Grandma again.'

'Yes, of course you do. So do we all. But we can only think and talk of her.'

There was a pause.

'She was very old, wasn't she?' said Muriel in a different tone. 'Do people who are quite so old, want to live?'

'They do not mind dying as much as younger people.'

'But they do mind it a little, Father? Grandma did mind a little?'

'I think she did not. She did not even know about it.'

'No one else will die for a long time, will they?'

'I should think not; it is likely that no one will.'

'Then we shall all be the same, except for not having Grandma?'

'Yes, but we shall not feel it the same.'

'No, it will be quite different,' said Muriel, and was silent.

'And except for not having Aunt Hetta,' said Clare. 'She is going to marry Dr. Chaucer, and go to live in his house.'

'Is she? Then does she like Dr. Chaucer?'

'Yes, of course she does, and he particularly likes her.'

'Well, he always looks at her, doesn't he?'

'That will do, miss,' said Hetta with a laugh.

'Then won't Aunt Hetta be in the house any more?'

'Not in the house, but she will come to see you, and you will go to see her.'

'Who will sit in Aunt Hetta's place?'

'Edith.'

'And who will sit in Grandma's?'

'I shall,' said John. 'It is time I grew up and was the head of my own house.'

'Then it wasn't Aunt Hetta's house and Grandma's?'

'It was. But now it is Edith's and mine.'

'Is that better?' said Muriel.

'No, but we shall try to make it as good as we can.'

'Well, houses generally belong to a husband and wife, don't they? Dr. Chaucer's house will now, won't it?'

'This is full power of speech,' said Victor. 'Grandma has not lived and striven in vain.'

'It has come too late, in the established manner,' said France.

'I always talk——' Muriel broke off.

'What a prospect for the future!'

'The speech is cast in the forbidden form of question,' said Edith.

'Here is a thing that Muriel can do for Grandma,' said Chilton. 'To learn the art of statement.'

'Will Aunt Hetta look after Dr. Chaucer's house?' said Muriel, resuming the art at her disposal.

'Yes. It will be her house as well.'

'Then what will happen to Miss Bunyan?'

'We must ask her to come back and look after you,' said John in jest.

'There is something in the idea,' said Hetta in a serious tone. 'Edith cannot go on teaching when I am gone. She will hardly have the time. She does not want to do too much.' Her concerned, almost propitiatory tone revealed her mind.

'I don't remember why she left,' said John, 'though I am naturally glad she cleared the way.'

'I remember,' said Clare.

'So do I,' said Chilton, 'though I did not know how far the memory would lose its sting.'

Muriel gave a laugh.

'Muriel has stated that she remembers, in what way she can,' said France.

'There was some scene with Mater, which meant nothing, but had that result at the time,' said Hetta, implying that scenes might easily be of this kind.

'Wouldn't it be all right for her to come back, now that

Grandma will not be here?' said Muriel.

'Well, it was your grandmother who did not care for her,' said John.

'Will the house be just Father and Edith and Miss Bunyan and us?' said Muriel, leaning towards Clare and using an anticipatory whisper.

Twelve

'I have a wonderful piece of news,' said Evelyn, entering the Marcons' drawing-room. 'I heard it in a way which makes it unjustifiable to repeat it, so I will only repeat it very little, much less than other people would. I will only tell it to you, whom it most concerns. Otherwise you would be the last people to hear it, and that does seem a very unfair custom. There is a rumour from the lawyer's office, which is almost a certainty. Mrs. Ponsonby has left all her money to Alfred.'

'What?' said Stephen.

'Yes, it is terrible, isn't it? Or it would be terrible, if Alfred were to keep the money. But he will have to give it up. There will be all the excitement for everyone and no money for Alfred.'

'It is true, I suppose?'

'Yes, I went myself to the office with a message from my father. The clerk could not understand how the leakage happened, but I do understand how leakages happen myself.'

'What did Russell himself say about it?'

'Nothing. I could not tell him the clerk had repeated it. I always talk to that particular clerk; he knows the kind of conversation I like. And he likes it himself too. One can always find something in common with everyone.'

'You can always find that in common.'

'Dear Alfred! What a tribute to him!' said Miss Marcon.

'What a predicament!' said her brother.

'No, it is surely not, is it?' said Evelyn. 'Not a predicament?

I am afraid it is rather a tribute. Alfred will have to relinquish the money, and too much as a matter of course, for him to have any credit.'

'He will have a certain amount of credit,' said Miss Marcon. 'After all, we can't force him to give it up.'

'But you may have to force him. Perhaps he will want to keep it, and force will be necessary. Then he won't have either money or credit.'

'You dislike him so much?' said Stephen.

'Well, you have to like people very much or be almost a stranger to them, to be glad for them to have money or credit. And I admit I should like Alfred to earn all that comes to him.'

'He may feel he has earned it by attending on Mrs. Ponsonby,' said Miss Marcon.

'Of course he may. That is when you will have to use force. Or perhaps kindness would be better. They say it is the surer way. Yes, that is when you will have to lead Alfred by kindness.'

'You won't earn all that comes to you,' said Stephen.

'No, so if Alfred does not either, I shall have no advantage over him.'

'Why do you want advantage over people?'

'I do not; I always give others the first place. It is only over Alfred, because of something in himself. But I know that people who speak against their relations, are up in arms if anyone else does it; and I see that is how it is with you and Alfred.'

'What is he in himself? Nothing to show.'

'Rotten at the core, I suppose,' said Miss Marcon. 'Dear boy!'

'He always comes in to you on Thursday,' said Evelyn, going to the window.

'It is his day off,' said Miss Marcon, 'but he has not come in lately. Since Mrs. Ponsonby got so old and frail, he has not left her.'

'He may come to-day,' said Stephen. 'She has got old and frail enough at last. But we must not tell him this rumour, if it is not to be repeated.'

'Of course we must not,' said Evelyn. 'Unless it is our duty to prepare him for the truth. If it came upon him unawares, there is no knowing what might happen. His baser nature might assert itself, and if you are to lead him by kindness and not by force, it is important to avoid that. I don't call that repeating it.'

'I don't suppose people ever repeat things really,' said Miss Marcon.

'You mean he might keep the money?' said Stephen.

'Yes, that is what I mean.'

'If he is rotten at the core, his better nature must be at the top,' said Miss Marcon.

'It is at the top,' said her brother. 'That is why Mrs. Ponsonby had it before her eyes.'

'I think that is so nice about Alfred. I do like people's better natures to be where they show. There is so much less good in them, if most people don't know they are there. What good would Alfred's have been to Mrs. Ponsonby, if she had not known about it? And now he has the comfort of feeling that he brightened her last days.'

'And has perhaps brightened more days of his own. He will find it a comfort.'

'No, no, no,' said Evelyn. 'Virtue is its own reward. I don't mind agreeing that Alfred has it, if it works like that.'

'You don't think he has,' said Stephen. 'It must be an anxious business.'

'Yes, it is dreadful to have uncertainty, though I don't agree that anything else is better. Here is Alfred, coming unconsciously towards his trial. I am glad his better nature is at the top; it is a consolation to feel he will stand the trial nobly.'

'It is not a proper thing to see,' said Miss Marcon. 'What is the good of a trial, if it does not reveal people?'

'That would not be a proper thing to see,' said Stephen, 'especially if their better nature is at the top.'

'Well, Aunt Charity! Well, Uncle Stephen! So you see me once more a useless person, wanted by no one.'

'Or we should not have seen you,' said Stephen.

'You have a duty to your pupils,' said Evelyn.

'Oh, yes, I am a governess,' said Alfred, throwing himself into a chair. 'I said I was wanted by no one. Why say it again in another way?'

'Sometimes there is something disarming about you, Alfred. It makes me hope the best of you.'

'I don't hope it of you, Evelyn. You have been speaking against me, as usual, to my uncle and aunt.'

'But only your uncle ever believes me. I have not disturbed a woman's faith in you. And I believe you are going to justify that faith, Alfred.'

'I wonder they listen to you.'

'Well, people do listen when people talk against other people,' said Miss Marcon. 'Or what would be the good of doing it? And people always seem to think it is some good.'

'To-day I have been telling them something not at all against you. Or I hope it will not be.'

'Something to your advantage, as the phrase goes,' said Stephen.

'No, no, it won't be to his advantage. Don't put his mind on to that line. It will make no difference to him.'

'Oh, a legacy is there?' said Alfred, hardly looking from one to the other. 'And Evelyn thinks I have no right to it.'

'Of course, you are quite indifferent,' said Evelyn. 'Who would think about such things at such a time?'

'It is a pity it is only at such times that they happen,' said Miss Marcon.

'We do pretend not to think of them,' said Alfred. 'But people don't intend them to be taken in that spirit. What is the amount of the legacy?'

'Surely the amount does not matter,' said Evelyn. 'It is the thought that counts. Oh, Alfred, is this the time to dwell on petty personal advantage?'

'Petty is not the word,' said Miss Marcon.

'I don't know who would think of my advantage if I did not.'

'I really don't know either,' said Miss Marcon. 'I think you are right to blame everyone. But here is someone who did think of it.'

'So that hard lump of bitterness may melt away,' said Evelyn.

'The old lady and I were great friends. I enjoyed her experience and thought she set a gallant example.'

'You have had the things that are most valuable.'

'So he has,' said Miss Marcon. So let us go on to the others.'

'I suppose the legacy is larger than you like, Evelyn?'

'Yes, it is. Much larger. But I don't know whether to say that. It may be better in that way. If it were not so large, you might take it. Then you would have something, and now you will have nothing.'

'You talk as if Mrs. Ponsonby had left me all she had.'

'Yes, I know I do. That is the way to talk.'

'Yes, that is it,' said Stephen. 'The news has leaked out from the lawyer's office. It should not by rights be repeated, but it must reach you soon. You are the old woman's sole legatee. That is your position.'

'Well, well, what can I do about it? I suppose I have to withdraw in favour of the family.'

'Yes, that is it,' said Evelyn.

'It can't be done in a minute,' said Stephen. 'The money is yours. You will have to make it over by deed of gift.'

'Yes, of course he will. Or he might change his mind. People have to be protected from themselves. They are often their own worst enemies.'

'It does seem that Alfred has to be,' said Miss Marcon.

'I shan't be beyond a point, Aunt Charity. I shall keep a sum equal to a possible legacy. I have a right to that.'

'You expected a legacy?' said Stephen.

'Oh, Alfred, on what were your thoughts running in Mrs. Ponsonby's last days?'

'Yes, I suppose I did, without thinking of it.'

'That was a very nice way to expect it,' said Miss Marcon. 'Much better than most people's.'

'Mrs. Ponsonby had about fourteen hundred a year,' said Stephen. 'John has six hundred, Hetta four. The expenses would be run very close if John did not earn.'

'Then suppose Alfred keeps five pounds,' said Evelyn. 'To buy him a ring.'

'Why are you so anxious I should keep so little?'

'Well, perhaps I cannot answer that. Perhaps my reason is not quite pure.'

'We know that Evelyn would give it all up in your place,' said Stephen.

'People never are in other people's place,' said Miss Marcon. 'It is Alfred who must have the credit of giving it up, not Evelyn.'

'If Alfred has to have so much credit,' said Evelyn, 'I would almost as soon he had the money.'

'Well, up to a point you will be gratified,' said Alfred, in a tone which did not seem to attach much importance to his words. 'For I shall keep some of the money and lose some of the credit.'

'You will lose all the credit,' said his uncle.

'Well, I should lose it all, if I gave up all the money. It would be taken as a matter of course. And I don't see any good in a will, if it is not to have any effect.'

'People will not see much good in this one.'

'You might keep a small sum which would not affect the family,' said Miss Marcon.

'But then it would not affect me either.'

'Every little counts,' said Evelyn.

'It does not count enough,' said Alfred. 'You won't have the pleasure of seeing me a penniless man.'

'Well, I admit it has been a pleasure. But I shall see the Ponsonby disturbance, and you in a most uncomfortable place. There is always compensation.'

'There will be for me,' said Alfred. 'The old lady shall have her way.'

'It does seem natural that she should do that,' said Miss Marcon. 'Of course, if you are doing it for her sake!'

'You must tell that to her family,' said Stephen.

'I hold no brief for her family,' said Alfred, almost with violence. 'I have had no kindness from any one of them, or I have had it from only one. I hold no brief for any family. I have had no kindness from you, Uncle Stephen, since I was a helpless boy. Family is no magic word to me.'

'It begins to be to me,' said Evelyn. 'Is this true, Stephen? Is it your fault that Alfred is what he is? That spark of good which is in everyone, was even in him once.'

'I did not make Mrs. Ponsonby's will. It is she who did the evil that lives after her. Alfred must do what he likes.'

'I can hardly do that,' said Alfred. 'I cannot keep the whole. I think I shall keep half, and propose to Clare. Then I shall be ensuring the future of one of the family.'

'The spark of good,' said Miss Marcon.

'The family will be ensuring your future,' said Stephen. 'Why Clare more than France?'

'France would not have me and I think Clare would. She need not do more than tolerate her deliverer.'

'The spark again,' said Evelyn. 'Sometimes I find myself almost liking you, Alfred, and Clare may feel the same. But you are not on the right path; try to turn aside in time.'

'I will go back and tell them what has happened and what I have decided.'

'We do see how things leak out.'

'You have the courage of your intentions,' said Stephen. 'You will tell them that in return for half Mrs. Ponsonby's money you offer yourself.'

'And add that it is all you have to offer,' said Miss Marcon. 'I believe people always say that, when they offer themselves. They don't seem to count themselves when they can offer other things.'

'Alfred did not count himself much,' said Evelyn.

'You are not on my side, Aunt Charity. But I must think of my own life. No one else will think of it. You are all thinking of the Ponsonbys and not of me.'

'Well, they do come into one's mind in connection with their family money, dear. Forgive me for not seeing all round the question. We shall leave our money to you and not to them.'

'What do you say to that, Alfred?' said Evelyn.

'With two lives in between, it is no good to think of that money.'

'Alfred, Alfred, this sad tendency of your thoughts!'

'Ought we to give our lives in this righteous cause?' said Miss Marcon.

'Poor, misguided, headstrong boy!' said Evelyn. 'He is his own worst enemy.'

'You are fond of calling him that,' said Stephen. 'I do not see it as the term.'

'We can't ever call people that,' said his sister. 'He may be the Ponsonbys' worst enemy: I should think he is.'

'Will you say it all before Hetta?' said Evelyn. 'How have things been since the other night? Turn your thoughts from yourself and tell us.'

'No,' said Miss Marcon, 'we have forgotten the other night. Our friends are safe with us. We like to feel that about ourselves.'

'And, Alfred, brought up like this, you can so go back on your training? Are your friends safe with you?'

'It is Mrs. Ponsonby who has done the deed. It is nothing to do with me. She did not ask my advice. I am going back to tell them the truth, and play fair and open from the first.'

'Yes, hold to your noble course, dear,' said Miss Marcon, raising her face for her nephew's kiss.

'I am doing nothing I am ashamed of, Aunt Charity.'

'I really can't understand that, though I know you have

explained it.' Miss Marcon turned to her brother as her nephew left them. 'I hardly think Alfred's better nature can be at the top after all, though he seems to think it is.'

'What is to be done?' said Stephen.

'Nothing, except watch Alfred possess himself of seven hundred a year and marry Clare. But it will be enough.'

'It is all my fault,' said Evelyn. 'If I had waited and let the truth come on Alfred before the family, he would have had to do the right thing. It all comes of being such a tittle-tattler. And I suppose he can earn something himself, so he will have more than seven hundred a year. And to think I have been the cause of it! That is the bitter part.'

'And we can't discontinue our allowance to him,' said Stephen, 'in case we seem to be driving him to his course. So he will have that as well.'

'I will go and walk it off,' said Evelyn. 'We can only try to look at the bright side. If he had given up the money, he would have been admired, and he will be despised for keeping half, as much as he would be for keeping the whole. So I will try to think it is all for the best.'

'Well, the boy has put us in a new position, Charity,' said Stephen.

'And we shall have to appear to be loyal to him through it all. And people are so dreadful, loving the sinner and hating the sin. I never thought to have to be one of them.'

'I can't understand his wanting or daring to keep the money.'

'I can't understand his daring to. Alfred is a brave man, Stephen. I daresay anyone would want to, perhaps everyone. I evidently don't hate the sin as much as you do, but then you hate the sinner more than I do, so the position is equally unfair on us both.'

Alfred had returned to the house and was facing the assembled family. He had asked them to come and hear him, with an air which was almost of authority. They thought he was going to resign his post because of the loss of Sabine, and were surprised by his exaggerated attitude.

'I have asked you to come and hear a word from me. I am going to say it once and not again. Some news has come out about Mrs. Ponsonby's will, and there seems no doubt about the truth of it. She has left all she had to me. I will give you a moment to realise it.'

He paused with his eyes on the window, hardly seeming to

disguise that his sense of his position gave him another sense of himself.

'My mother cannot have done that,' said John.

'She has done it.'

'Then you can make over the money according to the terms of the last will,' said Hetta. 'That is quite easily done.'

Alfred was silent, seeming to keep a smile from his lips.

'What were you thinking of doing yourself?' said John. 'Is there another method?'

'You are sure you have come to the moment to know?'

'This is the moment for that, surely.'

'You are sure?' said Alfred, putting back his head so that he seemed to look down on his audience.

'Yes, yes. Let us hear it. It must be a simple thing.'

'It is quite simple,' said Alfred more quickly, his mood broken by the words. 'I am the owner of all your mother possessed. Everything she had is mine. And I am going to keep half. The rest I will make over, as your sister said. That is my last word. Before you say your own words, remind yourself that what you will have, I shall be giving you.'

There was silence.

'No wonder he is nervous about our words,' said Chilton. 'But he will have to hear them. What are your reasons, Marcon, for such a purpose?'

'Your grandmother's wish, my own wish, the law of the land. By all those things remember I can keep the whole.'

'We can dispute the will,' said Hetta. 'We shall just have to do that.'

'The lawyer drew it up without question of your mother's reason. I believe you cannot dispute it.'

'My mother was a very old woman,' said John, 'and not herself in her last days. We all knew that, and you knew it best of all. You attended on her openly as if it was the case. We can all bear witness to it.'

'I waited on her as an old woman, but I enjoyed the quality of her mind to the last.'

'Well, well, we know it will not come to that. You can take a sum in place of the legacy you might have had, if she had kept her reason. We will consent to that and make an end.'

'It is the beginning, if you hold to what you say. But the end will come. I should advise you to bear it in mind. I have said I will take half: I could say something different.'

There was silence.

'There is one thing more,' said Alfred, coming a step forward. 'There is another word I want to say. I want to make an offer of marriage to Clare. I have no longer nothing to give. If she will face a simple life with me, I will make her a good husband. I know she wants a change in her life, and I should be glad to give it to her. I hope this, that must be between us all, will not embitter our relations as a family.'

There was faint laughter from Chilton and France.

'I think it will prevent much of a bond between us,' said Chilton.

'You can feel that the money is helping your sister.'

'That is not what we should feel.'

'Your having no longer nothing to give is hardly a recommendation,' said Edith.

'I would do almost anything to get away from home,' said Clare, not moving her eyes. 'I can't deny it.'

'You evidently can't,' said Chilton, as Alfred came to his sister's side.

'I don't think Alfred is right, but it makes no difference. I can't want him to give up the money. I want to get out of this house to another life. That is all I can think of. I have borne enough.'

'That is natural perhaps,' said John, turning from his daughter. 'We will leave Clare.'

'It is as wrong and deplorable as things said to be natural always are,' said France. 'But we must leave it, as you say.'

'You may have the law on your side, Marcon,' said Victor, his manner showing what he would be as a man. 'If Russell drew up the will without question, possibly you have. But you have no right, and you know it. If you think you have, why do you not keep the whole?'

'I can do that if it pleases you better. I see it would be more consistent, and it is what your grandmother wished.'

'You know it is not,' said Edith. 'You were not a stranger to her.'

'Perhaps I was the only person who was not.'

'You know that is not the truth.'

'What is truth?' quoted Alfred, throwing back his head.

'I cannot think Alfred means what he says,' said John. 'I cannot think he is the meanest of men. If I had thought it, should I have put him over my sons? The matter will not end like this.'

'So Father's judgement must have been sound,' said Chilton. 'I am sure I hope it must.'

'Of course it will not end like this,' said Hetta, in an almost pleasant tone. 'People cannot think, when they have had a shock. And it must have been a shock to Alfred to hear this news of the will. It has been hard on him and he has all our sympathy. But he will see his course when he has had time. And we shall forget all this, as it should be forgotten. Things have to be forgotten sometimes, when people have been living in chequered days.'

'You are taking the right line to make me change my mind. But I shall not change it. I will say it once more and never again.'

The family dispersed, seeing nothing else to do, leaving Alfred alone, leaving him, as they found, with Clare. John and Hetta went together to the library, and Edith did not follow them. This was a case for their old union.

Then the time went on in the ordinary way. Alfred did his duties and kept the brothers to their books, seeming to meet their coldness and distance as signs of grief for Sabine. Clare spent her time alone and was seldom seen. There was a sort of odd formality over the house. No one spoke of the future; no one knew how to speak of it; no one made it definite with words.

The day of the funeral came, came too soon, came too slowly, fraught with so much that threatened it as what it was. Sabine's son and daughter did not weep at her grave. She had outlived herself, had not done according to herself, and it was not herself they would weep.

Clare stood without expression, suffering Alfred to stand at her side. The women had gone as a matter of course to the funeral. It seemed hardly an occasion for emotion, seemed to deny itself. Hetta treated Alfred with courtesy and calm, having nothing against him until it was shown, seeming to hope to have nothing.

They returned to the house and assembled to hear the will. Their closer friends followed them into the library, walking uncertainly, glancing at each other, allowing their curiosity to conquer any sense of doubt. Hetta and John accepted their presence as a means of breaking the truth.

The lawyer was a man who atoned for an uneventful personal life by an interest in the lives of other people, a tendency indulged by his profession. His eyes roved about under motionless brows, as he produced and unfolded his parchment.

'This is the last will and testament of me, Sabine Henrietta Ponsonby, widow of John Chilton Ponsonby, being in my sane mind.' The listeners looked at each other, and caught up with the words further on. 'It is my wish to be buried with my late dear husband, John Chilton, and I direct that all my debts shall be at once discharged. I appoint my friend, Alfred Stephen Marcon, and my only son, John Victor, as executors and trustees of this my will. And I give and bequeath all my worldly goods, whatsoever and wheresoever, to the aforesaid Alfred Stephen Marcon and John Victor Ponsonby, to be held in trust for the members of my family in the shares to be hereinafter declared.' The stereotyped, stilted sentences rolled on, but were heard no longer. It was clear how the matter lay, clear what had caused the rumour, clear what was the truth. A legacy of five hundred pounds to Alfred was accepted with the other pieces of knowledge which reached and left the listeners' minds. The provisions in the main were what they had been, what had been from time to time revealed by Sabine. People were inclined to meet each other's eyes and to admit a smile to their lips. Eyes went to Alfred and rapidly withdrew. Alfred's eyes were on the ground. Mr. Russell rolled up the will and faced the room. The days fell back and left the family face to face with the loss of Sabine, with Sabine's place left for the first time empty.

'Isn't it fortunate that the rumour got about and revealed Alfred's true nature?' whispered Evelyn. 'My own true nature is still unsuspected. It gives me the unfair advantage I always wanted.'

'I can hardly believe young Marcon would have held to the purpose he professed,' said Chaucer, shaking his head.

'But he must believe it; that is most unfair,' said Evelyn. 'I see how it will be. It is too bad.'

'I shall not be able to act as executor,' said Alfred, turning his eyes fully to the lawyer, so that he kept them from everyone else.

'Well, well, it can be arranged. Your signature may be required at times. We can adjust matters,' said Mr. Russell, to whom Alfred was a human being and therefore a potential

232

client. 'You will let me know if I can make you any advance upon your legacy.'

'I want the whole at once; it is to be my start in life,' said Alfred in clear, easy tones. 'You can't imagine the relief it is to find I have not got nothing.'

'I daresay we can't,' said Chilton. 'It must be an odd relief.'

'Poor Clare!' said Jane.

'Not poor at all,' said Alfred. 'She gets rid of me as well as of the money. I have no longer anything to give, and do not hold her to her bargain.'

There was a silence.

'Poor Clare!' repeated Jane, her tone calling attention to the pertinence of the words.

John went to his daughter's side and found himself forestalled by Rowland.

'I am glad I had the delusion about the will,' said Alfred, in a distinct, rather drawling voice. 'It gave me a glimpse of what money would be, and though I did not find it as satisfying as I should have thought, I found it satisfying enough to resolve to do my utmost with what I have. It has been a salutary experience, though people did not think it was, while it lasted.' He gave a laugh. 'But I still do not think that wills should have no effect, and if this one had been made as was said, I would have held to my decision. I shall be going away at once, as I shall not like the house without its mistress. The boys are grown and I am not needed; they can go to Oxford at once. And I shall miss our ruler, if no one else will.'

He ended with a smile and turned aside, putting his hands in his pockets, but as if recollecting himself drew them out and stood in a normal attitude.

'Congratulations, Ponsonby!' he added, nodding to John.

'There is no need for them. We simply have what is our own.'

'You thought you were not going to have it,' said Alfred on a note of patience. 'And you are glad you are going to. That is what I meant, as you know.'

'How Alfred must wish he had given up the money!' said Jane.

'He must wish there had not been the rumour,' said Edith. 'As he has explained, it was not in him to give it up.'

'He must wish the rumour had been true,' said France.

'Was Mrs. Ponsonby failing in her mind at the last?' said Jane. 'It was odd to make Alfred executor.'

'People often appoint more than one person,' said John. 'Her grandsons were young and Alfred had shown her great kindness. But perhaps she had failed enough to be hardly seen as herself.'

'Why did she not appoint Hetta?'

John was silent, knowing that Sabine had once done so, knowing that Hetta also knew, knowing that the old woman's simple change of one name to another had put Alfred's name before his own, knowing that his mother would never have displaced the old Hetta.

His sister answered at once.

'She felt—we felt I had enough on my shoulders, and it is more usual to appoint a man.'

'It was wonderful to see Alfred trying to carry off his position,' said Miss Marcon. 'It is wonderful to attempt the impossible. They say that kind of failure is greater than success, and it is certainly very different from success.'

'Alfred has all the disgrace of accepting the money and none of the advantage,' said Evelyn. 'That is just what I should have chosen, but the pleasure has somehow lost its savour. I suppose the chief joy is always in anticipation.'

'It is sad that we none of us have any proof that we should have given up the money,' said Jane. 'And I really do believe I should have given it up! I am a person who in schoolroom language likes to be "right with myself."'

'It is hardest on Stephen and me,' said Miss Marcon. 'Because we believe we should have given it up too, and it may rather seem it is in our family to keep it. I think we must leave the neighbourhood and go among strangers, where the news will have preceded us, and try to live it down.'

'We are all fortunate in not having been tried,' said Rowland.

'We have been saying we are unfortunate,' said Edith, 'and I think that is best.'

'Alfred seems to have brought more shame upon us, now he does not have the inheritance,' said Miss Marcon. 'And yet it is better for people that he should not have it. But there is plenty in life left. Stephen will have no patients in a fresh place, and that will be compensation; and I shall go to the British Museum, with a new experience in my rather peculiar face, so that people will look up and speculate upon the odd but arresting figure.'

'Alfred has done ill by us, if it comes to that,' said Rowland.

'The consequences of people's sin do fall on other people.'

'We shall all have to go after you.'

'Then there doesn't seem to be any good in our going.'

'Would you really have gone?' said Jane.

'No, I don't suppose so. I expect we should have chosen the harder thing. People do choose what is harder.'

'After all, Alfred would have been in a way entitled to the money!' said Jane.

'He will always be able to say he might have had means of his own,' said Stephen.

'Ponsonby, my son is to speak for me,' said Rowland, coming forward with his hand on Clare's shoulder. 'I do not dare to speak for myself.'

'I should think not,' said Evelyn. 'It is for me to suffer the embarrassment. I have always been my father's burden bearer. He has asked Clare to be a mother to me, and she has consented.'

'What?' said his aunt.

'It is the strangest marriages that are the most successful,' said Rowland.

'A few minutes ago Clare was engaged to Alfred!'

'That is why Father could not propose to her. He had to wait until she was free.'

'She has soon transferred her affections! Is she sure of her mind now?'

'She got entangled, poor girl, entangled with Alfred. That must explain my odd hostility to Alfred, that I obscurely felt he was standing in my father's way.'

'He was not until quite lately. He and Clare were only engaged a few days.'

'But Father had a sense of his own unworthiness. Clare's being engaged to Alfred helped him. Anyone who could belong to Alfred for a few days, would belong to Father for life. It must have given him confidence.'

'Ponsonby, I am waiting for your word,' said Rowland.

'Well, my girl is clear that she wants to leave her home, and though her plans are confusing, I welcome one which keeps her in the place.'

'We all welcome it for that,' said Stephen.

'That is at once the most and the least we can say,' said Chaucer.

'And it was Stephen who said it,' said Miss Marcon.

'Congratulations, Seymour,' said Alfred. 'I seem to spend my time congratulating people on what I wanted myself.'

'They are the truest congratulations,' said Miss Marcon. 'You did want a good deal, dear. Think of the people who have it!'

'It seems to draw Alfred closer to me,' said Evelyn. 'I think he and I will be nearer than ever before.'

'I have never disliked you, Evelyn.'

'But I have disliked you, Alfred; yes, so much.'

'Why did Seymour propose to Clare?' said Chilton to France.

'He was sorry for her, and wanted to do all he could, so he offered her himself and everything he had.'

'Men do seem to do that to Clare,' said Victor. 'I must say I should not have thought it.'

'His attitude to his sister is still boyish,' said Chilton.

'It is fortunate that the match is as suitable as it is,' said Edith, 'considering she always accepts the men.'

'I should not have thought that either,' said Victor.

'Victor sees all round the question,' said Chilton, 'as he indicates to us. I think his emulation of us is wholesome: I think it will help him.'

'Well, I must make haste and be married,' said Hetta, 'to be free to arrange the same thing for Clare. Or shall I plan it the other way round?'

'Sir Rowland, you and I will not quarrel about it,' said Chaucer.

'But do let Father come first,' said Evelyn.

'Won't Edith arrange it for Clare?' said Muriel.

'Perhaps she will, if I am too absorbed in my own affairs,' said Hetta. 'I begin to feel that tendency coming upon me.'

'We don't really want two people to do things, do we?'

'Whatever you want, miss, you will not have two.'

'Edith is silent,' said Stephen to his sister.

'It is nice of you to notice that, Stephen. You are one of those people who are human like everybody else. And you ought to understand silence.'

'She is letting Hetta hold the first place until the last.'

'You see you understand it.'

'Well, our family is in the general eye!' said Jane. 'I shall be able to have the little house of my own I have always planned! I don't know why having it entirely one's own makes so much difference. It is very egotistic, but so it is. One feels that one's own personality will really be able to impress itself at last.'

'I am sorry for my aunt,' said Evelyn.

'Yes,' said Chaucer, shaking his head and taking a step towards him. 'It is a sad thing when people in fulfilling their own lives must do the opposite for other people's.'

'I mean I am sorry because she means what she says, and people will not believe her.'

'Ah, such generous deception is often practised by women.'

'How much does she mean it?' said Miss Marcon.

'About half.'

'That is an enormous proportion. Poor Jane! I did not mean it at all, when I said we would go away.'

'It must be wonderful to be a Ponsonby,' said Evelyn to Chaucer.

'It is,' said Rowland.

'I forgot Father was one. I somehow thought Clare would be a Seymour.'

'That was silly of you,' said Miss Marcon.

'It is even more wonderful,' said Chaucer, stepping forward to atone for his slowness in words, 'to make someone else a Chaucer.'

'You will all come and have some tea,' said Hetta. 'The business is over now.'

'It is dreadful of us to have stayed for it,' said Miss Marcon. 'But it was a dreadful thing we stayed for. I see we had to be punished. It shows the power of money.'

'We have seen that in the last days,' said her brother.

'We have seen so much in those days that I am quite confused. Something seems to have happened to everyone. But for me the day shall be simply the day of Mrs. Ponsonby's funeral. It is better than the day of our own public humiliation.'

'Ah, that is what it is for us all, Miss Marcon,' said Chaucer.

'What an untruth!' said Evelyn.

'Go in, go in,' said Hetta, lifting her hand in her old way. 'You need some tea, so go where it is to be found.'

'Miss Marcon, in someone Mrs. Ponsonby's spirit lives,' said Chaucer, smiling and indicating Hetta.

Muriel and Miss Bunyan were in the drawing-room, the latter dispensing tea as a member of the house. Chaucer observed her office and looked away, and on receiving a cup from her hand took it with full thanks, but with his eyes turning to his neighbour.

'I trust, Evelyn, that the new chapter in your life promises well for you?'

'Yes, very well. My father's happiness will have to be mine. So I am sure to have some happiness.'

'That, if I may say so, perhaps promises better than anything else has done for you.'

'You may not say so. I have always been an ideal son.'

'And how much younger will my future niece and your future stepmother be than you are?'

'About nine years,' called Jane.

'I do not know,' said Evelyn.

'About nine years,' called his aunt.

'I do not talk about people's ages.'

'You must be very thankful, Miss Marcon,' said Chaucer, 'of the outcome of this occasion. That your nephew is saved from himself.'

'It seems that other people are saved from him. I feel he has somehow lost all he had.'

'Alfred, would you like to be seen with me?' said Evelyn. 'I don't mind walking with you before everyone.'

Alfred seemed not to hear.

'Poor boy, his stumble was a bad one,' said Evelyn, looking round.

'It is a good thing you are a son, Evelyn,' said Jane. 'Or you might be in danger of being disinherited.'

'Like my poor Alfred,' said Miss Marcon.

'I wish Mrs. Ponsonby had lived to be my great grand-mother,' said Evelyn.

'You naughty boy, making fun of your father's engagement! Where is my bringing up?'

'Clare will go on bringing me up now. Men are always children.'

'Now is everyone provided with tea?' said Miss Bunyan, with the conventional briskness of someone guiding people back to life after a funeral. 'And no one ready for a second cup? Then I will have some myself in the interval.'

Muriel's eyes showed a light.

'Muriel, would you like to hand some things? That would be a help to me at the moment.'

Muriel laughed at the speaker's personal preoccupation.

'The occasion seems somehow to be a celebration,' said France to Chilton.

'Well, with Grandma in the churchyard, and Aunt Hetta in the vicarage, and Clare with the Seymours, and Alfred in the world, a new life will open up before us.'

'What do you think of the changes, Stephen?' said Evelyn.

'I think but poorly of them. The change for Mrs. Ponsonby is the best. The breakers are ahead, not behind.'

'I am sure there are some behind, dear,' said Miss Marcon.

'Change may be good for its own sake,' said Evelyn.

'It is, if these changes are good.'

'Hetta and Clare can always come back to this house.'

'If they do that, what is the good of their leaving it? And Hetta cannot come back.'

'Well, so we have had an engagement,' said Miss Bunyan. 'I have just been made aware of it. So we ought to eat and drink and be merry, although——'

She broke off at Muriel's laughter.

'You said we ought to be merry,' said the latter.

'I did not mean my words to be taken quite so literally on this occasion.'

Muriel looked at the cup and plate in Miss Bunyan's hands, and her sense that in one case the words had been so taken, aroused her further mirth.

'Muriel has not got out of her habit of laughing at nothing,' said Miss Bunyan.